IRISH
BRIGADES
Abroad

IRISH BRIGADES *Abroad*

FROM THE WILD GEESE TO THE NAPOLEONIC WARS

STEPHEN MCGARRY

The History Press Ireland

In memory of my father

First published 2013, reprinted 2014

The History Press Ireland
50 City Quay
Dublin 2
Ireland
www.thehistorypress.ie

© Stephen McGarry, 2013

The right of Stephen McGarry to be identified as the Author of this work has been asserted in accordance with the Copyright, Designs and Patents Act 1988.

All rights reserved. No part of this book may be reprinted or reproduced or utilised in any form or by any electronic, mechanical or other means, now known or hereafter invented, including photocopying and recording, or in any information storage or retrieval system, without the permission in writing from the Publishers.

British Library Cataloguing in Publication Data.
A catalogue record for this book is available from the British Library.

ISBN 978 1 84588 799 5

Typesetting and origination by The History Press

Contents

	Introduction	7
1.	The Recruitment of the Irish Regiments Abroad	15
2.	The Character of the Brigade	30
3.	The Jacobite War (1689–91)	46
4.	The Flight of the Wild Geese (1691)	63
5.	The Day We Beat the Germans at Cremona	73
6.	The First Jacobite Rising (1715)	84
7.	The Battle of Fontenoy (1745)	92
8.	The Second Jacobite Rising (1745)	105
9.	The Decline of Charles Edward Stuart	127
10.	The Waning Jacobite Cause	133
11.	Lieutenant General Thomas Lally's Expedition to India	143
12.	The War of American Independence (1775–83)	151
13.	The French Revolution (1789)	163
14.	The United Irishmen and France	175
15.	Napoleon's Irish Legion (1803–15)	191
16.	Conclusion	215
	Notes	226
	Bibliography	270
	Index	281

Introduction

From the time of King James II's reign over the three kingdoms of England, Scotland and Ireland, swashbuckling young Irishmen achieved great success and fought with distinction in most of the major battles in Europe and beyond. The prospects for the ordinary Catholic in Ireland in the eighteenth century were bleak and, perhaps not unlike modern emigrants, the best and brightest were often forced away. Many of those who left saw the undertaking of military service on the Continent as only a temporary condition. While contemporary Irish emigrants might look to Australia or Canada in search of a better life, during the eighteenth century the Irish turned to France and Spain, countries with well-established Irish communities. This book will look at how they fared, from the War of the Grand Alliance in 1688 right through to the Napoleonic Wars. What emerges is a picture of honour, chivalry and integrity, of self-sacrifice and, above all, of great adventure.

Irish troops displayed these qualities numerous times, such as when they volunteered to cover the retreat of the French army against the Germans in 1735; or their near-suicidal attack launched to capture George II's son, HRH the Duke of Cumberland, during the Battle of Lafelt. When Napoleon's Irish Legion proudly marched through the French town of Verdun, the legion band played 'Saint Patrick's Day in the Morning', aware that there were captured British POWs billeted in the town. One must also not forget their plan to rescue the French queen, Marie Antoinette, during the French Revolution, or the epic musketry duel fought during the famous Battle of Malplaquet between two Irish regiments, one in the French and the other in the British army. The Battle of Fontenoy (1745) was their highest battle honour, when six Irish regiments in the French army were largely responsible for breaking a British infantry advance and secured victory.

The formation of the Irish Brigade of France began with an exchange of nearly 6,000 French for Irish troops during the Jacobite War (1689–91), which became Mountcashel's Irish Brigade. The Irish supported the Catholic king, James II, in the war, which was fought in Ireland. James had been deposed and fought to regain his crown against the Protestant king, William of Orange, who had usurped him during the 'Glorious Revolution'. Conflict in eighteenth-century Europe was generally along religious lines and the Jacobite War was no exception. The Protestant countries of England, Holland and Prussia (including Catholic Austria and Portugal) were frequently at war with the Catholic countries of France and Spain. The war's repercussions resonated deeply in Northern Ireland, particularly during 'The Troubles' in the twentieth century, and are still felt today. Some sections of the Protestant Unionist community annually commemorate their victory over the Catholics at the Battle of the Boyne, fought over 300 years previously.

After the Jacobite War, the Irish army withdrew to France. This exodus became known romantically as the 'Flight of the Wild Geese', and spearheaded Irish migration to the Continent. The term the Wild Geese evoked the migratory flight of the birds in autumn and was used on ships' manifests for the secret transport of Irish recruits to armies overseas. The Irish followed James II, who had been forced into exile in France, and were known as Jacobites, from *Jacobus* (the Latin form of James). The Treaty of Limerick (1691) guaranteed Catholic rights after the war but these rights were removed by the Penal Laws. Catholics turned to military service abroad, which offered an escape and was frequently the launching pad into successful careers in government or in business. Land forfeitures by 1700 left only one-sixth of land in Catholic hands and the Irish took up the Jacobite cause in the hope that they would regain their rights and lands with a Stuart Restoration.

Irish migration to the Continent dates back to the golden age of the Irish Church (AD 600–800). In this period, Irish missionaries were credited with re-establishing Christianity following the collapse of the Roman Empire that had brought Europe into the Dark Ages. Ireland had remained independent of Roman rule and escaped the ravages that occurred after the Empire's collapse, due in part to its geographical remoteness on the periphery of Western Europe. The country had been a rebellious and troublesome colony since the twelfth-century English conquest and military links with the Continent were established after failed Irish rebellions. Many fled to France and Spain where they were perceived as soldiers of conscience, having similarities to the earlier crusaders. They adhered to their Catholic religion despite pressure to convert to Protestantism, preferring to serve abroad under arms and in so doing forfeiting their estates at home.

Irish military service in Spain dates from the Flight of the Earls in 1607, when Gaelic chieftains Owen Roe O'Neill and Hugh O'Donnell settled in Spain.[1] They established the Tyrone and Tyrconnell regiments but both were disbanded by the close of the seventeenth century. The Irish Brigade of Spain comprised the regiments of O'Mahony, Crofton, Fitzharris, Bourkes, Castlear, MacAuliffe and Comerford. In 1709 these were re-formed into the regiments of Hibernia, Ultonia (Ulster) and Irlanda who remained in Spanish service until 1818. The Irish had always capitalised on the shared Milesian origins between the peoples of Ireland and Spain, which they used to their full advantage to gain privileges at court or for support for their cause. The Milesians were the early Celtic people who invaded, settled and ruled Ireland in the first millennium BC. The Irish also owed allegiance to the House of Stuart, as they believed the Stuarts were descended from the old Milesian kings of Ireland.

Of all the Wild Geese who went to the Continent, those who went to France were the most successful and contributed most both militarily and politically during the period. France eclipsed Spain as their preferred destination, due to the ease of migration to France and Flanders from Ireland. 'The Flight of the Wild Geese' in 1691 also reinforced links in France over Spain, as 'the overwhelming majority of Jacobites in France were Irishmen in the service of France.'[2] France assisted Ireland in the

Jacobite War, and the French king, Louis XIV maintained James in Saint Germain, Paris which encouraged his followers to settle there. The Irish Brigades were the Jacobite army-in-waiting and were central to any plots for a Catholic Restoration. Paris became 'the chief centre of the various plots and conspiracies to restore the Stuarts, whose efforts to regain the ancestral throne found their most zealous supporters in the exiled nobility and gentry of Ireland'.[4] France was used by the Irish as a platform for invading the British Isles. The Channel ports were the preferred embarkation point due to the short run across, and the Irish regiments were frequently stationed there and threatened British national security. In 1728, Charles Forman, the English pamphleteer, observed:

> As long as there is a body of Irish Roman Catholic troops abroad, the chevalier [James III] will always make some figure in Europe by the credit they give him; and be considered as a prince that has a brave and well-disciplined army of veterans at his services; though he wants that opportunity to employ them at present, which he expects time and fortune will favour him with … they [the Irish] are British subjects and speak the same language with us, and are consequently the fittest troops to invade us with.[3]

The Irish regiments of France went through many changes in their history. The French formed a unit known as the Irish Brigade, comprising the Irish infantry regiments, for practical, cultural and linguistic reasons. The sole Irish cavalry regiment of Fitzjames' served alongside other French cavalry regiments.[4] In 1690, Mountcashel's Irish Brigade in France comprised the regiments of Dillon's, Clare's, Mountcashel's and Dorrington's. Shortly afterwards these were joined by Sheldon's horse, Albemarles', Galmoy's and Bourke's. When the French army was re-organised in 1715 only five Irish regiments remained: Clare's, Dillon's, Dorrington's, Lee's and Nugent's (later Fitzjames). In 1744, Lally's was formed along with the Scottish Royal Ecossais (Royal Scots) to support the Stuart claim. Lally's and Fitzjames' horse were disbanded in 1762, followed by the Scottish regiments. In 1775, the Brigade was reduced to three regiments – Berwick's, Walsh's and Dillon's – all of whom were disbanded after the French Revolution.

Irish soldiers were also active in other parts of Europe. For nearly forty years (from 1792 to 1833) a sixty-strong Irish bodyguard served the Italian Duke of Parma, and in the early 1700s, Irish officers comprised 8 per cent of the officer corps in Bavaria, in present-day Germany.[5] In Russia, several Irish officers served Catherine the Great's court, including Cornelius O'Rourke from Co. Leitrim, who rose to the rank of general. His son, Major-General Joseph O'Rourke, led an army that drove Napoleon out of Russia. Field-Marshal Peter de Lacy from Limerick took a leading role in reforming the Russian army, and his son Maurice de Lacy also attained a marshal rank in Austria. Irish military service in Austria began during the Thirty Years War in the 1600s, where they rose to the highest positions in the military and political life of the country. Additionally, twenty-five Irishmen received the Austrian army's most prestigious military decoration – the Order of Maria Therese – founded in 1757 to reward officers for exceptional acts of bravery.[6]

Austria was an ally of England until 1756, and was often at war with France and Spain, resulting in Irishmen opposing each other on the battlefield. Many Irish Catholic families preferred to serve in Austria (rather than in France or Spain) as advancement was based more on individual merit than to noble birth. In the 1690s, the first Irish regiment was formed from Irish soldiers who were imprisoned on the Isle of Wight during the Jacobite War. This regiment never saw action and many deserted, probably seeing service in the Austrian Imperial army as better than rotting in an off-shore prison. A second regiment was also raised from Irish prisoners, but was disbanded shortly afterwards due to sustaining heavy losses from illness. The Irish regiments in Austria did not remain in service for long. England had applied diplomatic pressure on their Austrian ally for their disbandment, as they distrusted Irish Catholics serving in the armies of their allies.

Catholic Ireland was effectively a nation in exile after 'The Flight of the Wild Geese'. Patrick Sarsfield's intention when leaving Limerick with the Irish army was to 'make another Ireland in the armies of the great King of France'.[7] The Irish established close-knit communities in Europe and brought their music, culture, books and religious relics with them.[8] The Gaelic order entered into a period of decline from the 1607 Flight of the Earls and the subsequent departure of many of the Gaelic nobility. The county lost much of its Gaelic culture and identity in its wake as the Gaelic nobility were patrons to roaming scribes, bards and musicians. From then on, key aspects of Irish culture were being forged in Europe. The first book printed using Irish character type was printed on the Continent. The Franciscans in Leuven, Belgium were so concerned that whole swathes of Irish history were being wiped out entirely due to the English conquest that they undertook their great work, *The Annals of Ireland of the Four Masters*, which recorded key aspects of Irish history up to the year 1616.

J.C. O'Callaghan's *History of the Irish Brigades in the Service of France* (1870) has remained the standard work on the Irish Brigades.[9] O'Callaghan undertook his book to restore the nation's honour as he was so incensed at Voltaire, who wrote: 'The Irish whom we have seen to be such good soldiers in France and Spain have always fought badly at home. There are some nations that are made to be enslaved by others.'[10] To complete his work, an effort that took him twenty-five years, O'Callaghan trawled through the dusty archives in France and Spain. Previous to this, no history of the Irish Brigades had been written, partly due to the vast amount of research involved.[11] In 1837 an English writer in *The Gentleman's Magazine* observed this and wrote:

> The Irish Brigade in France, a body of which I regret that no history exists, for the achievements of the various regiments of which it was composed, would well deserve a special narrative nor were those in the Spanish service less distinguished. A gentleman, Captain O'Kelly, now or lately who had been living in La Reole, in the south of France, had collected material for a history of the corps, as he told me some years ago, but what has prevented their publication I know not what.[12]

The famous French writer Voltaire believed the House of Stuart was cursed. The first of the Stuarts, James I, was assassinated and his son was killed at the age of 29, fighting the English. Mary Queen of Scots was executed, as was Charles I, and his grandson James II was also driven from his throne. His son, 'James III', and grandson, Bonnie Prince Charlie, devoted their lives to regaining the crowns of their ancestors until their hopes were ultimately dashed at Culloden in the Scottish

Map of Britain and Ireland.

Jacobite Rising of 1745 – commonly referred to as the '45'. Thereafter, with all hope of a Stuart Restoration fading, the Irish Brigades were deployed elsewhere. The Irish regiments served in the Seven Years War in Canada, and in Europe, in India, and alongside General Washington in the American War of Independence. The French Irish Brigade was disbanded during the French Revolution but Napoleon reestablished them as La Légion Irlandaise to spearhead an invasion in Ireland. This corps was disbanded in 1815, after Napoleon's defeat at Waterloo. The Spanish Irish Brigade were stood down three years later, formally drawing to a close Irish military involvement in Europe.

The Irish Brigade's exploits and triumphs have been largely forgotten. On a quick scan through a general study on Irish history, one can be hard pressed to find a reference to the Battle of Fontenoy or to the Wild Geese at all. *Irish Brigades Abroad* covers some of these missing pages of Irish history. I am grateful to the assistance I was given around the various battlefields and libraries here and abroad, particularly the services of the National Library and the Research Library in Pearse Street, Dublin. In their well-stocked reservoirs, scarcely any book was unavailable, no matter how old or how long out of print, whether this was the beautiful (slightly battered) leather-bound copy of Marshal de Saxe's *Memoirs* from 1757, to the little pamphlet signed by the English historian Francis Skrine on a lecture he gave on the Irish Brigades to the Irish Literary Society in London, in 1921. I recalled the achievements of my compatriots with pride but regret that conditions prevented them remaining at home where they could have prospered. As we approach the 2015 bicentenary of the ending of Irish military service in France, I hope you enjoy reading about these brave Irishmen and I hope I have done them some justice.

Stephen McGarry, Dublin, 2013.

1

THE RECRUITMENT OF THE IRISH REGIMENTS ABROAD

Eighteenth-century Ireland had harsh Penal Laws, which limited opportunities for Catholics at home and forced many to turn to military service abroad. The Penal Code prevented Catholics from carrying arms, then a matter of personal honour and protection. They also had to sell their horse to a Protestant for £5; a horse was a forerunner of the performance car today and was a status symbol at the time. Mixed marriages were forbidden. Catholics were deprived of the vote and were banned from the professions and from educating their children, although in many cases this was impossible to enforce, as Catholic hedge schools sprang up and children were sent to the Continent to further their studies.

The Act to Prevent the Further Growth of Popery 1704 was the most important single statute and was cleverly designed to break the power of Catholic families. The Act directed that when a landowner died, his land was to be divided equally (or gavelled) between all his sons to break up the estate. To ensure the eldest son inherited the estate intact, Catholics sent their younger sons abroad. Some entered the priesthood while others joined the Irish Brigade. The eldest son was also required to convert to Protestantism to inherit his family's estate, or would otherwise forfeit it.[1] 'The estimated fall in Catholic landownership decreased from 14 per cent in 1700 to 5 per cent in 1780 but this was not due to more Catholics losing their lands to Protestants, but to Catholics becoming Protestants to retain their land.'² In some families, to ensure estates remained in the family, a system existed for generations whereby the eldest son was brought up a Protestant and the other sons as Catholics. The younger sons were typically sent to France and joined the Irish Brigade. Far from suppressing Jacobitism, these laws assisted in pushing the sons of the gentry to France and into the army of James III, 'the Pretender'.

Ownership of land was the basis of wealth, social standing and power, as landlords received income through rent and gained respect in their community. Irish people have always had a special attachment to their land and passing it down to subsequent generations was always of paramount concern. The Wild Geese lost their ancestral estates by leaving and many cherished hopes of getting their estates back. Charles O'Brien, the 6th Lord Clare, Marshal of France and military governor of Languedoc, lost 80,000 acres but kept an exact rent roll, which he would find useful when his estates (he hoped) were restored.³ He also maintained close links with his native County Clare and 'knew all the private affairs of the local landed gentlemen as if he had lived among them'.⁴ The flamboyant Chevalier Charles Wogan from Kildare was governor of La Mancha province (outside Madrid), made famous by Cervante's early seventeenth-century novel *Don Quixote*. Walsh wanted to return home and claimed that even after achieving fame and fortune abroad he 'should have a better estate at home than ever his [Don Quixote's] fathers enjoyed and a tomb too where no man of honour may be ashamed to lie'.⁵ As late as 1786, the authorities in Ireland were alarmed when they learned that Chevalier Thomas O'Gorman, a captain in the French Irish Brigade, was collecting portfolios of confiscated Catholic estates dating from the time of Cromwell with a view to restoring them to their Catholic owners.⁶

Chevalier Thomas O'Gorman (1732–1809) was a native Irish speaker who came from a prominent Gaelic aristocratic family from Castletown, Co. Clare. He was educated in the Irish College in Paris and joined the Irish Brigade and was knighted by Louis XVI. He married into the French aristocracy and inherited vast vineyards in Burgundy. The colourful O'Gorman was a noted antiquarian and genealogist. He produced pedigrees by studying medieval Gaelic genealogical manuscripts (such as the *Great Book of Lecan* and the *Four Masters*) for many Irish gentry officers on the Continent who needed proofs of their nobility for advancement in society or in the army. O'Gorman lost his estate in Burgundy in the turmoil of the French Revolution and returned to Ireland to retire. In 1785 he arranged for the transfer from the Irish College in Paris of the fourteenth-century Irish-language *Book of Ballymote* and the *Book of Lecan* to the Royal Irish Academy in Dublin where they still remain.

In the eighteenth century, the economic power and prestige of many once prominent Catholic families had been virtually wiped out. In 1739, a pamphleteer declared that 'there are not twenty Papists in Ireland who possess each £1,000 a year in land'. Thirty years later in 1772, the Viceroy Lord Townsend noted that 'the laws against popery have so far operated that at this day there is no popish family remaining of any great weight from landed property.'[7] Their decline was also highlighted in the 1770s by Arthur Young's *Tour of Ireland*: 'The lineal descendents of great families, men possessed of vast property are now to be found all over the kingdom, working as cottiers',[8] although even with their land and wealth gone this 'underground gentry' were still held in high esteem by the local people. The wealth of the chief of the O'Connor clan from Roscommon (a direct descendent of the eleventh-century King of Connaught), Young stated, were 'formerly so great, are reduced to three or four hundred pounds a year, the family having fared in the revolutions of so many ages much worse than the O'Neils and O'Briens. The common people pay him the greatest respect, and send him presents of cattle … they consider him as the prince of a people involved in one common ruin.'[9] In 1790 the French consul to Ireland, Charles Coquebert de Montbret, mirrored Young's observations and 'was astonished to find on visiting Ireland that even French army families like Dillon and Lally were mere tenant farmers on Kirwan's estate at Cregg in Galway, while the Mullays were simply 'peasants'.[10]

The ordinary Catholic farm labourer lived a precarious existence, being exposed to bad harvests which led to several Irish famines in the eighteenth century. A soldier's life could be an attractive (but dangerous) option as one could lose life or limb – or both. Migration was always a complex social issue; some joined yearning for adventure or to escape family pressures or the law. Others joined the French and Spanish army to help liberate Ireland from British rule. Recruits received a cash bounty on joining and were paid around the same rate as a labourer. In many cases, uncles or other family members brought other relatives over into the Irish regiments.

There were also limited opportunities for the sons of Catholic gentry families. They could enter the Catholic Church, become a medical doctor (one of the few professions open to Catholics), or join an Irish regiment on the Continent. All three options necessitated leaving Ireland and all were expensive. Catholics were prevented from entering Trinity College Dublin until 1793 and as there was no seminary (until 1795) students had to train on the Continent. By contrast, the choices of their Protestant counterparts were wider; they could take a degree in Trinity; be called to the Bar; purchase a commission in the British army or navy or buy a seat in Parliament.[11]

For the Catholic gentry, an army career was attractive as entry into the officer class improved the family's social standing in their communities. The cash-strapped family, reduced to middlemen or tenants on their ancestral estates, could restore some of their former status, dignity and pride, by having a son serving as an officer on the Continent. Many were sent to France to acquire and cultivate the gentlemanly skills necessary for advancement in life: 'In terms of prestige, the finest career for the younger son of a Catholic landowner was that of a French officer.'[12] The sole cavalry regiment of Fitzjames' horse was the most prestigious; Dillon's was also highly prized as it was known for speaking the best French.

The younger son who was training to be an officer still had to be supplemented with money sent from home.[13] Officers could only afford to marry at the rank of captain, which yielded £100 a year but promotion was slow.[14] Officer cadets sometimes served as common soldiers until a commission became available. The Liberator Daniel O'Connell's uncle, Captain Maurice O'Connell and Captain Richard Hennessy of Cognac fame, served in the ranks for several years before their promised cadetships were procured.[15]

A career could be forged in the French *Marine Royale* for those with the right connections. A naval ensign or midshipman could rise in five years to lieutenant and then captain a small frigate. The more ambitious might even rise to the coveted rank of *capitaine de vaisseau*, commanding one of the three-deck battleships of the line.[16] John MacNamara from Co. Clare rose to vice-admiral and commander of the port of Rochefort. His aggressive naval tactics helped to ensure one of the few French naval victories during the War of the Austrian Succession. In 1745, he commanded the *Invincible* and successfully engaged four British ships of the line in a sustained sea-fight and beat them off.[17] Another kinsman, Count Henry MacNamara, commanded the French navy in the Indian Ocean. During the French Revolution, he was denounced as a foreign aristocrat and assassinated by revolutionary soldiers of the French garrison in the Ile de France, in modern-day Mauritius.[18]

Service in the Spanish navy, the *Armada Española*, was not as highly regarded as the French navy although it provided good promotional prospects for those with ambition. Captain O'Donnell, a nephew of Hugh O'Donnell the Earl of Tyrone, captained a man-of-war in the Spanish Mediterranean Fleet before being killed at the Battle of Taragonna in 1642 during the Thirty Years War.[19] In the 1750s, Daniel O'Kuoney from Co. Clare rose to the rank of admiral in the Spanish navy.[20] Enrique MacDonnell captained a Spanish man-of-war at the Battle of Trafalgar and also rose to admiral.[21]

The Irish even ventured into Catherine the Great's Imperial Russian navy, which had embarked on a series of expansion plans to rival its European neighbours in the 1800s and sought Irish acumen in building up her fleet. Several Irishmen became admirals and went on to enjoy illustrious careers there, such as Admirals Lacy, Kennedy, Tate and O'Dwyer, along with Commodore Cronin and Rear-Admiral O'Brien.[22]

The Irish not only served within their own Irish regiments, as thousands of footloose Irish swordsmen were scattered in various regiments throughout the Continent. In 1813, after the French defeat at the Battle of Nivelle during the Peninsular War, an English officer walking among the wounded French soldiers came across a dying officer of an elite French light infantry *Chasseur* regiment, who called out to him in English. He discovered that the officer was an Irishman, who asked him to pass some papers:

> If you are an English officer, you can give me comfort in my dying hour. Yesterday I had a son, we were in the same regiment, and fought side by side; twice he saved my life by turning aside the bayonet that had threatened it and when at last I fell, he tried to bear me to a place

of safety, but at the moment, the enemy bore down upon our ranks, and I was separated in the *mêlée* from my gallant boy. Should he be a prisoner in your army, for the sake of humanity, endeavour to discover his destination, and convey to him these papers.[23]

The English officer sought out the man's son among the French prisoners of war but found out that he had sadly died of his wounds the previous day.

Miles Byrne, who served in Napoleon's Irish Legion, also recalled the career of Dubliner Chevalier Murphy, who left his job as a clerk in Thomas Street, Dublin and emigrated to France. He joined a regular French regiment of the line and rose up through the officer ranks, was decorated with the Legion of Honour before rising to inspector general in the French army.[24]

British trade policies maintained Ireland as an economic backwater, reliant on England, on the pretence she might break away and ally herself to either Catholic Spain or France. English Navigation Acts placed embargos on French and Spanish imports, which only boosted smuggling and made it more lucrative for the Irish. Many notable Catholic families, such as the O'Sullivans, Gooths and O'Connells of Co. Kerry sustained themselves through some of the leanest years of penal times through this contraband trade; one of the O'Connell's quipped that 'their faith, their education, their wine and their clothing were equally contraband.'[25]

The well-established trading routes running from Galway and Limerick along the southern and western seaboards to the French centres of Bordeaux and La Rochelle had been brisk since the Middle Ages.[26] Illicit trade resulted in French wines, silks and tobacco being smuggled into Ireland, and counterfeit money, pirated copies of books, untaxed wool, salted pork and beef, butter and Wild Geese recruits smuggled out. This cargo was carried by handy, especially fitted-out armed sloops and cutters, which plied the coasts of Rush in Co. Dublin, Kerry, Clare and Galway. Privately owned armed vessels (known as privateers) operated under licence by carrying *lettres de marque*, legitimising the taking of enemy ships as prizes in wartime. A former officer of Dillon's Regiment, Luke Ryan from Rush, the famous captain of the *Black Prince*, was commissioned as a privateer carrying French *lettres de marque* in the American War of Independence.[27] Ryan was credited with the capture of 'more vessels belonging to Great Britain than any other single vessel during the war.'[28] In many cases, smuggling was combined with wrecking as ships with unknown colours sailed along the Kerry coasts at their own peril as wreckers would tie a lantern to the neck of a horse and set the horse out to graze. From a distance the light rising and falling was similar to a light in a distant ship, which had the effect of steering the ship onto the rocks, and then wreckers would steal whatever booty was onboard.

The British were also concerned about the high number of priests training on the Continent, many of whom had strong Jacobite sympathies and were suspected of being implicated in recruitment. The clergy in Ireland were an influential force and they promoted service in the countries of France and Spain, advocating that by serving in Catholic armies they were remaining faithful to their Catholic faith. Nicholas Taaffe addressed a petition to Maria Theresa and Emperor Francis of Austria, claiming that he was forced to leave Ireland

> Because he was afraid that his descendants pressed by the Penal Laws would not resist the temptation of becoming Protestants. He therefore took refuge to a Catholic country where his ancestors were well known by the military services they had rendered at different intervals to the House of Austria. He had abandoned his relations and his estate and the rank and liberty he had in his country to prevent his descendants from deserting a religion to which their Imperial Majesties so fervently adhered: he did not repent of having acted thus, but it would be a great grief to him if before his death he had not the consolation to see he had not ruined his family.[29]

There were around thirty Irish Colleges on the Continent from the sixteenth century and the largest and most influential one was the Irish College in Paris. The colleges not only trained the clergy, they also acted as unofficial embassies by liaising with the authorities at home and also educated the Brigade's children. They lobbied foreign courts and provided genealogical pedigrees and certificates of marriage and baptisms. In return, the Irish regiments financially supported the colleges, through bursaries and gifts, and many soldiers submitted a portion of their wages to them. They also supported the Irish language by teaching priests Irish, as they were required to be proficient in the language when they returned to their Irish-speaking parishes. The presence of Irish clergy choosing to remain on the Continent and bringing extended family members over through the uncle–nephew axis further fortified links between Ireland and the Continent.

Ambitious Irish parents groomed their children for emigration to France from a young age. It was quite typical for a 12-year-old child to be sent to an Irish college abroad and from there he might enter the priesthood or join an Irish regiment as an officer cadet.[30] After a few years' army service, an officer might venture into business. Irishmen could claim French nationality subject to ten years' satisfactory military service and they were given similar rights in Spain.[31] Naturalisation was an important privilege as it gave the recipient licence to engage in the lucrative French and Spanish colonial trade. An officer's Irish background was deemed by some to be politically neutral and with his linguistic skills he was ideally positioned to trade with the British Empire and the continental powers, especially with the opportunities presented in the New World. Many Irish trading families became successful and established themselves in the trading ports of Cadiz, Dunkirk, La Rochelle and Ostende, and elsewhere. They channelled trade into Catholic hands back home in Ireland and also used their wealth for political purposes and funded Bonnie Prince Charlie's expedition to Scotland in the '45'.

The bogeyman of the Protestant Ascendancy in Ireland for much of the eighteenth century was the Pope and the Catholic king, James III. The French Irish Brigade in particular 'remained the focal point of Catholic fantasies and Protestant alarms'.[32] The Protestants feared an invasion by these troops and the risk of losing their rights and lands to Catholics should James III claim the throne. In the early eighteenth century, France maintained 250,000 troops in wartime and in peacetime a standing army of 120,000.[33] When Britain was at war with France, the authorities in Ireland tried to prevent recruitment to the French armies, and in peacetime there was no great need for high numbers anyway. At the same time, they were keen to remove idle swordsmen from the countryside where it was feared they might question the political status quo and join the illegal militant Whiteboys; even worse, they might even get the landlord's daughter 'into trouble'. They were especially keen on seeing the back of those young bucks from dispossessed Catholic gentry families, who still held great sway with the local people. They recognised that not one in twenty returned, but despite this they were aware that those leaving might yet return as an invader.

Recruitment into the Irish Brigade of France peaked in the 1720s. For example, Dillon's Regiment received 800 recruits from Ireland when it was stationed in the northern French town of Sedan in 1729.[34] Dublin Castle frequently exaggerated the numbers recruited, which only increased hysteria, when even seasonal workers travelling to England were suspected of joining the 'Pretender', James III. This fear became so great that recruiting for the Irish regiments abroad became a capital offence. Prior to the Scottish Jacobite Rising of 1715, Joseph Sullivan, an Irishman in the French army, was hanged for paying two English soldiers to abjure their oath to George I and join the 'Pretender'. Irishmen were recruited into the Irish regiments abroad with the promise that they would be home within a year to expel the English. In 1715, the authorities arrested and hanged some of the 150 men who had gathered on the north Dublin Hill of Howth to board a ship to bring them to France. In 1726, Captain Moses Newland from Co. Carlow was publicly hanged in St Stephen's Green in Dublin for recruiting 200 men to join the Irish Brigade in Spain.

The British applied diplomatic pressure on France and Spain, calling for the disbandment of the Irish Brigades. This was stepped up in times of threat to Britain's national security. Protestant alarm often resulted in a knee-jerk reaction with additional anti-Catholic laws passed upon invasion scares. After Irish success at the Battle of Fontenoy, a law was passed preventing those serving in France or Spain from holding property in Ireland and military service in France was made a treasonable offence in 1756. Many officers and their families were very concerned and were reluctant to return home on leave. Some officers sought legal advice before they proceeded to set foot in Ireland, and Richard Hennessy gave this as a reason for leaving the army, before founding his cognac distillery.[35]

There has always been controversy surrounding the numbers of Irishmen who served on the Continent. By 1762, as many as 450,000 Irishmen died in the service of France, according to the Irish Brigade's chaplain, Abbé MacGeoghegan. Chevalier Richard Gaydon recorded that Dillon's lost over 6,000 men by 1738; applying this figure over the other Irish regiments in France, this suggests 40,000 casualties overall. In the same period, Sir Charles Wogan claimed 120,000 Irishmen died for France. However, it is difficult to estimate the numbers who served abroad, with the exception of the well-documented migrations of the Flight of the Wild Geese in 1690.[36] Recruitment into the Irish regiments in France numbered around 1,000 per year in the 1720s and 1730s, and tapered off thereafter.[37] A recent study suggested that just under 25,000 Irish-born rank and file served in the French Irish Brigade from 1690 to 1791.[38] Although these numbers exclude officers and the sons of Irishmen born in France who served, they nevertheless appear surprisingly low, considering they include Mountcashel's Brigade and Sarsfield's Wild Geese. Collectively, up to 50,000 Irish-born officers and men may have served in the armies of Spain, France and Austria, from 1690 through to the disbandment of Spain's Irish Brigade in 1818. By including the sons and grandsons of Irish-born soldiers these figures could be doubled. It is impossible to calculate how many died in service, but we can safely assume that many did not die in their beds.

The Irish Catholic gentry contributed around 100 officers yearly to the armies of Europe. At any one time, there were around 525 Irish officers serving on the Continent in the eighteenth-century; 500 in France and Spain and 25 in Austria.[39] The Irish would have exerted significant political influence, especially concerning any plans for an invasion of Ireland and a Catholic restoration of James. It was not surprising that the British authorities were alarmed. Putting this figure into perspective there were 2,000 commissions in the British army in the 1750s. Irish Catholics were not permitted to serve as officers or as private soldiers in the British army. However, even if Catholics had been allowed to join the officer ranks in the British army, they would have had to compete with Scottish, English and Irish Protestant families. Another important fact was that commissions in the British army had to be purchased. These would have been out of reach of cash-strapped families of Catholic gentry trying to keep their head above water and it would have been unlikely that they would have procured 500 commissions. On the Continent, commissions were not only purchased; kinship or recommendations also acquired them. This system was exploited well by Catholic gentry families in Cork and Kerry, who received commissions through the mediation of better-connected relatives. Even if Catholic gentlemen had been permitted to join the British army, opportunities would still have been better on the Continent.[40]

Wild Geese recruits came primarily from the south-western counties of Clare, Tipperary, Cork and Waterford. Recruiting sergeants developed various means to recruit young men to serve abroad, ranging from bribery to corruption to press-ganging. Some recruits were plied with drink, and were attracted by the flashy uniforms and stories of adventure and glory. The instant gratification of receiving a cash bounty when signing up quickly sealed the deal for many. Irish Catholics in the British armed forces, where military service was harsh with frequent floggings for minor misdemeanours such as tardiness, drunkenness and insubordination, were also recruited into the brigades among captured prisoners of war. The historian J.C. O'Callaghan tended to over-emphasise Irish recruitment from the British army, claiming that many had enlisted to gain passage to the Continent, to join the Irish Brigade of France.

Irish officers with good local connections back home in Ireland were also particularly valued on recruitment missions.[41] Irish recruits were especially valuable as they helped to preserve the Brigade's Irish ethos, now that foreigners increasingly filled the ranks. In 1745, due to high Irish losses after Fontenoy, Captain McDonough and Captain O'Brien were sent to their native Clare and recruited a couple of hundred men to fill up the ranks. The Irish Brigade's commander, Lord Clare, was delighted and wrote proudly to McDonough from Paris:

> With your assistance and O'Brien's the ranks are near filled up; the Brigade is now in a high state of discipline, and as fine a body of fellows as ever stepped on parade; I would not give up the command of them for any honours that could be conferred on me, it would delight you to hear another Irish shout from the Brigade.[42]

MacDonough subsequently married a local girl on this recruiting mission, and was permitted to remain in Ireland. He was one of the few Wild Geese to die in his native land and lies buried in the old graveyard in Killelagh in Doolin, Co. Clare.

The whole nature of recruiting changed during the eighteenth century. In 1726, the French army began regular medical examinations for recruits and as many as one-third were rejected as being medically unfit. In 1750, Lord Clare as Inspector of Recruiting implemented regulations on recruitment following the hanging of several Irish recruiting officers in London and Dover. Recruiting sergeants were stationed in Calais 'to enlist none but handsome men, not under 5 feet 2 inches in height, well limbed and at least 35 years of age.'[43] Spain, although an ally of France, competed for Irish recruits. The Spanish Embassy in London at times walked a fine diplomatic line: acting as recruiting agents while also maintaining cordial diplomatic relations with the British authorities; but recruitment into the Spanish army was at best irregular.

However, from the 1750s onwards the Irish contingent in France and Spain declined steadily in the ranks and plummeted dramatically in a generation. Out of a regimental strength of 3,742 men in 1729: 71 per cent were Irish, this reduced to 67 per cent in 1737 and only 5 per cent in 1776.[44] A controle of Fitzjames' horse in 1737 showed that 80 per cent were Irish-born.[45] New recruits raised after heavy Irish losses from the battles of Fontenoy and Lafelt were mainly non-Irish and changed the whole character of the corps. Irishmen formed the minority in the ranks thereafter due to disease, battle casualties and losses through natural wastage. Post-1747, mainly Belgian Walloons, Dutchmen, Germans, Flemish and Frenchmen filled the ranks, officered by Irishmen. Daniel O'Connor wrote home in 1756 declaring: 'in asking a survey of the state of things here I look upon myself as in a society of foreigners, perhaps there is not a tenth part of us Irish and our national enthusiasm is no more.'[46] According to the muster rolls of the *Annuaire militaire* of 1793 nearly all officers in the French Irish Brigade were Irishmen.[47]

It also did not help that the difficulties in transporting recruits overseas made it easier and cheaper to recruit from other countries sharing land borders with France and Spain. Service in the Irish Brigade of Spain had also lost some of its prestige, with poor promotion prospects, high desertion rates, bad food and irregular pay. The Irish regiments served all over Spain, North Africa and in Spanish America which made it difficult for the Irish to establish connections in a particular area. In 1740, the Spanish Irish Brigade mustered around 2,700 men. The Irish officer contingent numbered 200, and in the ranks numbered just 65 men as most recruits were Italian, French, Spanish and Portuguese. Despite this, in common with their compatriots in the French service, the Irish regiments in Spain were still officered by Irishmen or sons of Irishmen.

Other reasons can account for the decline in Irish numbers: 'The Great Frost' of 1739–40 which caused the subsequent famine wiped out nearly one-quarter of the Catholic population. The economy of Ireland improved steadily from the 1740s; wages rose and emigration to the American colonies was more attainable, and, though still expensive, the price of passage halved in the 1770s.[48] After Charles Edward's failure to restore the Stuart throne in the Scottish Rebellion in 1745, the chances of a Catholic Restoration retreated and military service abroad was no longer an attractive option. In 1762 Irish officers in the French service transported 334 Irish Newfoundlanders to France and proposed forming them into a new Irish corps – the Royal Marine Irlandaise, but only just over two dozen choose to enlist.[49]

By the 1780s an army career had lost much of its shine, as officers' complaints of the time centred on 'the fewness of promotion prospects and low salaries'.[50] This was exacerbated in peacetime when regiments were reduced and officers were retained on a half-pay footing; in this environment, progression to senior rank could be slow and unsteady. The exploits of the Brigade were closely reported in the Dublin press. The Irish were used as crack troops and were often chosen for the most dangerous missions. In 1735, while campaigning in the War of the Polish Succession, General Dillon volunteered the Irish infantry regiments of France to cover the retreat of the French army against the Germans, which they successfully carried out when other French regiments had refused to undertake 'so hot a service'.[51] Perhaps the high casualty rates put potential recruits off, when other options were becoming available.

The number of Irishmen serving on the Continent tapered off when the Catholic-ban in the British army was lifted in the 1750s. During the American War of Independence, the British were keen to yield to Catholic demands, as they feared revolution in Ireland. This led to the Catholic Relief Acts of 1778 and 1782 being passed which dismantled some of the legal discrimination against Catholics.[52] Several years later, the First Emancipation Act in 1793 lifted the ban which prevented Irish Catholics becoming officers in the British army. The British wanted to address Catholic grievances further and pressurised the Irish Parliament to allow them the vote and to enter Trinity, but these were met with resistance. However, they allowed Catholic recruitment when they needed manpower and especially when the regiments were posted far way. The British did not trust Irish soldiers serving in Europe as they had little allegiance to the British and when captured they frequently defected to the enemy. In 1705, a corps was formed in Lille in the French army from Irish deserters of the British army.[53] In the 1750s French and Indian War, the British Commander in the Americas voiced concerns that most deserters were Irish, who had defected. During the American War of Independence, 350 Irish Catholics who formed part of the captured British garrison in St Eustatius in the West Indies joined the French Irish Brigade. The Duke of Wellington wrote in his despatches during the Napoleonic Wars that 'the deserters from the British regiments are primarily Irishmen.' It cost a great deal of money and effort to recruit, pay, train, dress, arm and equip a soldier, and to transport these troops long distances overseas. If this soldier 'turned', it represented a double blow, not to mention the disclosure of sensitive military intelligence to the enemy, which was a serious threat to success in any campaign.

Napoleon was gravely concerned at the prospect of Irishmen joining the British army, as he was keen to tap into this manpower himself. When the Catholic question was first raised he wrote to his Irish doctor Dr O'Meara from St Helena that he 'would have given fifty millions to be assured, that it would not be granted for it would have entirely ruined my projects upon Ireland'.[54] Due to the easing of the Penal Laws, 36,000 Irishmen served in the British army against France in the French Revolutionary Wars (1793–1801) and many fought in the Napoleonic Wars (1803–15). The Irish regiments in the British army 'crowned themselves in glory' in the Peninsular War. Napoleon's Imperial Eagle was a prize on the battlefield and was irreverently referred to as 'the cuckoo' in the British army. In 1811, two Irishmen serving with the 87th (The Prince of Wales Own) Irish Regiment of Foot desperately scrambled and hacked their way through to take an Eagle during the Battle of Barossa, the first one taken by the British in the war. Ensign Edward Keogh was killed in this attempt; Sergeant Patrick Masterson, from Roscommon, bayoneted the eagle bearer, Frenchman Sous-Lieutenant Edme Gauillemin, and succeeded in snatching the Eagle, memorably quipping: *'Bejabers Boys! I have the cuckoo!'*[55] Two years later, during the decisive Allied victory of the Battle of Vitoria, the same Irish regiment, the 87th Foot, took the baton of a Marshal of France from the French commander, Major-General Jourdan, which Wellington sent back to the Prince Regent, the future King George IV as a prized trophy.

It is somehow ironic that the Irish contributed directly to Napoleon's downfall. Irishmen were over-represented within the ranks of the British army and under-represented in the officer class, reflecting the political status quo back in Ireland. For the ordinary Irish Catholic, joining the British army was an escape out of poverty as there were few other opportunities available in an undeveloped Irish economy. The ordinary redcoat in the British army was more often than not an Irishman. It has been estimated they comprised 40 per cent of Wellington's army at Waterloo, where the 27th (Inniskilling's) Foot, ordered to hold a strategic crossroads, were literally found dead in square there. For this action, Wellington praised them for saving his centre line at Waterloo.[56] Indeed, the Irish foot soldier and the self-loading rifle were credited with the expansion and security of the British Empire. In 1829, when the Catholic Emancipation Bill was before the British House of Lords, the Duke of Wellington acknowledged that it was 'mainly to the Irish Catholic that we [the British] owe our preeminence in our military career'.[57] Irish Catholic recruitment in the British army lacked a political ideology, and was fuelled by economic necessity, and by a lack of opportunities at home, not unlike Irish service on the Continent. Yet an essential difference remained, best encapsulated by the historian Richard Holmes who recognised that 'the uncomfortable fact remained that Ireland was a country under occupation by the very army in which Irishmen – officers and soldiers alike – played such an important role.'[58] Irishmen serving in the British army and navy from the Seven Years War in 1756 right up to the Battle of Waterloo in 1815 only maintained British bondage back home in Ireland by scuppering Franco-Irish designs for her liberation. England it seemed had the upper hand!

2

THE CHARACTER OF THE BRIGADE

The Irish regiments on the Continent had a great *esprit de corps,* and were a home away from home where family members brought others into the regiment. Many recruits had been sent abroad while they were still teenagers and they knew no other life; the regiment replaced family far away back home in Ireland. They were a close-knit community and tended to socialise and marry within their own circle, their offspring frequently continuing the family military tradition. The sons of serving soldiers joined the regiment alongside their fathers, sometimes from a very young age, where 'officers and men formed a band of brothers and no friction ever occurred between the regiments. Each was a home for homeless exiles; and it was quite common to find three generations serving simultaneously.'[1]

The Irish had their own drinking-dens in garrison towns, where they must have cut a distinctive figure in their dashing red uniforms, in contrast to French regiments of the line who were mainly dressed in the traditional *gris-mesle* or light grey. They were a cosmopolitan corps as they comprised many different nationalities. By the 1750s, with the Irish rank and file dwindling, the Brigade's Irish ethos was maintained by serving second- and third-generation Irishmen. Nationality was not just linked to place of birth but due to parentage; Colonel José O'Hare although born in France was 'a national of the Kingdom of Ireland born in the Kingdom of France'.[2] In the 1750s, the nationality of the

French-born Spanish Prime Minister Ricardo Wall, an ex-officer of Hibernia's Regiment of Spain, was also described as 'of the Irish nation'.[3]

The Irish were popular, and Irish culture, music and dancing, were very much alive in the regiments. They played the Irish game of hurling and introduced the game to their French allies: 'I stayed with Neil,' wrote the Marquis de Lostanges, 'who explained to me all the rules of your game of hurling.'[4] Two years after the Battle of Fontenoy, soldiers of the Brigade played a game on the battlefield in honour of their fallen comrades. The Irish regiments were presided over by a patriarchal proprietor-colonel, his wife at times playing a matriarchal role. The widows of fallen soldiers received a pension or were given a licence to beg from the king.[5] After long years of service, many entered the old soldiers' home, Les Invalides, in Paris. Eoghan O'hAnnracháin has calculated that 2,500 Irishmen were admitted to the Invalides between Louis XIV's reign in 1630 to the French Revolution in 1789. The old soldiers met in the Luxembourg Gardens in Paris and reminisced about their glory days in the Brigades. The Irish in France tended to retire to Cambrai, close to Flanders, where their friends and families in the Irish regiments were stationed. The Irish in Austria retired to Graz and Prague.[6]

It was prestigious for France to have foreign regiments in her service. By the 1750s, one-fifth of the French army comprised foreigners, spread over the foreign regiments of the Swiss, German, Italian, Irish and Belgian Walloons. Louis XV issued a royal decree, whereby commands in the Irish regiments were to be given in English, and the other foreign regiments were to use French, German and Italian. These English commands were, one supposes, interlaced with Irish and French. Research available indicates that the Irish language was widely spoken, as Richard Hennessy claimed to have learned a lot of his Irish while serving in the Brigade.[7] Count Thomas Lally, the son of an Irishman and although born in France, roused the Brigade at Fontenoy with cries in Irish: '*Cuimhnígí ar Luimneach is ar fheill na Sasananch!*' ('Remember Limerick and Saxon perfidy!') prior to their charge at Fontenoy.[8] Many rank-and-file recruits emanated from remote Irish-speaking regions where they would only have spoken English as a second language, if at all.

The Irish language was always the language of the old Gaelic aristocracy but it had become the language of the poor at home in Ireland. However, it was spoken in the company of generals and emperors in palaces across the Continent. In a classic example of a *faux pas*, the celebrated Irish tenor Michael Kelly provided the following anecdote. In 1783, recently arriving from Ireland, he was in the company of Major-Generals Henry O'Donnell and James D'Alton, together with General Maurice Kavanagh and Emperor Joseph II of Austria at the Imperial Summer Palace in Schonbrunn, Vienna. D'Alton was a native Irish speaker and mentioned that no other language was a better accompaniment to music than Irish, with the exception of Italian. Kavanagh then said something in Irish to Kelly, which Kelly did not understand. The Emperor turned to him and asked, did he not understand the language of his own country? Kelly replied: 'Please, your Majesty, none but the lower of the Irish people speak Irish.' The Emperor laughed loudly. Kelly immediately recognised he had put his foot in it and luckily the high-ranking Irish officers in his company did not overhear, or pretended not to.[9]

After Mountcashel's Irish Brigade arrived in France in 1690 the Irish gained a reputation of being the crack troops of the Continental armies. The French Irish Brigade was the best fighting-unit of all the foreign regiments, and was considered one of the best in the French army as a whole. In terms of reputation, the Spanish Irish Brigade was not far behind them. 'For the first half of the 18th century, France had the largest army in Europe, but its troops were poorly trained and had too many officers who owed their rank to patronage rather than personal skill.'[10] This was in contrast to the culturally separated Irish Brigades who operated semi-independently within the larger, generally inefficient armies of France and Spain. This autonomy enabled them to organise themselves into efficient well-trained units as they controlled the promotions, based on merit, of their most capable officers below the rank of colonel.[11]

What were the attributes that made them successful soldiers? The Irish had traditionally been a hardy, proud, war-like people since Celtic times and they were by nature tribal and loyal to their Gaelic chieftains. They extended this sense of fidelity to the colonel-proprietor of the Irish regiments and to the Catholic King James. They were warmly called *les oies sauvages* (Wild Savages) and French mothers in Provence and Brittany were said to threaten their children for misbehaving by bringing them not to the bogeyman-but to *les Irlandais*. Those Irish troops who were demobbed out of the French army following the Peace of Ryswick (1698) joined the ranks of the Bavarian army and were accused of introducing 'a spirit of brutality, gambling, drunkenness and pugnacity which had never before been seen in that army'.[12] The French observed during the Jacobite War that none of the Irish musketeers was shorter than 5 feet 6 inches in height, with the grenadiers (heavy infantry) and pikemen being even taller. They recognised that, with proper training and leadership, they could be depended on to show courage, and their background of rural poverty helped them to withstand hardship and the rigours of military service.[13] Twenty years earlier in 1669, France supported the Greeks against the Turks in the Cretan War. After the besieged city of Candia (modern-day Heraklion) fell into Turkish hands, the French commander, Marshal de Bellefonds regretted that his Italian troops were not replaced with 'more solid and better trained' Irish regiments, but he had not enough time to ship them from Flanders.[14] It would have just been the kind of holy crusade the Irish would have relished.

Irish peasants worked the land, reared on a diet rich in potatoes, milk, bread and oats and ate more meat than the French. In the 1780s, Arthur Young observed that children in Ireland were better fed than in England, but walked bare foot and were dressed in rags. The Irish were physically fit, and stronger than the average Frenchman and were 'taller than the English'.[15] In 1798, French uniforms sent with General Humbert were too small for many of the Irish rebels. The ancient Celts were famous for their horsemanship and a mounted Irish trooper with Fitzjames' Horse must have appeared a formidable sight to the average Frenchman.

The Irish further developed their military expertise built over years of campaigning. 'The Irish soldiers' knowledge and practice of military discipline along with their possession of a specific technical knowledge of artillery, engineering or sanitation meant that they were highly valued and they played a significant part in the reorganisation of antiquated continental armies.'[16] The battle-scarred Lieutenant General Alexander O'Reilly from Co. Meath played a major role in modernising Spain's antiquated army. He established the Spanish Military School in Avila, which studied war as a science by focusing on engineering, infantry and cavalry tactics. He also adopted Prussian training methods for the entire Spanish army. These included creating a constant musket barrage by means of companies marching up in line three-deep; the first rank would fire, and then step behind, enabling the other two lines to discharge their muskets efficiently.[17] In 1728, the acumen of the Irish soldier was recognised by the English pamphleteer Forman, who advocated the disbandment of the Brigades in France and Spain:

> They are season'd to dangers, and so perfected in the art of war, that, not only the Sergeants and Corporals, but even the private men, can make very good officers, upon occasion. To their valour, in a great measure, France owes, not only most of what trophies she gain'd in the late war, but even her own preservation.[18]

The Irish were obsessed with their genealogical pedigrees, as social advancement in France and Spain depended on proving one had noble birth and so officers had to prove a noble pedigree to get on in the French army. 'The lesser, usually untitled nobility filled the lower levels of command, but everywhere the senior posts were the preserve of the titled, and often the court, aristocracy.'[19] To gain entry into this elite court circle, a candidate had to prove his family ranked among the nobility for at least 300 years.[20] In 1780, the highly ambitious General Daniel O'Connell (then serving as a colonel in the French army) wrote to his brother, Maurice, in Derrynane, Co. Kerry explaining his predicament:

> There is a matter of the greatest consequence to promoting my fortunes and expectations. I mean that of my genealogy. This is a point so much looked at in this society that without it a man, whatever his merit or capacity, will scarce ever rank among the great. It's indispensably necessary to be present at Court, to roll with the nobility and to be admitted to that honour a genealogy must be produced.[21]

There were numerous requests made by the Irish in France to the Heraldic King of Arms in Dublin for certificates of noble pedigree, which peaked around 1750. After the failure of the Jacobite Cause in the Scottish Rising of 1745, the Irish realised their estates at home would never be recovered and resigned themselves to pursuing their lives abroad. The Cabinet L'Ordre du St Esprit (the French Herald's Office) and the Juge d'armes (the verifiers of French noble titles) rejected some Irish pedigrees prepared by the Dublin Herald. This may have been due to the lack of supporting evidence, caused by the ravages of time, war and the confiscations of estates. The O'Connells were among the smaller clans in County Kerry who had been absorbed into the more powerful MacCarthys and therefore had no clan pedigree. The lack of documentation verifying a noble lineage could sometimes be overcome by possession of an estate. Bernard Cherin, the French Herald, spent four years examining O'Connell's pedigree before attesting it genuine. He recognised that 'the bit of unconfiscated property held by Count O'Connell's direct ancestors without any title-deeds, by the mere prescriptive tenure of immemorial possession, was their only proof of ancient lineage, but in this country it was the most conclusive of all proofs.'[22]

Title deeds of confiscated estates written on old parchment did survive and were kept safely and were passed down to subsequent generations in the hope they would someday be recovered. Reynaldo McDonnell, the 3rd Earl of Antrim (a former colonel in the Irish Brigade of Spain) kept the title deeds of his confiscated estate of 8,500 acres in Glenarm, Co. Antrim in an old tin box. In 1763 he passed these lands 'which belong to my family and were those of my grandparents in the Kingdom of Ireland' to his children in his will. His estate was confiscated after McDonnell went to Spain in 1691 and was then owned by the Hollows Blades Company, one of the London guilds.[23]

Military service was harsh with recruits signing up for six years. This was extended to eight when the French army was reorganised in 1762. But in reality, service could range from a few weeks to several decades.[24] In general, soldiers ate better than in civilian life with daily rations of wine, meat and bread, although the quality was at times poor. The Irish were paid better than other French or foreign regiments (with the exception of the Swiss). After 1762, privates were paid eight sous daily, before stoppages, and deductions for food, uniforms, horses, etc.[25] However, payment was frequently late and in arrears, sometimes for many months, especially when on campaign.

Uniforms were made from cheap cotton, providing the wearer little protection from the elements, and were more showy than serviceable. They were supposed to be worn for three years but were frequently made to last many more; most were reduced to rags while on campaign. It has been said that there were three types of uniforms worn: those that were displayed on the uniform plates; those specified as per the regulations; and those that the soldiers actually wore. The Irish regiments of Spain wore their distinctive red uniforms (the Stuart colours), designating their allegiance to the Stuart cause. The Regiment of Hibernia wore red uniforms with facings (cuffs and collars) in green and Irlanda was faced in blue, as was Ultonia but with a black collar.[26] The battleflags or colours of Irlanda's, Ultonia's and Hibernia's were white with a red saltire cross of Burgundy and a crowned harp on a blue shield in the four cantons. They carried the following device on their colour for their bravery in 1744 during the Battle of Velletri: *'In Omnem Terram, exhivit sonos eorum'* ('Their sound hath gone forth into all the earth').

The Irish regiments of France also wore red uniforms in common with their compatriots in the Spanish service. Clare's were faced with yellow; Dillon's (black); Bulkeley's and Lally's (green); Fitzjames' and Rooth's (blue), and Berwick's (white). Each Irish regiment was named after its colonel-proprietor who owned the regiment and earned an income through granting commissions. The colours of the Irish infantry regiments of France reflected their origins in the Jacobite War. They also maintained the mottos and devices of the flags flown at the Boyne and at Aughrim. These consisted of a cross with a crowned Stuart harp, with the motto of the Earl of Antrim's Regiment *'In Hoc Signo Vinces'* ('In this sign we shall conquer').[27] The Irish flags were some of the most beautiful in the French army. Dillon's, in particular, was red and black with a crowned gold harp in the centre, sporting a white cravet in the hoist (to aid recognition on the battlefield) in common with other French regiments. The second flag was the Colonel's colour with the same devices as the regimental flag but on a white background. The sole Irish cavalry regiment serving abroad (the celebrated regiment of Fitzjames) carried a golden standard on a royal sun inscribed with the motto *'Nec Pluribus Impar'* ('Not unequal to many') similar to those carried by French cavalry.

Cavalry troopers wore heavy jackboots, which restricted movement and made them vulnerable when dismounted. They also wore the metal breastplate known as the cuirass, one of the last relics of medieval armour.[28] Troopers were heavily armed with basket-hilted cavalry sabres, carbines and a brace of pistols in the saddle holsters. Regulation footgear provided little protection from trench foot and frostbite. White linen gaiters were also hard to keep clean and were ill-suited to rough terrain. Heavy headgear of the period (usually in the form of the distinctive tricorn hat) was uncomfortable and ill-suited to the rain, and offered little protection from grapeshot and musket balls. To add to their misery, they marched lugging 64 pounds of heavy kit around, carrying their cumbersome five-foot French issue Charleville musket. Officers in contrast, lived in the lap of luxury as was typical of the excesses in the eighteenth century. They drank the best claret and dined on the best cuts of meat on elaborate campaign furniture complete with silverware. They were kitted out from head to toe in exquisitely tailored uniforms, made from the finest materials, adorned with gold or silver lace, with dapper, custom-made jackboots. They lived an opulent, extravagant lifestyle, even while on campaign.

Irish troops were also at a distinct disadvantage to foreign or regular line regiments, as they were unable to return home on leave when Spain or France was at war with England. France was at war with England for much of the eighteenth-century. It was easier for Irish soldiers in the Austrian army to return home, as they were allies of England. In peacetime those in the French and Spanish service could return home on leave, many, one supposes, parading an insolent swagger to their Protestant overlords. This leave could last from a few weeks to one year. Some received a royal pardon for being in foreign service and did not return at all. After years spent abroad, the Irish having grown accustomed to the comforts and grandeur of cities on the Continent sometimes got quite a shock when returning to the 'old sod'. In the early eighteenth century, parts of Ireland remained war-torn and scattered with ruins from the 1650s Cromwellian conquests and the Jacobite War.[29] In 1725, Major Gerald O'Connor of Clare's Regiment returned home for the first time in 35 years and was struck with the 'squalid aspect' of the country: 'The presense of foreign rule', observed

O'Connor, 'and of the domination of sect and wide-spread and appalling poverty were the distinct and characteristic features of Dublin.'[30] After spending several months at home and disillusioned with the distressed plight of the enslaved Catholic populace he was glad to get back to France.

> The French officer who had returned home on leave or retirement, was far more a man of the world than his stay-at-home elder brother, on the lookout for a well-endowed heiress, sporting slightly part-worn Parisian fashions, interlacing his speech with French expressions and his conversation with anecdotes of soldiering in Flanders, Italy and the Indies. He was a familiar figure in Ireland and the object of dark suspicions by the authorities, who saw his fell hand in every enterprise without relish of salvation.[31]

Homesickness and the boredom of garrison life also caused many desertions, especially when confined to winter quarters. Recruits received a bounty on enlisting and some hoped to desert and maybe re-enlist under a false name and obtain another premium.[32] However, research suggests that desertions from the Irish regiments were comparable to those from other regiments in the French and British armies. 'For the soldiers of the eighteenth century desertion was the most common response to delays in payment or to the general conditions of service, whereas in the seventeenth century desertions were mostly due to mutinies.'[33] Deserters were sent to the notorious hard-labour prison ships (which were open to the elements and powered by oarsmen) known as the Mediterranean galleys. Records indicate that 165 Irishmen were sent to the galleys, of whom 80 per cent had been court-martialled due to desertion. Mutilation prior to being sent down was not uncommon. In 1705, Patrick Murphy had his ears and nose cut off, before sent to these ships.[34] Men were sentenced for a particular length of time and the hard labour was designed that prisoners would redeem themselves to their country and 'expiate their service to the King'.[35]

After the Irish army withdrew to France following the Jacobite War they continued the struggle under French and Spanish patronage as Catholic Ireland's army in exile. Their service in the armies of Europe was motivated by political and religious reasons, and in particular, loyalty to the Catholic Stuart king. Many chose exile with the aim of returning as an army of invasion. Captain Rutherford writing to Mary Modena, James II's wife, asserted: 'Our duty to our king will make us serve the French king with all the zeal and faithfulness that he can expect.'[36] Service in the Imperial army, as Austria were adversaries of France, presented the Irish with a dilemma, and some had refused to fight against King Louis of France: 'They had never wished to enter the imperial service ... but ... they were bound to their King James, and therefore could not offer themselves to the imperial service because his imperial majesty was waging war against the king of France, their king's ally.'[37]

In 1702, Irishmen in the French army defended the Italian town of Cremona when it was attacked by their compatriots in the Austrian army. When the Austrians surprised the Spaniards in Sicily in 1718, the Irish troops in Spanish service tipped the scale of victory against them. In 1744, an Imperial Austrian army commanded by Field-Marshal Browne, together with other Irish officers, crossed swords with and nearly wiped out two battalions of the Irish Brigade of Spain who were guarding the headquarters at Velletri, outside Rome. This attack cost over 400 Irish casualties, including the Regiment of Irlanda's colonel, Daniel MacDonnell.[38]

By the 1750s, the gap between officers and the ordinary soldier was at its widest. The officers generally came from the nobility, because there was no other career open to them but, as one of them quipped, 'to go and get themselves knocked on the head, like fools, in the king's service'.[39] It was said that for much of the eighteenth century only one officer in a hundred was a commoner.[40] The common soldier emanated from the lowest strata of society and were generally seen as the scum of the earth, consisting of vagabonds, criminals and opportunists. What better place for an individual escaping the arms of the law then to lie low for a few years and join an Irish regiment in the French or Spanish army? Many recruits were social outcasts; others had mental problems and were unable to make it in 'Civvy Street'. In 1756, Daniel O'Connor, a recently arrived young officer cadet in the French Irish Brigade, wrote home disconsolutely that the rank and file were recruited from 'robbers and criminals from all parts of the world' that had congregated in Lille, in northern France where the Irish regiment was based, and consequently he wanted to leave the corps.[41] A disproportionate number of Huguenots also joined the army, as there were few other careers open to them. Some Irish Protestants also served and religious bigotry did not appear to be an issue with these hard fighting men. The Irish Catholic gentry sent their younger sons into the officer class to improve their prospects in life. Insubordination, indiscipline, excessive drinking and gambling (which relieved the boredom of garrison life) were the main reasons cited for lack of promotion. Where an officer's mastery of the Spanish or French languages was weak this also curtailed advancement.[42] The newly arrived cadet had a hard time before he received rank. An enthusiastic Irish cadet in the French Irish Brigade recalled his basic training:

> We were divided into two parties. One represented the English who were supposed to make a descent; the other to beat them back to their ships. Though I have only been five days learning the exercise, Captain O'Conor permits me to march in the ranks and carry a gun. I fired seventy cartridges and the next most dexterous member of my party fired but fifty, upon my honour. Our second colonel happened to pass by and saw us charge, fire, and jump over hedges and ditches, and was told by Barry, our officer, how many cartridges I had fired, talked with admiration of the dexterity of so fresh a soldier.[43]

High levels of military training and discipline were also required. A recruit had to be well trained to remain in line while being exposed to an artillery barrage or in the face of a deadly enemy volley, which would often wipe out the entire first line of a column. Troops were drawn up three-deep in linear formations (like in an elaborate game of chess), which aided command and control on the battlefield. Muskets were inaccurate outside short range, and soldiers were drilled to march calmly in line up to an enemy and volley fire at seventy-five yards. They had to train to a level so that they could form from column to line wheeling through ninety degrees on demand, and vice versa. The Prussian army was recognised as the harshest and the Prussian soldier as the best drilled and disciplined in the period. In 1785, 'a Prussian army of 23,000 men approached in column and on a single cannon-shot, wheeled in seconds into a line two and a quarter miles long.'44 As Napoleon's light infantry Irish Legion lacked cavalry support they trained extensively to form square to repel enemy cavalry attacks, and to keep this combat formation while manoeuvring in battle. The famous Prussian general Frederick the Great also deduced that it took five years of military service and training before a soldier would not flinch in the frontline.[45] A lieutenant wrote that newly trained officers were sent out

> to drill with a squad composed of peasants from the plough and other raw recruits, first learning the facings, marchings and the companies' evolutions. That being completed, the officer put on cross belts and pouches and learnt the firelock exercises then again he marched with the same; and when it was considered that the whole was perfect, with and without arms, they began to skirmish in extended file, and last of all learned the duties of a sentry, and to fire ball cartridges at a target.[46]

Weapon handling in the period caused many accidents. A recruit had to complete a whole series of manoeuvres to load and fire his musket calmly in all weathers, and especially in the face of an impending enemy bayonet charge:

> Bad weapon handling constantly caused accidents. When front ranks knelt to fire and then sprang up to load they were often shot by careless rear-rank men; the Napoleonic Marshal Saint-Cyr reckoned that one-quarter of French infantry casualties in his career were caused in this way. Soldiers were terribly burned when cartridge boxes blew up; eyes were poked out with bayonets as ungainly soldiers bungled drill movements and ramrods were regularly fired off by men who had forgotten to remove them from the barrel of their musket, causing injuries and broken windows during practice, and difficulty in battle, where a spare ramrod might not be at hand.[47]

The greater accuracy of modern firepower made cavalry especially vulnerable on the battlefield. A British infantryman recalled a French cavalry charge during the Battle of Dettingen (1743):

They rode up to us with a pistol in each hand, and their broad swords slung on their wrists. As soon as they had fired their pistols they flung them at our heads, clapped spurs and rode upon us sword in hand. The fury of their onset we could not withstand so they broke our ranks and got through; but our men immediately closed [ranks] and turned about, and with the assistance of a regiment who were in our rear, the French horse being between both, we killed them in heaps.[48]

A soldier's lot was more often than not an unhappy one. Wolfe Tone's favourite expression comes to mind; 'Tis but in vain, for soldiers to complain.'[49] Medical expertise was in its infancy in the eighteenth century, and this was especially so in the treatment of battlefield casualties. Military hospitals were established but they were often overcrowded and dirty, with many treatments, such as tapping (the draining of blood) to cure ailments, causing more harm than good. Engagements were fought honourably between gentlemen, some officers still preferring to chivalrously carry swords or spontoons instead of firearms. These spontoons or halbards imposed discipline and while positioned horizontally behind the men served to keep them 'in line' and not flinch or break when receiving an enemy volley.

It was common for an officer in battle to challenge his opposite number to single combat with swords. Swordmanship required a combination of strength, skill, balance, timing, agility and stamina and was not just confined to the battlefield but was essential for self-defence in 'affairs of honour'. Serial duellers abounded in the eighteenth century and one was 'wise to be extra vigilant in keeping good manners lest they offend someone with even the most seemingly innocent word or gesture'.[50] The hotheaded Irish, known for liking a 'jar', already had a notorious reputation for duelling where 'hot words at night often led to cold steel in the morning.'[51] The Irish penchant for blazing or duelling became such a concern that an organisation was established in Ireland, the Society of Friendly Brothers, whose members wore a knot of green ribbon to show that although gentlemen, they would neither issue nor accept challenges. Where a challenge was given and accepted there was often no going back. On one occasion in 1814, a young ensign was 'called out' while attending the theatre in an evening in Bordeaux, and refused. A court-martial was convened and for failing to defend the regiment's honour he was thrown out of the regiment.[52]

Saxe exaggeratingly remarked that a sign of good general was to go through one's entire career without having to fight a single pitched battle.[53] Battles in the eighteenth century were often referred to as 'petticoat wars' and were long drawn-out affairs with commanders manoeuvring troops away, preferring sieges and marches and counter-marches, to spare their expensive troops from conflict.[54] However, war in the period was brutal, as grapeshot and musketry reduced hand-to-hand combat and increased casualties enormously, resulting in limbs and heads being blown clean off. Regiments could be lost in moments and were expensive to replace as they were raised by colonel-proprietors at their own expense. A seasoned French officer had exclaimed at the horror he observed at the Battle of Fontenoy where the regiment of the Garde Francaises was cut down in seconds after receiving a tremendous British musket volley. The wounded were sometimes left for long periods of time on the battlefield (without food or water), where many bled to death, although, in 1743, the Dettingen Agreement provided largely for the treatment of wounded casualties on the battlefield. Medical personnel were recognised as noncombatants and were to treat the wounded from both sides, who were to be returned to their units when their injuries had healed.

Soldiers feared abdominal wounds the most as they resulted in a high mortality rate. Musket balls or the bayonet caused most wounds. Bayonets went in deep and sometimes required a boot to be placed on a chest to retrieve from an abdomen. Some bayonets had a triangle-shaped blade, which caused excessive bleeding and complications (these bayonets were later banned from use). Engagements fought at sea were often fought at close quarters within pistol shot. Cannon balls decapitated and cut men in two and unleashed deadly sprays of wooden stakes and splinters when hitting a ship's hull. Low-velocity, soft, leaden musket balls shot from unrifled muskets sometimes ricocheted when impacting bone and bounced about through internal organs, causing a variety of internal injuries.

Amputation without anaesthetic was the preferred procedure for wounded soldiers suffering from broken or shattered bones because there was little chance of saving an injured limb. This procedure had a high death rate, as the patient suffered from shock and infection, caused by non-sterile medical instruments such as saws to cut through bone. It has been estimated that only 35 per cent of persons who underwent this procedure survived this ordeal. The wounded were held down by surgeon's mates and had to 'bite the bit' while a surgeon would tie a tourniquet around the limb and cut the skin with a knife, and saw through the bone, which a skilled surgeon could accomplish in under a minute. Sometimes the patient was given alcohol to numb the pain and the surgeon hoped the patient would pass out from the shock. The arteries were then sewn up and loose skin was pulled over the stump and stitched. The surgeon would wipe his bloody hands on his apron and start on the next patient, and by so doing would transfer infections, although this was seen as a normal part of the healing process. When a musket ball penetrated the body, it carried articles of the soldier's clothing into the wound, which caused infections. In many cases, the surgeon would root around in the wound to remove the musket ball or grapeshot, and if it was out of reach of his fingers it was deemed safer to leave the projectory there. Many carried grapeshot around in their bodies for years, no doubt curtailing life expectancy.

Post-combat stress (diagnosed today as post-traumatic stress disorder) was not properly understood or diagnosed at the time, although a condition called *mal de curazon* (sickness of the heart) in Spain and *la nostalgie* or *mal du pays* (homesickness) in France was recognised as a serious military medical disorder right through to the Napoleonic Wars. It was first identified in 1688 by Dr Johannes Hofer as 'the sad mood originating from the desire to return to one's native land'. The symptomatology of *la nostalgie* is comparable with depression and particularly affected the many foreign troops serving outside of their own countries, as it was also known as 'the Swiss disease' due to its proliferation among the many Swiss troops serving in France. One supposes that Irish troops in a state of perpetual exile would have experienced more of their fair share of this disorder.

Disease caused more deaths than battle casualties. Cholera, dysentery, diarrhoea, typhus, malaria, smallpox and yellow fever were rife. Inadequate accommodation and poor-quality food (especially while on campaign) made regiments susceptible to ailments; sunstroke, dehydration and exhaustion, and exposure also took its toll. It has been estimated that during the Peninsular War only one death in ten was due to enemy action. When troopers of Fitzjames' horse were captured en route to Scotland in the 1745 Jacobite Rising, many were reported to have smallpox scars on their faces. This disease killed one out of every two afflicted. Ships' crews and marines suffered from scurvy, which was not recognised as a vitamin deficiency or treated until the close of the eighteenth century when crews were given a daily ration of lemon juice. Disease decimated whole regiments, especially when they served in the tropics. Non-immune Europeans were especially susceptible to tropical diseases such as malaria and dengue fever spread by mosquitos, whose role as carriers of disease was not understood in medical circles at the time.[55] The lucrative sugar islands of the Caribbean needed to be heavily garrisoned to protect national interests, and when a regiment was posted there it often meant a death sentence. Taking the year of 1796 as an example: some 41 per cent of European troops succumbed to disease within a year of arriving in the Caribbean.[56] As we shall see, the Irish Brigades suffered terribly when they were posted there.

3

THE JACOBITE WAR (1689–91)

The Jacobite War was fought in Ireland between Williamite supporters of the Protestant King William and Jacobites of the Catholic King James. The war was part of the broader European conflict of the War of the Grand Alliance (1688–97) in which France was at war against an Anglo-Dutch coalition. When the Protestant King Charles II of England died in 1685 his brother James succeeded him, but James had converted to Catholicism ten years previously, which was a despised religion to many English Protestants. Matters came to a head three years into James's reign when James's son (James Francis Stuart) was born and was baptised a Catholic, which appeared to secure the Catholic succession. Prior to the birth of James's son, the throne would have passed on James's death to his Protestant daughter, Mary, who married the Protestant Prince William of the Dutch House of Orange.

King James II was the first Catholic to be crowned in England in over a century. His enemies considered him an imposter, 'a Pretender' on account of his religion, and were especially concerned about his close links with France. In November 1688, William of Orange was invited over to England by James's enemies, and, carried by favourable 'Protestant winds', landed safely in the south of the country. Protestants still celebrate William's arrival to this day as a cornerstone of their religious freedoms in the 'Glorious Revolution'. James was determined to hold onto his crown and sent loyal Irish and Scottish regiments to England to oppose William. This backfired as it provided propaganda for James's enemies, who resented the presence of Irish Catholic troops on English soil. When James finally lost the fight for his crown, these Irish troops were imprisoned in England and their loss would prove a major blow to the Jacobite war effort in Ireland. James fled to France where he established his shadow court in exile in the palace in Saint Germain (outside Paris), which would become the centre of Jacobite political intrigues for the next hundred years. The House of Stuart were absolute kings, in common with many Continental monarchs, believing in their divine right to govern, which many people accepted at the time. The Sun King, Louis XIV of France, was keen to support James in reclaiming his crown, as William's power grab was a serious blow to French ambitions and prestige.

Ireland was used as the main base in the war to reclaim James's crown, as loyal Irish Catholics formed three-quarters of the population. The Catholic gentry had risen in the Irish Rebellion of 1641 and established the Catholic Confederation, a breakaway government free of English control. Cromwell, determined to re-establish English rule, landed his 12,000-strong New Model Army in Ireland and laid much of the country waste. His name is still synonymous with savagery, particularly for his sacking of Drogheda where he massacred the entire town of men, women and children. The Irish were removed from their lands and sent 'to Hell or to Connaught'. In the 1650s over 50,000 men, women and children were sent as indentured labourers to Barbados and Virginia in the Americas.[1] Cromwell granted land to his soldiery in lieu of cash and many common soldiers received land from the old Gaelic and Hiberno-Norman aristocracy and formed the backbone of the Irish Protestant Ascendency.

When Cromwell died in 1658, Charles II's accession was widely supported by Irish Catholics, who were confident he would reverse some of Cromwell's land confiscations, but these were only partially resolved. When his Catholic son, James II took the throne he finally restored Irish Catholic rights and lands. He removed Protestants from key positions of power and replaced them with loyal Catholics; Justin MacCarthy (Lord Mountcashel) was appointed Lord Justice and James created Richard Talbot the Earl of Tyrconnell and gave him command of the Irish army.

Talbot came from an old Norman family that had settled in Ireland in the twelfth century and he succeeded in rallying the Gaelic Irish and the 'Old English' or Hiberno-Norman to the Jacobite cause.[2] By 1689, Tyrconnell hastily raised a Jacobite army of 7,000 to fight for James's restoration, but for any chance of success, he needed help from France. The French were keen to relieve pressure in the war on the Continent by supporting James in a campaign and willingly provided uniforms, equipment and money for James's cause. Ireland was now becoming a Jacobite stronghold and a rogue state in English eyes. William could not stand idly by and watch James's growing support in Ireland threaten his kingdom. He promised concessions to Irish Catholics if they would stand down, but they refused. As a result, he mobilised a multinational army made up of English, Dutch, German, Swiss and a large contingent of Danish troops from the war on the Continent to invade the country.

Tyrconnell wanted to secure Jacobite control of all the garrison towns in Ulster and in April 1689 ordered Lord Mountjoy's Protestant regiment to withdraw from Derry, but instead the apprentices of Derry shut the gates upon the advancing Earl of Antrim's Catholic regiment. The town then prepared for a siege, which is celebrated today in loyalist tradition.[3] The Jacobite army at the time was largely comprised of raw recruits and lacked adequate siege equipment, so they ineffectively dug entrenchments outside the town and waited.[4] The town held out for three months before the Royal Navy came to its relief. The Jacobites' failure to take Derry provided the Williamites with a bridgehead in the north of the country.[5]

King Louis XIV provided James with 6,600 French troops for the war in Ireland but part of the deal was that a comparable number of Irish troops were to be shipped to France in exchange. These troops formed the first Irish Brigade in France. In April 1690, 5,387 Irish troops arrived in France from war-torn Ireland, disease-ridden and in ragged condition. They were re-formed into three regiments known as Mountcashel's Irish Brigade: the Regiment of Mountcashel's led by Justin MacCarthy, the Regiment of Clare's under Daniel O'Brien, and the Regiment of Dillon's under Arthur Dillon.[6] After drilling in Nantes and clothed in their new French grey tunics, they were dispatched under the Marquis de Sainte Ruth's command to Savoy, in southeastern France. They marched 500 miles in the heat of summer to garrison Chambéry, which had been abandoned due to a shortage of French troops, and they quickly gained a reputation as first class soldiers.[7] They won their first laurels in an assault against Italian troops who were holed up on a mountainous slope, which was deemed impassable until the Irish 'burst through headlong through the trenchworks and routed the enemy'.[8] They continued their successful campaign, earning the respect of their commander, who praised them for having 'done marvels'. They also saw action in Germany and took part in the Siege of Hiedelberg. The following year, they won further acclaim in Spain when they captured the Catalan town of Urgel, which had been stoutly defended by a large garrison of elite Spanish troops. Their reckless 'do-or-die' style of soldiering greatly appealed to the French, 'for they were always in good spirits', observed the Duc de Noailles, and 'always first in the breech'.[9] The success of Mountcashel's Irish Brigade as an experimental force convinced the French war office that Irish troops would be invaluable in larger numbers.[10]

Vernet Horace's, *La Bataille du Fontenoy, 11 Mai 1745*. This features the Irish Brigade presenting a tattered British flag to King Louis XV. (Courtesy of Réunion des Musées Nationaux, Paris)

The Jacobite army 'depended heavily on the expertise of approximately 200 Irish officers with continental experience'.[11] James Fitzjames the Duke of Berwick (James's illegitimate son), Patrick Sarsfield and Justin MacCarthy (Lord Mountcashel) gained valuable military experience in Flanders during the Franco-Dutch War in the 1670s. Justin MacCarthy emanated from a once-powerful Gaelic aristocratic family from Co. Cork, who were 'out' in the 1641 Rising and lost their estates under Cromwell. The MacCarthy's were exiled to France and raised a regiment of foot in support of Charles II.

Patrick Sarsfield is one of the most romantic figures in Irish history and was the best-known Irishman at the time of his death. Sarsfield represented the 'new Irishman', as he came from both Gaelic and Norman backgrounds. He was educated in France and served as an officer in a French regiment. When war broke out, he was promoted to colonel and commanded a dragoon troop. He was Hiberno-Norman on his father's side and Gaelic Irish on his mother's and spoke Irish, English and French. Sarsfield was described as 'a man of amazing stature, utterly devoid of sense, very good-natured and very brave'.[12] James recognised his popularity amongst his men, promoted him to major-general and created him Earl of Lucan. In common with many of his contemporaries, Sarsfield saw the advantages a Catholic king could have on improving their fortunes. Sarsfield was young and had advantages over Tyrconnell, who had no Gaelic background, lacked military experience and was well into his sixties.

Many commands in the Jacobite army were given in French, a language the Irish gentry officers were familiar with.[13] They had gained fluency through military service in France after the Cromwellian wars, although there was a shortage of skilled officers in the Jacobite army at battalion- and company-level, due to the exclusion of the Catholic gentry from military service under the recently deposed Protestant regime.[14] The Jacobite cavalry were raised from the Irish gentry, and were widely lauded as 'the flower of the army'. These gentlemen troopers had most to gain as they had lost their ancestral estates under Cromwell and fought with most conviction.[15] They were 'better mounted than any gendarmes [French cavalry] I ever saw,' observed the French Brigade commander, the Duc de Lauzun. The Irish charger, due to breeding with the

Arabian horse, was considered the best in the world. The Arab horse was introduced into Ireland in the first millennium through trade with Spain and was later bred with the English horse in the twelfth century. The Irish horse also benefited from a temperate climate combined with good quality pasture due to the high limescale content of the Irish subsoil.[16]

Unfortunately for the Jacobites, no such accolades could describe the outgunned and outnumbered Irish infantry, who lacked both discipline and military experience. William's army were equipped with the latest flintlock muskets while the Jacobites carried the older French-supplied matchlock. The flintlock delivered heavier firepower and was more reliable; misfiring every third shot opposed to the matchlock which misfired, on average, every second one.[17] The Williamites could also rely on well-armed battle-hardened troops from the war on the Continent.

In March 1689, James himself landed in Kinsale in the south of Ireland with arms, supplies and 6,600 troops of the French Brigade under the Duc de Lauzun. Several Irish regiments who served with James in England and had escaped to France accompanied him. James's army marched triumphantly into Dublin to the bagpipe tune of 'The King Shall Enjoy His Own Again' and he 'was so overcome by emotion he wept'. In less than a year, the entire country was under Jacobite control, except for the northern province of Ulster, which still held out.[18]

William landed in Carrickfergus, in the north of Ireland in June 1690 with 15,000 troops, £2,000 in coin and an artillery train from Holland. His army marched south towards Dublin and supporters swelled it to 35,000. James marched confidently out to block William's advance to Dublin and choose the natural boundary of the Boyne River, which was the most defensible position if James was to make a stand in eastern Ireland.[19] The Boyne may not have been the best choice to stage a set-piece battle, as a Jacobite defeat would mean abandoning Dublin; 'we are of the opinion that the Boyne is the walls of Dublin,' noted one of William's advisers.[20] The Jacobite army, comprising 19,000 Irish troops and 6,600 troops from the French Brigade, arrived at the Boyne, with William's army arriving the next day on the opposite riverbank. William's army headquartered a few miles from the Boyne, in the twelfth-century Cistercian Mellifont Abbey, which lay in ruins as Henry VIII had suppressed it in 1539 along with the other Irish monasteries.

The Battle of the Boyne was nearly over before it had started. The Jacobite gunners could not believe their luck when were able to fire at William on the opposite riverbank prior to the battle. He was hit but the wound was not serious. The Jacobites realised they were outnumbered and could not risk an open pitched battle, therefore they took up a defensive position at Oldbridge and hoped William would attack here. On the morning of 1 July (Old Style)[21] the battle began when William's second in command, the Duke of Schomberg, led 8,000 men in a flanking manoeuvre to Rossnaree, 10 miles up-river from Oldbrige. James dispatched Gordon O'Neill's 500 mounted dragoons to confront them but they were overwhelmed and forced to retreat. Fearing he was being outflanked, James consulted with Lauzun and ordered half his army and most of his cannon to counter Shomberg at Rossnaree. However, when this large Jacobite force arrived there they were unable to attack Shomberg's army due to a boggy morass that separated the two armies.[22] This manoeuvre had cost James dearly as the bulk of the Jacobite army remained in position here and literally sat out the battle.

Lieutenant General Hamilton's Jacobite infantry, supported by the cavalry under Major-General Sheldon and the Duke of Berwick, held the line at Oldbridge. To the tune of 'Lillibulero' William's elite Dutch Blue Guards waded waist-high across the river, beating back the Jacobite infantry with their superior firepower.[23] Hamilton's infantry were lined up four men deep and opened fire at 50 yards with their matchlocks, but failed to stop the Williamite advance, taking with them any chance they had of winning the battle. The last hope now hinged on the Jacobite cavalry, who, fortified with brandy as per the custom of the day, charged and returned numerous charges and finally halted the Dutch Guards crossing the river. However, they were unable to beat back the general advance and the Jacobite cavalry were forced to retreat and fall back to Dunore. The ferocity of the fighting was so fierce that Sheldon and Berwick both had horses shot under them; Berwick luckily escaped alive by being rescued and riding pillion with a trooper. William's second in command, the Duke of Schomberg, was killed by a cannon ball by the Jacobite gunners in this phase of the battle, as he was singled out in the field and was mistaken for William.

Realising all was lost, the Earl of Tyrconnell rode to Duleek to direct the Jacobite retreat, which was initially well organised. Several regiments had not even fought yet, such as Sarsfield's dragoons who had seen no action as they had been deployed to counter Shomberg at Rossnaree. The Jacobite cavalry counter-attacked to screen the Jacobite infantry's retreating manoeuvre from the enemy. But the ordered retreat became a rout as William's cavalry cut them down, leading to individual soldiers dispersing in panic. 'Viewing the hills about us I perceived them covered with soldiers of several regiments all scattered like sheep flying before the wolf,' described an officer in William's army.[24]

Tyrconnell urged James to leave the battlefield to evade capture, because although they had lost the battle the war could yet be won. He arrived in Dublin on horseback the same day, escorted by Sarsfield's 200 dragoons and bringing the news of his own defeat. A legend arose that he complained to Lady Tyrconnell that the Irish betrayed him and ran, 'but your Majesty won the race,' she replied. When the Jacobite army arrived in Dublin the next day, they found James, the garrison and the governor gone. James had wasted no time, and had ridden all night to rendezvous with a frigate in Waterford, which brought him to Kinsale and onwards to France. The flight of the king did nothing for Irish morale and he tarnished his reputation by fleeing. 'James the Coward' was the sobriquet given by Gerald O'Connor, one of the Jacobite officers present at the battle.[25] Berwick defended his father, claiming that he fled to muster French support for an invasion of England. When the Jacobites evacuated Dublin, the relieved Protestants took control, plundered Catholic homes and sang celebratory *Te Deums* in St Patrick's Cathedral.

The Jacobite army were ordered to fall back to Limerick on the river Shannon. To rally their troops for the forced march, each regiment planted its colours on high ground, attracting the stragglers with bagpipes. James's army was not only accompanied on their long march by some of their families but were joined by a motley crew of prostitutes and hangers on. William mistakenly believed the Jacobites had been decisively beaten and issued terms, which became known as the Finglas Declaration, which pardoned the ordinary Jacobite soldier but excluded the officers. This proved to be a major mistake as it strengthened the Jacobites' resolve to continue fighting, since William intended offsetting the cost of his campaign by confiscating Catholic estates. The historian J.G. Simms argued that if William had repeated his promise that Catholics could retain their estates and enjoy free exercise of religion (as he had done early in 1689) it is likely the Jacobite military effort would have collapsed.

The fate of Europe hung in the balance at the Battle of the Boyne, with two kings fighting for their thrones over an Irish river. Losses were comparatively light though, with 1,000 Jacobites and 500 Williamites killed. The Jacobites were blamed for not having dug entrenchments on the river bank and choosing to engage a much more numerous enemy in front of a river fordable by infantry and cavalry. One wonders if the French were keeping their better commanders for the Flanders campaign. Berwick described the French Brigade commander, the Duc de Lauzun, as follows:

> When he came to Ireland, at the head of the auxiliary troops he made it clear that if ever he had had any knowledge of the military profession, he had by that time totally forgotten it. At the action at the Boyne, I was with him when the enemy passed at Slane, he said, we must attack them, but while he was endeavouring to find out a proper spot to attack upon, the enemy had time to get into the plain and form themselves. After which I observed to him, that there was no possibility of charging them. In Ireland he showed neither capacity nor resolution though on occasions he was said to be a man of great personal bravery.[26]

James arrived back in France and visited Louis XIV, in the hope he would pledge more troops, but he was unwilling to provide any more support, even though a Williamite army had just been routed at Killiecrankie in Scotland. After the death of the Jacobite commander Viscount Dundee in Killiecrankie, James appointed an Irish officer, Major-General Cannon, to lead the Jacobite army in Scotland, supported by 300 Irish officers and men from the Irish campaign. James compounded his poor image from fleeing, as he publicly blamed his failure in France on the unwillingness of the Irish to stand and fight. This was politically naive as it made the war unpopular in France and compromised French support in Ireland. As a result, Irish merchants in France were accosted in the street, but Irish reputation would soon be restored with their admirable defence of Limerick.

The Williamite army pursued the Jacobites steadily as they marched towards Limerick, and took the Jacobite-held towns of Drogheda, Wexford and Clonmel along the way. The Jacobites adopted the age-old scorched-earth policy by burning crops and houses, and local Irish outlaws known as raparees ambushed the Williamite rear-guard with hit-and-run attacks, a favourite Irish tactic since ancient times. In July 1690, a Williamite force under Major-General James Douglas was ordered to secure the bridge over the Shannon and take the strategic town of Athlone. The Jacobite garrison was ordered to surrender or otherwise no quarter would be given. But the town's prickly old governor Colonel Richard Grace was defiant; while firing his pistols in the air, he shouted; 'when my provisions are consumed, I will defend until I eat my old boots.'[27] The subsequent siege dragged on and, faced with stiff resistance and with ammunition low, the Williamites abandoned it. They expected Athlone to fall in time, once the bigger prize of Limerick fell into their hands.

William was pursuing the Jacobites at such speed that his 100-carriage siege train (containing artillery and siege equipment) was running a few days behind the army. Sarsfield saw his opportunity and set off with 800 horsemen to locate the siege train, assisted by a local raparee leader called Michael 'Galloping' Hogan.[28] The siege train was spotted outside Cashel and Sarsfield waited for nightfall beside the ruins of Ballyneety Castle (which is now called 'Sarsfield Rock') before ambushing the escort guard. The gunpowder barrels were lit in a circle, and the subsequent boom was said to have been the loudest man-made noise in Ireland, shaking nearby Ballyneety Castle, a portion of whose ancient walls came tumbling down. The moonscape holes cut into the ground by the explosion are today still visible and the castle is still standing. Destroying William's siege train was a great propaganda coup for the Jacobite war effort and boosted Irish morale in Limerick as it was also rumoured that a large French force had landed. It became the war's highlight and secured Sarsfield's reputation throughout Europe, as it was reported in the French newspaper, the *Mercure de France,* and helped to maintain French support for the Jacobites.

After nearly a week on the march, the weary Jacobite army, numbering 15,000 men and their followers, finally arrived in

Limerick. Finding few provisions made for their upkeep and maintenance the Irish and French officers convened a council of war and debated whether to defend the city or not. The French were tired of the incessant rain and endless fogs and wanted to go home. Their supplies were running low and they knew that by surrendering they would be repatriated back to France, but the Irish had to continue fighting as they risked losing their few remaining estates. The Jacobite high command was split between the Gaelic and Hiberno-Norman leaders. Those who advocated continuing the war generally came from Gaelic backgrounds, such as the prominent families of O'Neil, Maguire, McGuinness, McMahon, O'Farrells, O'Reilly and O'Garas.[29] They were supported by the Irish bishops and by Sarsfield and by the common soldiers. Those who advocated peace tended to come from Hiberno-Norman backgrounds, led by Tyrconnell, together with the families of Hamilton, Nugent, Dillon, Burke, Butler, Plowden and Sheldon. It is thought that the Gaelic Irish were no longer interested in supporting James and wanted to break the English connection entirely and set up a semi-independent Ireland under French protection.[30]

The difficulty in defending Limerick was that the city lacked exterior defences that could withstand a siege. The city had no ramparts to position cannons and lacked other fortifications. Her old walls were constructed to repel longbows, not late seventeenth-century cannon. The French Brigade's commander, Lauzun, famously stated that it could be taken by pelting it with roasted apples. He promptly withdrew his French troops to Galway, taking a great deal of arms and ammunition with him in the hope of convincing the Irish that defence was futile. The French lacked commitment in the war and had only three objectives in Ireland, according to Berwick, which was 'to get there, to fight, and to return'.[31] In the end, the decision was made to defend Limerick, with or without Lauzun's French Brigade. The Marquis de Boissleau of the French Guards was appointed town governor and the city walls were fortified with huge ditches dug outside. The Irish were fortunate to have such an able officer as he had experience in the latest warfare techniques and had participated in some of the major sieges on the Continent.

The Duke of Berwick and Patrick Sarsfield were the young bucks of the war. The 20-year-old Berwick (despite his young age) was already an experienced cavalry commander with battle experience gained on the Continent. He was unimpressed with the elderly Tyrconnell's strategies and proposed launching a series of hit-and-run raids involving 3,500 cavalry racing to Dublin. He planned to attack William's garrisons swiftly before drawing off and galloping back to the safety of Athlone and Sligo, which were still in Jacobite hands. The sixty-something Tyrconnell was not in agreement. He commanded the army and was not going to be dictated to in his management of the war by a young upstart, and so Berwick's daring plan came to nothing. He was equally unimpressed with Sarsfield's proposal to capture William, as they received intelligence that William lacked a proper security detail and could be easily taken, and this plan too was abandoned.

In August 1690, William's army of 25,000 marched towards Limerick, which at the time was divided into Irish and English towns connected by Balsbridge. William dug in outside the city and his gunners battered the old walls with artillery, which soon crumbled as they had already been weakened and badly damaged in the 1641 siege. Sarsfield's taking of William's siege train proved to be more of a propaganda coup as the effect of its loss was minimised with fresh supplies of guns and mortars brought up from Waterford. After heavy bombardment, a breach was made in the walls near St John's Gate. The Irish constructed an inner wall and erected barricades supported by cannon to defend against William's storming party when it would inevitably make its way through. When a storming party of Danish troops ran through the breach it fell into the trap and sought cover among the broken city walls while taking fire from the Irish troops positioned on the ramparts. There was also a barrage of rocks hurled down from the ramparts by hundreds of civilians. Elite German Brandenburgers were rushed through the breach but they too were destroyed. The assault ended in a Williamite massacre as they suffered a staggering 3,000 casualties, with some of William's best troops lost in a couple of hours. The Irish finally got some retribution for the eighth-century Viking plunder of Irish monasteries and towns by the dreaded Danes.

William's officers convened a council of war and decided to withdraw into winter quarters. If another attack failed, they would be leaving Limerick as a defeated army. One can only imagine the cheers of delight as William's army marched away. There was a shortage of draught horses and carts as so much had been needed to take the wounded to Cashel and beyond and one of the defenders observing, 'the cannons were hauled through the mud by teams of oxen. Large quantities of military stores, including grenades and bombs had to be left behind, what the English could not take with them they burnt.'[32] The following month, William was back in England and told Parliament that continual rainfall forced him to raise the siege, but 'not a single drop of rain fell for above a month before, or for three weeks after', claimed Berwick.[33] But this was a dubious assertion in the west of Ireland, even in August.

Limerick's heroic defence restored Irish valour and was the greatest victory of the war. Lauzun's French Brigade remained in Galway as inactive spectators and took no part in the city's defence, believing it would fall. In September, the French Brigade sailed for France, and Generals Sarsfield, Sheldon and Gamloy were invited to join Mountcashel's Irish Brigade there but they declined. He would continue the war, stated Sarsfield, even if this meant pursuing a guerrilla war without French support. Tyrconnell sailed with Lauzun as he was anxious to explain the course of events and to curry favour with James and he also desperately needed fresh supplies and reinforcements for the army. The French court were greatly impressed by Limerick's defence but could not understand why Lauzun and his French Brigade had returned knowing that Jacobite prospects were now much improved.

The Jacobites launched a series of sporadic attacks towards the end of 1690. Berwick besieged Birr Castle but arrived too late to relieve Cork, as it fell to a large Williamite army under John Churchill, the Duke of Marlborough. The Williamites now controlled much of the country although Berwick and Sarsfield waged a successful guerrilla campaign from County Clare and prevented William's army from crossing the Shannon. In May 1691, a French fleet arrived under the Marquis de Sainte Ruth carrying several hundred French officers and engineers. Sainte Ruth was given command of the Jacobite army and had experience leading Mountcashel's Irish troops in Savoy. The now battle-hardened Jacobite army were resupplied and kitted out in their new red tunics, the Stuart colours since the 1660 Restoration. Although the French off-loaded supplies, they also undermined the Jacobite war-effort by requisitioning tents, saddlery, ammunition, blacksmiths and armourers, which they required for the war in Flanders.[34]

William was now anxious to finally put an end to the war as his army was desperately needed in Flanders. England massively increased its resources to break the war's deadlock by landing wave after wave of supply convoys, which resulted in the greatest collection of artillery ever assembled in Ireland.[35] England could always tap into its commercial wealth and increase taxes for the war, whereas the Irish war effort relied on sporadic French support, combined with 'a hand to mouth effort based on Ireland's cash-strapped, agrarian economy'.[36] William remained in England and appointed the Dutch general, Godard Van Ginkel, as commander of the army in Ireland. In June, Athlone finally fell to Van Ginkel's army, which opened the way for them to cross the Shannon and forced the Jacobites to withdraw, leaving Galway and Limerick as the only two substantial towns still in Jacobite hands. Sainte Ruth now chose to make a stand and halt Van Ginkel's advance at the small hamlet of Aughrim, in Co. Galway. He drew up his Jacobite army at Kilcommodon Hill, close to Aughrim Castle and prepared for battle on a damp and hazy day on 12 July (Old Style), both armies fielding 20,000 troops. Sainte Ruth drummed up the Jacobites with speeches to inspire them. His reputation was at stake and he knew he could not return to France without achieving at least some glory, and he was confident of victory.

At first light, the Irish troops laid themselves flat on their faces to avoid Van Ginkel's superior fire and sharpshooters lined up behind stonewalls and bravely repelled Van Ginkel's advances. Danish and Huguenot troops led an attack on the Jacobite right on a sunken area of ground, known as 'Bloody Hollow' due to the ferocity of the fighting that took place there. Van Ginkel's infantry succeeded in gaining a foothold on the hill but were routed by a force under Gordon O'Neill that captured a gun battery. The Jacobite left was overpowered and Van Ginkel's army made a crossing near Aughrim Castle, but still the Jacobites had gained the upper hand in the battle when disaster struck. While Sainte Ruth was exclaiming how he would push the Williamites back to the walls of Dublin, he was decapitated by a stray cannon ball. This caused such confusion that the Jacobite cavalry left the field. Sarsfield's cavalry was held in reserve and he tried to rescue the situation and launch a rearguard attack but it was all too late as the battle was already lost. The Jacobite infantry were left exposed by their cavalry's flight and were cut down by enemy cavalry. Sarsfield managed to fall back to Limerick, unlike many of the other regiments who were slaughtered when the retreat became a massacre. Charles O'Kelly, a colonel in the Jacobite army, observed how the Irish 'lost the flower of their army and nation' at the apocalypse of Aughrim, where the fields ran slippery with blood. A Williamite account gives some indication of the horrors of war:

> As dusk fell the cavalry began to move away and take flight, abandoning the infantry who in turn threw down their arms, left their colours and ran. Terrible scenes followed as the English fell on the rear of the fugitives. Stricken with terror we saw them fleeing in all directions across the countryside, into the mountains, woods, bogs and wilderness. Like mad people, the women, children and Waggoner's filled every road weeping and wailing … some, mutilated and in great pain, begged to be put out of their misery, and others coughed out blood and threats, their bloodied weapons frozen in their hands as if in readiness for some future battle. The blood from the dead so covered the ground that one could hardly take a step without slipping. This grisly scene of slaughter remained untouched and unchanged for several days, the horror of which cannot be imagined except by those who saw it.[37]

The Jacobite army split into two; a detachment marched to Galway and the other to Limerick and regrouped. As the Jacobites could not stop and bury their dead, the bodies remained at the battle site for months, and from a distance the rotting, bleaching carcasses resembled thousands of sheep pasturing on the mountainside. Monks from a monastery finally undertook the burial of the fallen. Although the Boyne is the most famous battle of the war, some have described it as a mere skirmish, with relatively few casualties, compared with Aughrim, which was the bloodiest battle in Irish history with over 7,000 men killed. There were more soldiers killed at Aughrim than the combined casualties of the battles of Clontarf, Kinsale, the Boyne, Vinegar Hill and the 1916 Easter Rising.

The next Williamite target was the coastal city of Galway in the west of Ireland. The merchants of Galway represented what was known as the 'new interest' and had grown wealthy by trading with Spain and France. They were no longer prepared to accept payment for their goods in 'gunmoney', which were brass tokens with King James's head on them, as it was doubtful if these would ever be redeemed.[38] The war had destroyed the city's commerce and the Galwegians were happy to see peace at any price and surrendered without much resistance and even welcomed Van Ginkel and his officers with a civic reception in the city. Securing Galway was a major strategic coup for Van Ginkel as it divided the Irish beyond the Shannon. The French were disgusted that Galway had not put up much of a fight. J.G. Simms noted that the Irish condemned the town for preferring private gain to the general interest of religion and country.

Irish morale was lifted when nearly a thousand men under Hugh 'balldearg' O'Donnell sailed up the Shannon from Spain. O'Donnell had served in the Spanish army and saw the opportunities a Jacobite victory presented in the form of land acquisitions. The Jacobite high command had not supplied O'Donnell with arms, neither had they taken up his offer to reinforce the Jacobite garrison in Galway and instead his men were assigned to menial duties. Tyrconnell did not trust O'Donnell and suspected him of trying to re-establish an independent Gaelic kingdom, to the exclusion of the Hiberno-Normans. Many believed in an ancient prophecy that an O'Donnell with a red mark (*balldearg* is Irish for 'red spot') would defeat an English army outside Limerick, which further lifted morale. However, O'Donnell wasn't returning to Spain empty-handed and, as a mercenary soldier, he recognised the better opportunities presented by the Williamites and joined forces with them on the attack on Sligo. It seemed that Tyrconnell's distrust was warranted after all, and the prophecy too rang hallow. The town shortly afterwards capitulated, permitting the garrison to march out with full honours of war and join the Jacobite army at Limerick, which was again to be the last Jacobite stronghold.

The main Franco-Irish army in Limerick, numbering 18,000 infantry and 3,000 cavalry with 2,500 dragoons, geared up for their second siege. The breach in the city walls had been fully repaired, and the city was now better defended than ever, with strong outworks built around the walls complete with earthworks. Morale, however, was close to cracking and the French reluctantly distributed funds to stop desertions. Tyrconnell died in August, which was a serious loss to the Jacobite cause and also affected morale. Sarsfield and many of the Gaelic Irish had lost confidence in him and blamed him for the defeat at the Boyne. They had done everything to discredit him, although Berwick commended Tyrconnell in his *Memoirs*. The English circulated rumours that Tyrconnell was poisoned – pointing the finger at the French commanders and in particular at Sarsfield, as there had been history between the two men, but no evidence suggests foul play was involved.

Van Ginkel bided his time before appearing with his army outside Limerick. He predicted a bloodless end and hoped that the Jacobites would now surrender and agree terms, just like Sligo and Galway had done. However, the Protestant lord justices in Dublin were keen on retribution against the Catholics. They were in no mood to offer favourable terms, and pressured Van Ginkel to besiege the city rather than choosing the longer drawn-out option of a blockade. They were also concerned that a French relief force was expected to arrive at any time, and Van Ginkel was unable to patrol the coast and prevent a landing. Late in August 1691, Van Ginkel's army bombarded Limerick's walls and took possession of two nearby forts. The siege dragged on for nearly a month before a turning point occurred when the Williamites routed a large Irish force protecting Thomand Bridge. The Irish recoiled back towards the city walls, chased by William's troops, but the French officer commanding the main gate panicked and raised the drawbridge too soon, shutting out 800 troops. Many tried to surrender but no mercy was shown. One can imagine the horror, as the Irish along the parapet walls witnessed the massacre at close hand. This last action was a major blow to morale; relations between the French and the Irish had at times been strained, and this was the last straw. The Irish convened a council of war the same night at which it was decided to call a truce, and a white flag was raised over the city. On 24 September 1691, Lieutenant General Sarsfield and the Scottish Jacobite Major-General Wauchope rowed across the Shannon to parley with Van Ginkel to negotiate terms that would become the Treaty of Limerick, marking the end of the Jacobite War in Ireland.

4

THE FLIGHT OF THE WILD GEESE (1691)

As Patrick Sarsfield crossed the Shannon, he was to make a decision that was to have major ramifications on Ireland's destiny to the present day. He had only agreed to arrange a capitulation if the Irish army were permitted to go to France. The terms of capitulation were divided between military and civilian articles. The military articles dealt with the conditions permitting the Irish army to leave and the civilian ones dealt with Catholic rights and the restoration of confiscated estates. It was Sarsfield's intention to design the treaty to tide the Irish people over, until James was eventually restored to his throne.[1] Van Ginkel had granted favourable terms to Catholics in Galway and Sligo and the Irish were confident he would do likewise in Limerick. A total of 42 Articles were finally agreed in what became the Treaty of Limerick. The first Article was as follows:

> The Roman Catholics of this kingdom shall enjoy such privileges in the exercise of their religion as are consistent with the laws of Ireland, or as they did enjoy in the reign of King Charles the second: and their majesties, as soon as their affairs will permit them to summon a parliament in this kingdom, will endeavour to procure the said Roman Catholics such farther security in that particular, as may preserve them from any disturbance upon the account of their said religion.

Sarsfield instructed his lawyers to focus fully on the military articles. The Jacobite army was to leave Limerick as an undefeated army with all the honours of war: fully armed, with flags flying, bagpipes playing and drums beating. They were also to be permitted to take their horses and their personal property with them. To ensure the Irish would not change their minds, Van Ginkel's army occupied Limerick and the Irish marched out of Balsbridge and onto King's Island and fouled the town for William's troops as they left. Van Ginkel tried to persuade many to stay and join William's army and told them that if they went to France they would never again be permitted to set foot in the Kingdom of Ireland. 'About seventy per cent of the infantry was to go to France and of those who elected to stay, less than a quarter volunteered their services to the English. Apart from this minority, the Irish remained loyal to King James.'[2]

Many officers lost their estates by leaving. Patrick Sarsfield forfeited his land in Lucan, West Dublin, and the Dillons lost vast estates in Counties Meath and Roscommon. Charles O'Brien the 5th Lord Clare's 80,000 acres were also forfeited in Co. Clare. There was much soul searching and many were having second thoughts, realising they might never set foot in Ireland again. It was to be a difficult decision; face a bleak future in a Williamite Ireland or go into exile.[3] Sarsfield locked his men on King's Island to prevent desertions, but Van Ginkel was furious when he learned of this and threatened a resumption of the war directing that the men had to leave of their own free accord. The Irish were given brandy and were persuaded by the influential clergy that by going to France they could uphold their religion and would return triumphantly in a year. They were further coaxed with the promise of higher rates of pay than were usually paid in the French army. Those who decided to go to France marched across Thomand Bridge to line up in County Clare, and from there they marched to Cork. Sarsfield designated his most loyal troops – the 1st Royal Regiment – to march out first, and nearly all of the 1,400 troops agreed to go. Those marching past Thomand Bridge had chosen France and there was now no going back.

On 3 October 1691, the Treaty of Limerick was signed. Patrick Sarsfield let the French officers sign first to pre-empt any issue in the future of him having acted without proper authority that might question the treaty's validity. It became clear early on that the Irish would not go without their families. The reality for many soldiers was that their families did not know of their whereabouts, whether they were alive or dead. Some were not keen to go abroad as many came from isolated rural villages and had never left their own district. Fresh reports from France that the first arrivals were badly treated caused some to change their minds. The Jacobite Colonel Charles O'Kelly poignantly described the feeling and plight of many at the time:

> Those who resolved to leave it never hoped to see it again; and those who made the unfortunate choice to continue therein, could at the same time have nothing in prospect but contempt and poverty, chains and imprisonment, and in a word, all the miseries that a conquered nation could naturally expect from the power and malice of implacable enemies.[4]

The Irish army marched to Cork to be shipped to France, and this event became romantically known as the 'Flight of the Wild Geese'. While the bulk of the Irish army was awaiting embarkation at Cork, Admiral Chateau-Renaud's French relief fleet arrived up the Shannon one month after Sarsfield sued for peace. Twenty transport vessels, containing 3,200 officers and men with stands of arms and supplies accompanied his eighteen-ship fleet. Limerick was now only lightly garrisoned as most of Van Ginkel's army had already left and could easily be taken. But Sarsfield had already departed for Cork and it was argued that the treaty would be honoured as it was already signed, sealed and delivered. So, instead of relieving the beleaguered Irish garrison, the French relief fleet was used to ship the remaining Irish army to France. The first to depart Cork were the remnants of Dominic Sheldon's cavalry. Later on, panic broke out when a couple of hundred relatives were left behind in a last-minute rush to the last boats. George Story, a chaplain in William's army observed the chaos at the quay:

> Accordingly a vast rabble of all sort were brought to the waterside when the major-general, pretending to ship the soldiers in order according to their lists, they first carried the men on board, and many of the women at the second return of the boat for the officers, catching hold to be carried on board were dragged off and through fearfulness, losing their hold, were drowned; but others who held faster had their fingers cut off and so perished in the sight of their husbands and relations.[5]

Patrick Sarsfield sailed for France towards the end of December 1691, three years since Prince William of Orange had usurped James. The war that followed had claimed as many as 100,000 lives and cost the English Treasury as much as £18 million. There has been much speculation as to why Limerick capitulated so easily. There was plenty of food, the approaching winter season was putting pressure on Van Ginkel to withdraw into winter quarters and he was as far from taking the city at the end of the siege as he was at the start of it. French reinforcements were expected to arrive any day and Van Ginkel was short of ammunition, even though Berwick maintained that 'the Irish being in absolute want of provisions, proposed to surrender.'[6] Curiously, neither Berwick nor Colonel O'Kelly mention anywhere that a French relief convoy was expected any day and one wonders if the Irish were aware of their impending arrival at all. Van Ginkel received intelligence from English spies on the French coast that a relief convoy was on its way, and thought the Irish could have held out:

> It may appear very strange that a numerous garrison, not oppressed by any want, should give up a town which nobody was in a condition to take from them, at a time when those who lay before it had actually drawn off their guns and were preparing to march away, and when that garrison did daily expect a squadron of ships to come to their relief, if they had needed any.[7]

If the French convoy had arrived five weeks earlier, Limerick would not have fallen, as Van Ginkel had already indicated that he was unable to prevent an amphibious landing. The Protestant lord justices were still reeling from their humiliating treatment under the recent Jacobite government and were in no mood to grant favourable terms to Catholics. From the army's point of view, allowing the restoration of estates would have been a reasonable request that would have brought things along and enabled William's army to transfer swiftly to the Continent – where it was badly needed. But the Irish were weary of war, the Boyne, and the appalling casualties sustained at Aughrim and the death of Sainte Ruth and Tyrconnell, together with the recent capitulations of Galway and Sligo may have weakened their resolve to continue the fight. Many believed the war was already lost as Limerick was the last stand and by surrendering it might have been possible to achieve favourable terms, and officers may yet be able to save their estates.

The Irish signed the treaty with few of their original requests being granted; Sarsfield abruptly excluded Colonel O'Kelly from negotiations mid-stream, probably because he would not have agreed to them. O'Kelly stated that Limerick's defences were stronger than ever, and if Tyrconnell had lived, he would never have agreed to those terms. Sarsfield and his officers thought James would be restored to the throne within a year and some of the civil articles were vague and lacked clarity. But they were designed to be an interim measure only. We can blame Sarsfield for the absence of any contingency plan and for selling out too cheaply. Colonel O'Kelly thought that Sarsfield should have held out for a better deal. Berwick and Sarsfield were disillusioned with the army's low morale and wanted to pursue their careers and gain fame and glory in the grander European theatre in Flanders. In the end, Sarsfield got what he wanted – good promotion prospects in the French army in Flanders accompanied by the Irish army. William gave generous grants of confiscated lands to his Dutch followers; Bartolomew Van Homrigh was appointed as long-serving Lord Mayor of Dublin, and Lord Clare's estates were given to Joost Van Keppel. Many sold their newly acquired estates at huge personal gain to other Protestants, who become the new Ascendency. William honoured the treaty and was fair in his treatment of the Irish and returned half of the forfeited estates and pardoned many others, although the treaty was broken shortly afterwards as many were baying for revenge, which Berwick described in his *Memoirs*:

> It is beyond the scope of these pages to relate the outcry which the Articles of Limerick called forth. Those who would know how mouths, watering for forfeitures, roared at the treaty – how Bishop Dopping mounted the Christ Church pulpit to expound to the Lords Justices that Protestants were not bound to keep faith with Papists – how William was assailed in the English Parliament for lenity to Irish 'rebels' – how the Articles were violated, the trade of Ireland destroyed, and her creed persecuted.[8]

The collapse of the Jacobite war-effort can be blamed squarely on insufficient French support. Tyrconnell wrote to Louis after the 'shipwreck' at Aughrim requesting further aid as otherwise the Irish would be forced to sue for peace. The French high command were focused elsewhere on the European theatre and hoped to keep William's army occupied in Ireland as long as possible. 'This war in Ireland it may be said, that in London it was considered as the business of the day; and the capital concern of Great Britain,' observed Berwick, 'and in France, it was looked upon as a war carried on from motives of particular attachment and decorum.'[9] Limerick's capitulation was of course a serious setback for James as it temporarily scuppered his hope of regaining the throne, but all hope was not lost, as he still had 15,000 Irish veterans at his command. James departed Paris for the French coast of Brittany to welcome the Irish army in person:

> We are extremely satisfied with your conduct and of the behaviour of the soldiers during the siege; and most particularly of your and their declaration and resolution to come and serve where we are. And we assure you, and order you to assure both officers and soldiers that are come along with you, that we shall never forget this act of loyalty, nor fail when in a capacity to give them above others a particular mark of our favour.[10]

The future was quite uncertain for the Irish troops in France. Many ended up sleeping rough in the Breton towns. The luckier ones were billeted in villages amongst unwelcoming inhabitants. Sarsfield reassured his officers before leaving that they would retain their rank, but the French re-organised them while Sarsfield was tied up at the coast superintending the troop transports, with some officers demoted to private. The 15,000 troops became 'nine regiments of infantry of two battalions each, two of dismounted dragoons, two of horse, and two troops of life-guards'.[11] The Irish were resupplied in their new red uniforms, denoting their allegiance to the Stuart king. Sarsfield was also unable to honour the promises of higher pay, as the French were paid less. The Irish were under King James's commission as his private army, but they were paid and maintained by the French treasury.

James received the higher pay from the French but did not pass this onto the Irish, agreeing to make up these arrears when he was restored.[12] By this time, many, even at this stage, were sorry they hadn't stayed in Ireland, yet worse was still to come.

The exiled Stuart court lobbied King Louis for two years that England was ripe for invasion. James was confident of being welcomed by English Jacobites when landing in England. He also relied on the loyalty of flag officers in the Royal Navy who were expected to defect to the Jacobite side. In the end Louis caved in and agreed to finance the project. In the spring of 1692, a 20,000-strong Franco-Irish army assembled in La Hogue, Normandy. Berwick and Sarfield commanded nearly all of James's Irish army of 15,000. The cross-Channel transports were to be escorted by Admiral Tourville's covering fleet of forty-four ships. Royal Navy patrols swarmed the Channel as they were aware of an imminent invasion and were on high alert. Tourville departed port even though he was aware of an Anglo-Dutch ninety-ship fleet lurking off the Isle of Wight. He steered into the Channel and bore down on the centre of that fleet. For more than five hours the Dutch, English and French three-masters unleashed their deadly raking broadsides, the enemy broke the French line and Tourville was forced to disengage and ordered a withdrawal. The British flagship *Brittania* was severely damaged and an attempt was made to board Tourville's flagship, *Le Soleil Royal*. Although crippled she escaped with a number of other ships but they were beached in Cherbourg Bay pursued by the enemy. Berwick, and the other Irishmen, watched the high drama unfold from the port:

> We had heard the sound of the guns very distinctly, and the next morning we decried a number of ships advancing to our coast. At first we distinguished only the French colours, and thought that our victorious fleet was come to transport us to England; but our joy was of short duration, for soon after we discovered the English flag, which convinced us but too fully, that the allies were in pursuit of our ships.[13]

British sailors brought their longboats alongside and set fire to thirteen grounded ships in the sands. Others were towed away as prizes.

Tourville had been outnumbered two to one and should never have engaged this larger fleet, and his decision changed Ireland's destiny. James's intelligence was faulty as no English ships defected. As the Irish viewed the ferocious fires of the beached three-deckers, it was high on symbolism that they would never return home. The English saw the Battle of La Hogue as their greatest triumph over the French since Henry V's victory at Agincourt. The Irish Jacobites were devastated; they had gambled everything and redeemed nothing. They had fought a just war they thought they would win, but had suffered horrendous losses at Aughrim, where they had left their comrades' bodies rotting on the mountainside. The French had let them down, supplied them too late and even drew the drawbridge early at Limerick, which cost hundreds of Irish lives. They were compelled to capitulate at Limerick, were reduced to sleeping rough in Brittany and were prevented from returning to the Kingdom of Ireland on penalty of death. Instead of returning home triumphantly at the head of an army within a year, they were now to fight for France. They had never wanted to live their lives in exile and they were now lost to Ireland forever. What would become of their families, their parents, wives, sons and daughters living under the penal yoke in a Williamite Ireland? They should have stayed in Limerick and held out a little longer. This was their greatest regret.

With the invasion of England scrapped, the Irish troops were regrouped into the French army on the same footing as Mountcashel's Irish Brigade. Many joined the French army in Flanders (the main theatre of operations) and served under the famous hunchback general, Marshal Luxembourg, and the renowned French engineer Marshal Vauban. Others joined the French campaign in Germany and around 1,000 joined the French Marine Royale and were lost into history. The French had plans for both Sarsfield and Berwick, who retained the rank of Maréchal de Camp (the equivalent of lieutenant general). In the summer of 1692, they joined Marshal Luxembourg's staff in the Flanders campaign accompanied by members of the French royal family. In August, Sarsfield commanded the 'Golden Troop' of Horse Guards at the Battle of Steenkirk, not far from Brussels. William's Anglo-Dutch army attacked and scattered several French regiments and Luxembourg sent in his 'Golden Troop' with great losses but succeeded in halting

William's advance, leading to a French victory. Sarsfield and Berwick fought gloriously in the engagement and Luxembourg, one of the greatest French soldiers of all time, was lavish in his praise to King Louis:

> The Duke of Berwick was present from the commencement when we proceeded to reconnoiter the enemy and behaved during the entire combat as bravely as in the last campaign, of which I informed your Majesty at the time. With him was the Earl of Lucan [Sarsfield] in whom we have particularly noticed the valor and the fearlessness of which he had given proofs of in Ireland. I can assure your majesty that he is a very good and a very able officer.[14]

When the campaign ended, Sarsfield was created a Marshal of France, and received his baton, the highest rank in the French army. Sarsfield now had everything he wanted. His 19-year-old wife was fast gaining popularity at court and they had a son whom they called James; but a place called Landen in Flanders would soon change everything. In July 1693, Sarsfield served alongside Luxembourg in the Battle of Landen, where the French scored a clear victory against the Anglo-Dutch. In the village of Neerwinden, the French attacked three times, were forced to retreat as they were exposed to so much fire, but counter-attacked and drove the enemy back. While Sarsfield was leading a French cavalry charge on the Allied position, he was shot in the chest, and died three days later at the age of 37 years, allegedly gasping 'Oh, that this were for Ireland!'[15] Berwick was luckier; he was taken prisoner and marched to Antwerp to be sent to the Tower of London as a 'rebel', but before he was shipped to England he was exchanged for a high-ranking English officer.[16]

Sarsfield's widow married the Duke of Berwick, who after a brilliant military career was killed accidentally by a cannon ball from his own side, which blew his head off while he was directing the siege of Philipsbourg in 1734. Patrick Sarsfield's only son, James, inherited his father's title of Earl of Lucan and rose to colonel in Nugent's horse of France. He took part in a Spanish-led Jacobite invasion of Ireland and landed there in 1719 but died childless at 27 years shortly afterwards of cholera. Sarsfield's land in West Dublin eventually came back into the family through his niece, Charlotte Sarsfield, and the title Lord Lucan is still held today.

Under the terms of the Peace of Ryswick in 1697, Louis XIV was forced to recognise William III as king of England at the expense of James II, who never again left France and consoled himself in religion. Peace resulted in a major downsizing of the French army, leading to 10,000 Irishmen having to fend for themselves.[17] The demobbed Frenchmen returned to their home districts and to their farms, while the thousands of banished Irish were left destitute, unable to return home. James wrote to Louis asking for support in maintaining the Irish, but nothing was done. The district of Montmartre in Paris became notorious for being a favourite Irish haunt for assailing and robbing passers-by. Pope Innocent XII sent James 37,500 livres (of which 35,000 was given to the Irish). James and his wife treated the Irish generously and sold many of their jewels to maintain them, including many personal items; such as 'diamond buttons, a diamond girdle, diamond shoe buckles and diamond attaches'.[18]

In 1701 James II had a stroke and died shortly afterwards. He was not only considered a king, but was also revered as a champion of the Catholic faith and a religious symbol throughout France. He made his son James Francis Stuart (James III) promise that he would never abandon the Catholic faith, even for the throne of England. The following year, William broke his collarbone after his horse, Sorrel, stumbled on a molehill (subsequently giving rise to Jacobite toasts to 'Sorrel') and died of complications two weeks later. William left no heir and was succeeded by James II's daughter, Queen Anne. After her death, the Protestant succession was secured by inviting King James's cousin, George I of the House of Hanover to take the throne. The Treaty of Limerick was mostly swept away by the all-Protestant Irish Parliament of 1697 and Catholics were subjected to the continuous oppression of the Penal Laws that discriminated against them right up to the nineteenth-century.

5

THE DAY WE BEAT THE GERMANS AT CREMONA

The ink on the Treaty of Ryswick was scarcely dry when the Irish were called to serve in the War of the Spanish Succession (1701–14). When the heirless King Charles II of Spain died, he named the Bourbon Philip V (Louis XIV's grandson) as his successor, thereby creating one Bourbon monarch in France and Spain. The Grand Alliance of England, Holland, Austria and a number of German states took issue with this as they feared a powerful Franco-Spanish alliance, which would have drastically changed the balance of power in Europe. The subsequent war was fought in Flanders, Spain, Italy and in the Mediterranean and was significant as it was the first war in which England played a major role in European military affairs, and the last and bloodiest war waged by King Louis XIV of France.

The war involved some of the great military minds of the day: John Churchill, the Duke of Marlborough (an ancestor of Sir Winston Churchill) commanded the Allies and was supported by one of the most successful military commanders of his time, the Austrian Prince Eugene. On the Franco-Spanish side were the last of Louis XIV's great generals; the accomplished Duc de Vendome and the Duc de Villars and 'the most eminent of the Jacobite generals' the Duke of Berwick (James II's illegitimate son).[1] The Irish Brigades distinguished themselves in most of the battles of the war, and particularly for their heroic defence of Cremona.

The campaign opened in Italy in 1701, where Vendome led a French army to drive Prince Eugene's Austrian army out of the country. Eugene entrenched his large army in the well-fortified town of Chiari and prepared for battle. Vendome's 38,000 French troops also comprised 1,500 Irishmen drawn from the Irish infantry regiments of Berwick's, Galmoy's, Bourke's and Dillon's with two squadrons of cavalry from Sheldon's horse, formed mainly from men from County Westmeath.[2] The Austrians had embedded themselves in several farmhouses and mills and the Irish were ordered to dislodge them, which incurred heavy losses. The French were driven from the field after four hours of fierce fighting with 2,000 casualties. Later on in the campaign, Sheldon's horse clashed and cut through a large body of Austro-German cavalry near the town of Burgofort and according to dispatches neither gave nor expected quarter. Louis XIV rewarded his Irish troops by raising their pay and increasing their complement of 'half' and 'full-pay' officers across the entire Irish Brigade. These 'half-pay' officers were volunteers from the disbanded 1698 regiments, following the Peace at Ryswick, who had joined the Italian campaign.

Towards the end of the year, the French army retired to winter quarters in the walled city of Cremona on the banks of the river Po, close to Milan. The French garrison there included a 600-strong composite battalion of Irish troops drawn from Dillon's, Bourke's and Galmoy's. Eugene's Austro-German army planned to surprise the town in a *coup de main*, as by securing Cremona they would compromise French control of Italy. To add to the Austro-German numerical advantage of 10,000 men over the Duc de Villeroi's Franco-Irish 4,600 in the town they also had the element of surprise. An Italian priest whose residence overlooked the town's walls provided the Austrians with a map complete with troop quarters. This enabled 4,500 Austro-Germans to gain entry into the city through a sewer. At the same time, 2,000 men were to capture a fortified position leading onto the Po gate. In the dead of night, the first force of several thousand troops swarmed through while the town slept. They occupied the town square and thought victory was theirs. Even Eugene himself entered in triumph. One can imagine the confusion with soldiers scrambling semi-dressed, musket shots, houses in flames and blood spilling through the freezing cobble streets.

The difficulty facing the Austrians was that a fifty-strong detachment of Dillon's under Captain Stuart held their second force back at the Po gate. An Austro-German force prepared to storm through but the Irish musket volleyed them from behind bars of palisades and held them in check. The call to arms was sounded and the remaining Irish troops rushed forward in their nightshirts to bolster their compatriots and forced the enemy to withdraw. The Germans then prepared to bring forward 24-pound cannons to clear the way. Meanwhile, the French commander, the Duc de Villeroi, was pulled to the ground and would probably have been killed if an Irish officer in the Austrian army called Captain Francis MacDonnell hadn't rescued him. Villeroi offered him a generous pension and promotion in the French army if he would defect but McDonnell refused and brought him to his commander Prince Eugene.

The entire city was now in Austrian hands except for three places: the fortress, the Po gate and the convent (the latter two were still held by 400 Irish troops). Eugene, fearing that the assault was being lost, sent Captain McDonnell to ask his countrymen in the French army to surrender with a promise of 'higher pay, and rewards more considerable, than you have in France'.[3] McDonnell also reminded them that they were heavily outnumbered and that their commander had been taken prisoner. 'We wish to gain the esteem of the Prince by doing our duty,' the Irish replied defiantly, 'not by cowardice or treachery, unworthy of honour', before taking McDonnell prisoner.[4] McDonnell was promoted subsequently by the Austrians to major but was killed six months later in the Battle of Luzzara where he fought his own countrymen again, as the Irish Brigade of France fought on the opposite side.

Meanwhile, Captain McDonagh of Dillon's Regiment rallied a small body of French troops and sent word to the Irish troops guarding the Po gate to launch an assault on the two other enemy-held positions. The Austro-Germans were now determined to break through and attacked again. Baron Freiburg (of the Sligo-born Francis Taafe's Regiment of Austria) led the assault and charged through the Irish with mounted dragoons. The Irish formed square and fierce hand-to-hand fighting took place with heavy losses on both sides. Major Daniel O'Mahony from Co. Kerry captured Freiburg by grabbing his horse's bridle and offered him mercy but Freiburg bolted away and was fired at and killed. Later that afternoon, the Austro-Germans withdrew and the town was secured.

Cremona was one of Eugene's few defeats and was 'taken by a miracle and saved by an even greater one', he later recalled bitterly. 'The Irish performed there the most important piece of service for Louis XIV, that, perhaps, any King of France ever received, from so small a body of men,' concluded the English pamphleteer, Charles Forman. 'This action by the Irish, by an impartial way of reasoning, saved the whole French army in Italy.'[5] The Austrians failed to take the town, argued Arthur Conan Doyle, 'for better men were there, from Limerick and Clare'.[6]

Just under half of the thirty-nine Irish officers were rewarded for bravery, and Cremona sealed their reputation throughout Europe. This came at a heavy price as the Irish suffered heavily with 350 men killed or wounded.[7] Major O'Mahony was honoured by carrying the dispatches to King Louis XIV in a private meeting in Versailles, who thanked him and again raised Irish pay. O'Mahony received a knighthood from King James II in St Germain and was promoted together with the other Irish officers. He was known thereafter as *le fameux Mahoni* for his exploits and went on to enjoy an illustrious career in the Spanish army, rising to lieutenant general.[8] The battle at Cremona was later commemorated with an Irish bagpipe tune (reportedly to the same Gaelic air played by Irish bagpipers during the battle) called; 'The Day We Beat The Germans at Cremona'.[9]

In the late summer of 1702, the five infantry battalions of Berwick's, Bourke's, Dillon's, Galmoy's and Fitzgerald's and two squadrons of Sheldon's horse continued their Italian campaign with the French army under Vendome's command. The French launched an attack on the Austrian-controlled Duchy of Mantua where General Sheldon (while acting as aide-de-camp to Vendome) was wounded, and he, along with only three officers, were mentioned in dispatches to the French king. Irish troops served in the Battle of Luzzara (where McDonnell of Cremona fame was killed) and sustained heavy losses and although forced to retreat 'fought bravely'.[10] The Irish Brigade then helped rout the Austrians from Bondanello, where Lieutenant Colonel Barnewell from Galmoy's took a leading part in the assault.[11] Maréchal de Camp Arthur Dillon from Co. Roscommon led 1,500 French troops and dislodged an enemy force from Riga and later besieged Brescello, which surrendered shortly afterwards. Colonel Daniel O'Mahony was then installed as the town's governor.

The following year, 1703, the Irish Brigade was deployed to the campaign in Germany. Sheldon's horse distinguished itself at Speyer along the Rhine when 180 Irish troopers 'routed 2 regiments of Imperial cuirassiers and recovered the fortunes of the day, and thus led the way to the victory', according to an Allied source.[12] When the French besieged the fortified towns along the Rhine, Irish engineers under Major-General Lee's command joined them. An engineering officer called MacSheehy gained access through a breach during the siege at Kehl, which other French engineers thought was inaccessible. A body of troops from Clare's Regiment suffered heavily when they formed the storming party and pursued the fleeing German troops deep into the nearby woods.

August 1704 opened up the famous Battle of Blenheim, resulting in the worst defeat suffered by the French in the entire war. An Allied army of 40,000 men force-marched 400km from Flanders and cornered the Franco-Bavarian army on the banks of the river Danube, close to the German village of Blenheim. The French heavily defended the villages of Blenheim and Lutzingen at the opposite ends of the battlefield but only lightly fortified their centre at Ogerlau with fourteen battalions, three of whom were drawn from Clare's, Lee's and Dorrington's under Lord Clare. Vendome thought it unlikely that Marlborough would risk advancing here due to the boggy ground, but Marlborough boldly led an assault on the Irish position, which cost many Irish lives.

> The Prince of Holstein-Beck, had with eleven Honovarian battalions, passed the Nebel to Ogerlau, when he was utterly routed by the Irish Brigade which held that village. The Irish held the Hanovarian's back with heavy slaughter, broke completely through the lines of the Allies, and nearly achieved a success as brilliant as that which the same brigade afterwards gained at Fontenoy. But at Blenheim their ardour at pursuit had led them too far. Marlborough came up in person, and dashed in upon their exposed flank with some squadrons of British cavalry. The Irish reeled back and as they strove to regain the height of Oberglau, their column was raked through and through by the fire of three battalions of the Allies which Marlborough had summoned up from the rear.[13]

In the end, the Franco-Bavarians were overwhelmed and forced from the field. Clare's Regiment sustained their retreat by holding the enemy back. Major Gerald O'Connor from Clare's wrote in his memoirs how he was pursued on horseback by three enemy troopers and escaped certain death by plunging into the River Danube with his horse and scrambling to safety on the other side.[14] The battle was the greatest land victory under an English commander, leaving 40,000 men dead on both sides, while 14,000 Franco-Bavarians were captured, including the French Commander Marshal Tallard. The Irish Brigade who 'nearly turned the battle in favour of their master, King Louis XIV' luckily escaped to fight another day.[15]

However, the French redeemed some of their lost glory with success in Italy, defeating Eugene's Austrian army at Cassano. The Austrians countered this defeat by surprising the French at the river Adda. This engagement cost over 10,000 men on both sides, many of whom were drowned. Dillon's, Bourke's and Galmoy's guarded the bridge there and prevented the enemy from crossing the river. Galmoy's lost forty officers when they swam the river and destroyed an enemy battery by wading through up to their waists to get a clear shot at the enemy.[16] When a battalion of Prussian troops attempted to cross, they were musket volleyed by Bourke's, which forced their withdrawal. The French commander wrote a glowing report to Louis that 'the Irish had fought in this affair with an exemplary valour and intrepidity and that they formed a band, whose zeal and devotion might be relied upon, in the most difficult emergencies of war.'[17] Shortly afterwards, a French army under Arthur Dillon's command gained victory at Castiglione and was recommended for promotion to lieutenant general, for 'he is a foreigner of merit and of valor,' wrote Comte de Medavi to Louis, 'who on every occasion has always served your majesty well.'[18] In 1706, Bourke's, Dillon's, Fitzgerald's and Galmoy's formed part of the French army that placed Turin under siege, but were forced to withdraw upon the arrival of a larger Austrian relief force. The French army were then driven out of Italy for the remainder of the war.

The Wild Geese continued their arduous campaign in 1706 when the Allies attacked the Franco-Bavarians in Ramillies (in present-day Belgium). Both armies fielded 120,000 men and the Irish were heavily engaged. When the Irish advanced through Ramillies village, 'the scarlet coats of the regiments of Lord Clare, Lee and Dorrington appearing among the houses and gardens,' according to an Allied account, 'beheld the presense of the famous Irish Brigade and foretold a desperate resistance.'[19] According to Captain Peter Drake, an Irish officer in the French army, the French 'left the field in infinite disgrace, except Lord Clare's, which engaged with a Scotch regiment in the Dutch service between whom there was much slaughter'. The remaining Irish regiments were sent in to support them but when they were 'within pistol-shot' of the enemy, they were ordered to retreat.[20] Although Clare's lost 22 officers and 303 men they managed to capture the only two Allied colours taken in the face of this French defeat. One flag came from a Scottish regiment in the Dutch service which was 'nearly totally destroyed' and the other one came from the English Regiment of Churchill (known later as 'the Buffs'). These trophies were then lodged in the chapel of the Irish Benedictine Convent at Ieper (Ypres) in Belgium.[21] The 36-year-old Colonel Charles O'Brien, the 5th Lord Clare, was mortally wounded and died three days later and was interred in the Irish Dominican College in Leuven, together with Major John O'Carrol.[22] The shattered remains of the French army marched all night without resting and arrived 'dispirited and weary' in Leuven the following dawn.[23]

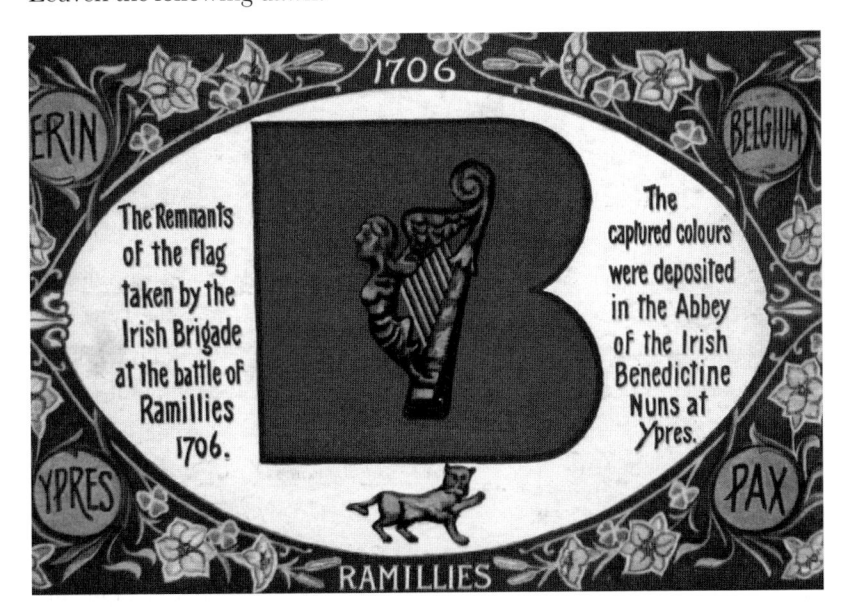

Post First World War postcard displaying the harp segment of the English Royal Standard of the Ramillies flag. (Author's collection)

Successive French defeats in Gent, Antwerp and Brugge finally led France to lose its grip on Flanders. Vendome defeated the Austrians at Calcinato in Italy, which partly made up for French defeats there. The French commander wrote to Louis commending Irish bravery there.[24] Chevalier Gaydon described how a company of Dillon's bayonet charged the Austrians in the battle.

> 'We marched on the enemy with fixed bayonets … the enemy gave us a volley with all the fire power that they possessed but with little success … our infantry had orders to hold their arms at the present while mounting the hill and not to fire a shot, under pain of death … we closed in on them … [and] threw them on top of one another with slaughter.'[25]

The spoils of war included several panniers of champagne, which the Austrians had left behind. Lieutenant General Dillon no doubt improved his popularity by distributing them to his brother officers.[26]

By 1708, the French had suffered a string of defeats in Flanders and needed a breakthrough to stave off an allied invasion of France herself. In July, the Allies launched a titanic attack with 80,000 men and defeated 95,000 Frenchman (together with Fitzgerald's, Clare's and Nugent's horse) at the Battle of Oudenaarde. The Allies went on to besiege Vauban's star-shaped fortress at Lille, which was defended by a large French garrison along with an unnamed Irish battalion. Lieutenant General Lee was also present and was wounded and received the Order of St Louis for bravery.[27] Lille was the grandest fortress in Europe at the time and was thought to be impregnable, but it finally fell into Allied hands after a four-month siege. This victory opened up the corridor to France to the Allies.

Eighty-six thousand Allied troops besieged Mons in Flanders in late 1709. Villar's 75,000-strong French army was marched to relieve it and they took up a defensive position in the village of Malplaquet. The Irish regiments of Lee's, O'Brien's, Dorrington's, Galmoy's, and Nugent's horse were assigned to Villar's army. The Battle of Malplaquet would become the most famous and bloodiest battle in the war. The Allied army comprised veteran troops whereas the French relied on unblooded new recruits due to heavy French losses suffered earlier. The French infantry were embedded in and around the woods of Malplaquet, where allied light mortars and heavy cannon pounded them in an attempt to flush them out.[28] The Irish, Swiss and French regiments succeeded in repulsing three enemy charges before they counter-attacked. 'With the aid of these reinforcement,' wrote the Duke of Marlborough in his memoirs, 'a furious charge was made into the wood of Tasniere upon the British and Prussians who recoiled a considerable way before the onset of the Irish.'[29]

Several French and Irish regiments took up position in Sart Wood around Malplaquet. A detachment drawn from an Irish Royal Regiment of foot in the British army (under the Protestant Captain Robert Parker from Co. Kilkenny) exchanged musket volleys with the Irish Regiment of Dorrington in the French army (under the Catholic Lieutenant Colonel Michael Rothe, also from Kilkenny). Both red-coated regiments were unaware at the time they were fighting their fellow countrymen. 'Forward, brave Irishmen!' yelled the Irish troops as they charged, 'Long live King James III and the King of France!' But the Anglo-Irish regiment succeeded in pushing them back and were astonished after the firefight to learn they had been fighting against another Irish regiment. Captain Robert Parker recorded that this was due to their increased firepower from using heavier musket balls and by creating a 'rolling' volley through firing by platoons, as opposed to firing by single ranks. 'We advanced cautiously up to the ground which they had quitted,' wrote Parker, 'and found several of them killed and wounded; among the latter was one Lieutenant O'Sullivan, who told us the battalion we had engaged was the Royal Regiment of Ireland.'[30] The Stuart king, James III, was also present and led the French Regiment of the Maison du Roi in the battle, and although under heavy cannon fire made twelve charges penetrating Allied cavalry lines. He received a sabre wound to his arm and was mentioned in despatches as having behaved with 'all possible bravery and vivacity'.[31] The Allies eventually forced the French from the field, leading to an Allied pyrrhic victory, due to nearly 20,000 killed on both sides. Around 10,000 Irishmen fought in the battle and over one-third were killed.[32]

After the French defeat in Flanders, Germany and Italy, the war's focus turned to Spain, where the Wild Geese of France and Spain would spill much blood. In 1703, Philip V of Spain transferred several Irish regiments from the French into the Spanish service.[33] In 1709, the long-serving Irish Regiments of Irlanda, Hibernia and Ultonia (Ulster) were formed and served with distinction at the battles of Zaragoza, Brihuega and Villaciosa the following year. In 1704, the Irish Brigade of Spain served on 'the rock' of Gibraltar before it capitulated following a heavy Royal Navy bombardment. The same year, the Duke of Berwick led a large French expeditionary force to Spain and Portugal to remove the Allies there. Berwick captured the fortress at Castel-Branco, which was strategically located close to Lisbon, but he was forced out of Portugul the same year. In 1707, he led the Franco-Spanish army in the Battle of Almanza (the most decisive battle fought in Spain) where the Irish troops played a significant part in the Allied defeat. Several Irish battalions were reported to have marched up to an English infantry line and at thirty paces bayonet charged the English who recoiled and gave way. After the battle, Berwick was decorated with the Order of the Grande Fleece and was made a Grandee of Spain by the Spanish king. Towards the end of the year, the French army supported by Lieutenant General Arthur Dillon commanding thirty French battalions besieged Barcelona, which fell after two assaults were made on the city. The newly formed Hibernia's of Spain augmented by Dillon's, Lee's, Berwick's and Burke's of France formed part of the storming party that rushed through one of the breaches. Patrick Sarsfield's son, James Sarsfield, then a captain in the Spanish army was also wounded in the mêlée and received the Order of the Golden Fleece for bravery there.[34]

France was eager for peace as she lacked resources to continue the war. This was finally decided with the Treaty of Utrecht. The War of the Spanish Succession settled the various power struggles between the European powers. It reduced French power and accelerated Spain's decline. Spain lost Spanish Flanders to the Austrians and only gained the crown of Spain for the Bourbon Philip V. With the demise of the Netherlands as a major world player, England embarked on her vast imperial course and emerged as the dominant naval power. The Irish regiments of France and Spain distinguished themselves in the war and established their reputation as elite troops. Their background of extreme poverty growing up in a harsh Irish landscape was well suited to the 'hard hand of warfare' and the vicissitudes and rigours of military life. It is impossible to calculate how many survived since Mountcashel's Irish Brigade and Sarsfield's Wild Geese first arrived in France in 1691. Rank-and-file casualties are uncertain but were likely to be very high. The Irish were frequently used as storm troopers in the vanguard

Artist unknown, engraving of Justin MacCarthy, Lord Mountcashel, the first commander of the Irish Brigade in France. (Author's collection)

for the most dangerous missions. Justin McCarthy (Lord Mountcashel) died convalescing from wounds while serving at the Rhine. Patrick Sarsfield was killed at Landen. Colonel Fitzgerald died of wounds received at Oudenaarde. Richard Talbot fell at Luzzara and Colonel Magennis was killed at Speyer. Daniel O'Brien, 4th Lord Clare, died at Marsiglia and his son Charles O'Brien, the 5th Lord Clare, at Ramillies. Lord Galmoy's only son was killed at Malplaquet. The intention of the Wild Geese when they left Limerick was to return triumphantly within a year; not to be used as pawns fighting their own countrymen in European dynastic conflicts with little relevance to Ireland's cause.

6

THE FIRST JACOBITE RISING (1715)

Another attempt was made to reinstate the Stuart king to the throne in the early eighteenth century. The Jacobite community in France and Spain were acutely aware of Scottish discontentment after the 1707 Act of Union between England and Scotland. The Union reduced Scotland's autonomy and power and was seen by many of the fiercely independent Highlanders as a 'slavish subjugation'. Anti-Union sentiment was so strong that Scottish swords of the period were provocatively inscribed with 'Prosperity to Scotland – No Union'. Jacobites capitalised on this discontent in a plan to repeal the Union and reinstate James Stuart. The Irish Jacobite Nathaniel Hooke was sent to Scotland to gather intelligence, returning with news that 30,000 would rise if France pledged 20,000 troops and sufficient stands-of-arms. James's wife, Mary of Modena, sent an Irish Catholic priest called Father O'Connor to Ireland on a fact-finding mission. He discovered that many leading Irish Jacobite leaders were imprisoned but he was assured of support, particularly in the south-western part of the country, where they had capitulated so quickly twenty-five years earlier.

The Jacobites in France finally persuaded King Louis XIV to pledge 6,000 French troops for a rising in Scotland. The French were not confident of success but let the expedition take place anyway as they saw it as a convenient diversionary tactic to remove troops and pressure from the war in Flanders. In 1708 an Anglo-Dutch fleet blockaded Dunkirk and pinned in the supporting fleet, but owing to heavy storms the blockade was temporarily lifted, enabling the French expeditionary force of thirty ships of the line, accompanied by a number of smaller frigates and 6,000 troops, to sail for Scotland. The French fleet successfully anchored at Inverness, in eastern Scotland, but failed to make contact with any prominent Jacobite leaders. The fleet was chased by the Anglo-Dutch fleet all around the north of Scotland and lost as many as half of their ships, which were either captured or lost due to heavy storms.

Several years later in 1714, another opportunity arose when Queen Anne of England died childless, but James was precluded from inheriting the throne due to the Act of Settlement 1701, even though he was Anne's half-brother. Timing and circumstance instead smiled down on the Hanoverian Prince George Ludwig (Queen Anne's closest Protestant relative), who was proclaimed King George I of England, Scotland and Ireland. Notwithstanding, James was still confident of regaining the crown as many prominent nobles in England supported his claim. His strongest support was in the mainly Catholic enclave of the Scottish Highlands where the Stuarts had ruled for centuries. He was recognised as James III and knew he could rely on the Highlander's feudal loyalty, support and bonds which passed from clansman to chieftain to king.

In 1714, the War of the Spanish Succession was concluded and the difficulty facing the French-based Jacobites was that Louis XIV could no longer support an invasion, as France and England were no longer at war. After Louis's death the following year, the regent Philippe d'Orlean's claim to the French throne hinged on maintaining peace with England. He said he could only supply volunteers from the Irish Brigade and French half-pay officers – otherwise the Jacobites were on their own. James ordered the colonels of the Irish regiments in France and Spain to be ready to select officers and men for an expedition to Scotland.[1] An Irish Brigade officer called Sir John Forrester spent three months in Scotland gathering support and distributing funds to the Scottish clans to purchase arms for an impending rising.[2] The opportunity to support the 'old cause' in Scotland was welcomed by the Wild Geese for a number of reasons:

Quite apart from the ideological commitment many of the officers and men of the Irish Brigade felt towards the Stuarts they now had the prospect of material advantage to incline them towards active support of any uprising in the British Isles. With France clearly exhausted militarily there were unlikely to be any wars involving France for some time to come and thus a much reduced chance of promotion and preferment, and the impending disbandments and transfers meant uncertain career prospects for many officers and men. It was, therefore, natural that the army of Catholic Ireland overseas would respond positively to what looked like a golden opportunity.[3]

The invasion plan involved launching a two-pronged attack. A prominent Irish Jacobite, James Butler, the Duke of Ormond, was to land in south-west England and march to London, and the Scot John Erskine, the 6th Earl of Mar, was to initiate a rising in the Highlands. It was then expected that English Jacobites in the north would rise and join the insurrection. The Duke of Ormond landed with French troops, in south-east England, along with an Irish cavalry detachment drawn from Nugent's horse, but they lacked support and they were forced to return to France. With Ormond's departure, the campaign focused on Scotland. The Earl of Mar led operations there and proved to be a resourceful leader in mustering support from the clans and raised 12,000 volunteers. He relied on creating anti-Union feeling to gain support from the mainly Presbyterian lowland Scots, who would not necessarily have been supporters of the Stuarts but were nevertheless reeling from the Act of Union, which they saw as grossly unjust. As the Earl of Mar was a politician and lacked military experience, the Duke of Berwick was expected to relieve him of command when he arrived in Scotland. However, the presence of such a high-profile general as Berwick would have implicated France in the plot, and in the end Berwick never joined the expedition.

In September 1715, the royal coronation took place in Braemar, attended by the Earl of Mar and around sixty others. The Stuart standard was unfurled, described as being blue 'on the one side, the Scottish arms, wrought in gold, and, of the other, the Scottish thistle, with these words underneath, *No Union*'.[4] James was proclaimed James VIII of Scotland

The First Jacobite Rising (1715)

and James III of Scotland, England and Ireland. The Highlanders were a superstitious people and were always watchful of omens, and observed as a bad sign that as the pole was planted in the ground the gilt ball fell down from its summit. Prayers were said, the clans assumed the white cockades symbolising their support for the Stuarts and, according to custom, a cross in flames was sent throughout the Highlands calling for a gathering of the clans.

The Jacobite army mobilised quickly and took control of Inverness. They tried to take Edinburgh Castle in a surprise attack but the plan was foiled. Whitehall suspended *habeas corpus*, mobilised 7,000 troops and offered £10,000 reward for 'James the Pretender', dead or alive. At this point in the campaign, arms and money necessary to sustain the rising were urgently required but the French fleet remained blockaded by the English Channel Fleet in Le Havre and Dieppe. It was now looking increasingly unlikely that the rebellion could spread outside of Scotland as the fledgling Jacobite army now lacked discipline, supplies and able military leadership. They overestimated support for their cause in the northern English counties of Lancaster and Northumberland. Catholic landowners did rise up there but they were heavily outnumbered and poorly equipped. On 14 November a government army decisively defeated the English Jacobites in the Battle of Preston in Lancashire, where many high-ranking Irish Jacobites were arrested. James Talbot and Charles Wogan later made a daring escape from Newgate Prison. With a price of £500 on their heads, Talbot was captured in London while Wogan made it safely back to France and would later emerge as a key figure in the Jacobite Cause and 'the most famous knight in Europe.'[5] Just the day before the English Jacobites' defeat at Preston, the Jacobites in Scotland confronted John Campbell the 2nd Duke of Argyll's government army at the Battle of Sheriffmuir in Scotland, and fared better than the Jacobites at Preston. At one point in the battle the Highlanders were forced over the river Allan where many drowned. The Stuarts of Appin and the Cameroons of Lochiel retired without striking a blow but the famous Scottish folk hero Robert 'Rob Roy' McGregor fought well. The Jacobites gained the upper hand in the battle but failed to defeat Argyll's army decisively, resulting in a stalemate. Some Highland clans were accused of being lukewarm and lacking conviction at the battle. One of the Highland chiefs cried out, 'Oh, for an hour of Dundee!' as he was so indignant at the sluggish Mar for drawing off his troops. This exclamation became famous and was a reference to the leader of the Jacobite army, Viscount Dundee, who was killed in the Battle of Killekrankie during the Jacobite War (1689–91). The Earl of Mar was accused of displaying his military ineptitude by withdrawing his forces to Perth instead of finishing Argyll off.

Thereafter, the Jacobites were a spent force and government strategy centred on containing them in the Highlands and preventing their march south into England. The rising was ultimately doomed to fail due to a lack of French support, and by December, they were close to capitulation when James himself landed in Scotland. He arrived with six nobles in Peterhead, along with a number of high-ranking Irish officers; Lieutenant General Sheldon, Brigadier Nugent and Brigadier General Francis Bulkeley. James's entourage pushed on towards Perth, where he received the news that things were not going in their favour. James was known colloquially among the Highlanders as 'old mister meloncholy' as he lacked charisma, and was received coldly by them. 'I must not conceal that when we saw the man whom they call our King, we found ourselves not at all animated by his presence,' recalled one of the Highlanders, 'and if he was disappointed in us, we were tenfold more so in him. He never appeared with cheerfulness and vigour to animate us. Our men began to despise him.'

The Jacobite army withdrew from Perth as defences there were inadequate to withstand a siege and a large government army was fast approaching. To make matters worse, James received rumours that several Highland chiefs were considering handing him over to the government and wanted to abandon the enterprise. When the army marched towards Aberdeen, James secretly departed from Montrose for France, ordering the Highlanders to fend for themselves. This was the second time a Stuart had made a run for France when things were not going well. The demoralised Jacobite army, now dwindling in numbers trundled on to Aberdeen and beyond to Badenoch and Locheer and gradually dispersed. The common soldiers eventually made it home and the Jacobite leaders escaped to the Orkneys and then boarded ships to France.

Throughout the 1715 Jacobite Rebellion, the British government had been aware of the Irish Brigade swelling the French Channel ports to spearhead the main invasion. Several Irish regiments were recalled from active service along the Rhine and were ordered to march to the French ports of Calais and Boulogne. The Irish were the preferred troops for the invasion as they were less politically provocative than French troops on British soil. They were accustomed to the food and the Highlanders' hardy way of life and knew the two languages, Gaelic and English.[6] Ireland traditionally maintained close links to Scotland. The Irish spoken in County Donegal in Ulster is similar to Scots Gaelic, and a particular dialect known as 'Highland Irish' was still spoken in County Antrim by the mid-1800s.[7] This connection extended back to the sixth and seventh centuries when an Irish tribe of settlers called the Scoti established the Gaelic kingdom of Dal Riata, which extended from western Scotland to Ulster.[8]

Catholics in Ireland failed to rise in 1715 as the country was relatively quiet in the period. Local Irish raparees continued to launch sporadic attacks on government forces in Ireland. There was even dissent among Irish Protestants who also harboured clandestine Jacobite sympathies, some of whom were converted Catholics. In 1708 a student of the all-Protestant Trinity College in Dublin was expelled for comparing William's *coup d'etat* to the behaviour of a common highwayman, and three years later several students were thrown out of Trinity for defacing King William's statue in College Green, Dublin.[9] On another occasion, a raucous Protestant mob marched through the streets of Dublin celebrating James III's birthday.[10] It was widely believed the Irish Brigade was landing with Lieutenant General Arthur Dillon leading 6,000 troops, but any invasion of Ireland was a diversion. The real goal for a restoration was always London. Historians have argued that the Jacobites should have opened another front in Ireland where support was strong. They could have pinned down the British army's 3,000 troops stationed in Ireland, which were shipped to Scotland and helped quell the rebellion there.

Spain did not play a major role in the 1715 Rising. Captain Marcus Magrath of the Spanish Irish Brigade organised to sail for Scotland with ninety officers, but abandoned the mission when they learned of the

Jacobite defeat at Preston.[11] The détente between France and England held for the following fifteen years, forcing the Jacobites into engineering alliances with other Continental powers. James Butler, the Duke of Ormond, approached Peter the Great of Russia to gain support for an expedition to England with 10,000 troops in an alliance with Charles XII of Sweden. An Irish agent in Spain called Peter Lawless travelled to Sweden to broker support for an invasion of the British Isles with a combined Russian–Spanish force the following spring.[12] However, these cloak and dagger plots ultimately collapsed and came to nothing.

Four years later, in 1719, it was their old friends France and Spain to whom the Jacobites turned in their time of need. Philip V of Spain openly supported the Stuart claim, as he was eager to restore Spanish power and prestige after losing possessions in the Treaty of Utrecht. Philip invited James to Madrid where he was received as King James III of England, Ireland and Scotland in a lavish royal reception. The Spanish Court sanctioned the sending of three expeditions to Ireland, Scotland and England. The expeditions to Ireland and Scotland were again diversionary manoeuvres to divert attention from the main landings in England. Colonel James Sarsfield of Nugent's horse (the famous Patrick Sarsfield's son) landed in Connacht in the west of Ireland with a number of Spanish and Irish officers to incite a rising there. The young Sarsfield had a price of £1,000 on his head and was a popular leader because of his famous name but received little active support and he eventually escaped capture sailing from Kilcoglan in Co. Galway. Around the same time, the main invasion force led again by the Irish Jacobite, the Duke of Ormond, sailed for Bristol with twenty-two ships carrying a large body of troops, along with a large contingent drawn from the Spanish Irish Brigade.[13]

This fleet was the largest Spanish force to invade England since the Spanish Armada of Elizabethan times, but just like the Armada this fleet too was dispersed by heavy storms and was forced to return to Cadiz. In April 1719, the diversionary Scottish landing, carrying Spanish-Irish officers also encountered heavy storms en route to Scotland, resulting in only two ships carrying 300 Spanish troops arriving safely in Kintail, Scotland. They then joined up with several hundred Highlanders under Lord George Murray, Cameron of Lochiel, and other highland chiefs. However, they were defeated by government forces at the Battle of Glenshiel and shortly afterwards, with support lacking from the Lowland Scots, the rising petered out. The rebels returned to their homes, the Spanish surrendered and were later repatriated and thus ended the 'Little Rising' of 1719.

The authorities recognised that the Highlands needed to be properly garrisoned to keep them in check. The commander of the British army in Scotland, the Irish Protestant General Wade, oversaw the construction of a chain of fortresses and a military road in the Highlands, facilitating the speedy movements of troops in times of unrest (similar to the Military Road in Co. Wicklow that was constructed after the 1798 Irish Rising). Wade also formed local independent companies of militia, made up of loyal clans known as the 'Black Watch'; with their kilts, broadswords and Highland feudal origins, they would prove to be a feared force while serving in Ireland and on the Continent.

7

THE BATTLE OF FONTENOY (1745)

The French Irish Brigade's reputation was copper-fastened in Fontenoy when six Irish infantry regiments broke a British infantry advance and, in doing so, snatched victory from the jaws of defeat. Fontenoy was a major battle of the eighteenth century and was one of the greatest French victories. It was also famous for the bravery of the British foot soldiers through their steady half-mile march while under heavy bombardment. The battle was fought close to Tournai (in modern Belgium) during the War of the Austrian Succession (1740–48). France wanted to secure success in Flanders, the cockpit of Europe, and assembled her army there. The Duke of Cumberland, William Augustus, George II's favourite son, was appointed commander of the Anglo-Dutch-Hanoverian army said to be the finest in Europe, and was sent over with a large force from England to confront the French army.

Marshal Maurice de Saxe commanded French forces from a two-wheeled wicker sedan chair as he suffered from the medical condition known as dropsy and was unable to sit on horseback for more than a few minutes. He was one of the great generals of his day and was at the height of his genius.[1] In 1709, when just 14 years old, he witnessed the bloody Battle of Malplaquet, which cost 40,000 lives, of whom 3,500 were Irish.[2] He was horrified at the carnage and was determined to conduct his battles in another manner, avoiding the costly mistakes of his predecessors.

His opposite number was the minnow, the Duke of Cumberland, who was subsequently known as the 'Butcher of Culloden' for his ruthlessness in suppressing the Second Jacobite Rising of 1745. Cumberland was 23 years old and a relatively inexperienced commander, although he had fought with valour and was wounded in the Battle of Dettingen two years previously and gained promotion to lieutenant general.

Saxe manoeuvred his battalions like a chess master would his pawns in a chess game. He marched his 76,000 men south and besieged the fortified city of Tournai, whilst Cumberland mobilised his army to relieve it. Saxe left a large tranche of his army to maintain the siege at Tournai and marched 45,000 men 10km to the village of Fontenoy. He took advantage of a slight rise in a strong position and hastily prepared earthwork defences waiting for Cumberland's Allied army to arrive. The battle was the affair of the day, where the famous French writer Voltaire, and even King Louis XV and the Dauphin arrived four days later with an enormous royal entourage. The French constructed five gun-batteries (built of wood protected by earthworks) equipped with four cannons, located between the villages of Vezon and Fontenoy to bar the Allied advance. The most important one was known as Redoubt d'Eu and was placed near Barri Wood to provide enfilade fire onto the enemy.[3] Saxe wanted to channel the Allies into this open ground between the wood and Fontenoy and suck them into the trap.

The six Irish infantry regiments of the Irish Brigade, one battalion each of Clare's, Dillon's, Berwick's, Bulkeley's, Lally's, and Roth's, commanded by Lieutenant General Charles O'Brien the 6th Lord Clare, were at full strength, numbering 3,870 bayonets.[4] The Irish infantry occupied the left flank at Barri Wood, and were to block the Allied advance there. The sole Irish cavalry Regiment of Fitzjames (four squadrons of 270 sabres) was posted in the centre together with other French cavalry. Total Irish strength at Fontenoy numbered 4,140 men. This was the only major engagement in the Brigade's history where all seven Irish regiments were fielded together. The Brigade's chaplain, Father Charles McKenna from Co. Monaghan, gave general absolution to the men before the battle, as did the other French regiments. The Scottish regiment of Royal Eccossais (Royal Scots) of France was not present, as it is thought they comprised part of the garrison besieging Tournai, where they remained

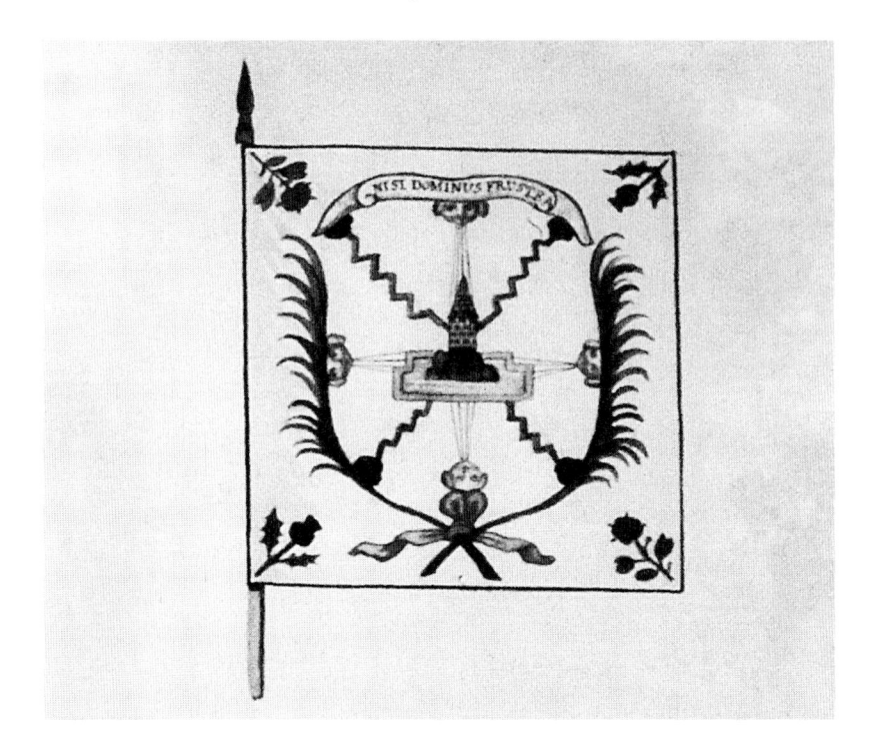

The Fontenoy flag, surmounted with the motto: '*Nisi Dominus Frustra*' (Without the Lord It Is In vain). Evidence suggests the flag is from Sempill's Regiment of Foot (later the King's Own Scottish Borderers) and not from the Coldstream Guards as was previously thought. (photo taken from La Bibliotheque Nationaux, Paris)

positioned in their trenches, and fought bravely.[5] The night before the battle, Colonel Thomas Lally of Dillon's Regiment reconnoitred the ground between the villages of Anthoing and Fontenoy. It was previously thought that this area was impassible, but Lally recommended additional cannon to be placed here.[6]

When dawn broke on 11 May 1745, Cumberland's 50,000 men mobilised in front of the village of Vezon and Saxe waited. The Allied cavalry advanced but were driven back as they received too much fire. At the same time, the Dutch attacked Antoing on the right flank, but a French battery of six 12-pounders opened up on them and forced their retreat. The Scottish Highland Regiment of the Black Watch took part in the second wave but was also repulsed with around 1,000 casualties. The Black Watch received its baptism of fire at Fontenoy and fought bravely. A French officer described them as 'Highland furies

Trooper of Fitzjames horse, 1758. (Courtesy of Het Legermuseum, Nationale Bibliotheek Van Nederland)

who rushed in on us with more violence than ever did the sea driven by the tempest'. A clansman killed nine Frenchmen and decapitated a horse with his broadsword, before his own arm was carried off by a cannon ball.

As his initial attacks failed, Cumberland marched his Anglo-Hanoverian infantry through the exposed open ground between Barri Wood and Fontenoy to the delight of the expecting French. As his 15,000 troops marched in ordered formation, his advance was stalled early due to enfilade fire from the d'Eu battery which was cutting swathes through his ranks. He ordered Brigadier Ingoldsby to storm this position but French light-infantry sharp shooters forced the attackers back. As a result, Cumberland was forced to make his attack while under constant enemy barrage and marched in parade order up the hill towards the enemy, drums beating the advance.[7] The Allied column quickly crowded into one, as it sustained such heavy enfilade fire, in what became known as the 'infernal column' and stopped 300 paces from the French first line. The discipline of the Allied column in keeping formation was a testament to good military training and coolness in battle.

They now faced four battalions of the premier infantry regiment of the eighteenth century, the Gardes Francaises and two battalions of veteran Swiss Guards. An English officer, Lord Charles Hay, sprang out in front of his line, doffed his hat, and shouted; 'We are the English guards and we hope you will stand till we come up to you, and not swim the Scheldt river as you swam the Main!' He was referring to an earlier engagement when the retreating Gardes Francaises tipped one of their boats and many were drowned. Hays then turned to his own men and called for three cheers, and the astonished French officer, Count d'Autoroche, counter-cheered. The Gardes Francaises fired a volley first. The British responded by firing off a 'rolling' volley by platoons down their line and in seconds over 800 men fell.[8] After sustaining such heavy casualties, the French regiment broke and ran; leaving the officers exposed who were nearly knocked down by the retreating troops. The column closed ranks and continued their advance and cut through the second French line of the Regiment of Roi. They were now well within the French position and no longer felt the enfilade fire that had swept the crest it had just passed over.

Meanwhile, the six Irish infantry regiments waited nervously out of sight behind Barri Wood, where couriers reported developments of the battle. Saxe ordered several combined infantry and cavalry counter-attacks to gain precious minutes. The column had now lost one-third of its strength and retired, but 'dressed its ranks and advanced again, sweeping all before it by sheer force of impetus'.[9] It is during these counter-attacks where confusion arises in the role the Irish Brigade played. Dillon's attacked together with the Regiments of Normandie and Vaisseaux and all three were repelled with substantial losses. Colonel James Dillon was killed leading his regiment in the charge. Fitzjames' horse lost seventy-five horses, cut to pieces by enemy cannon. The French thought the battle was lost and Louis was urged to leave the battlefield. But he was persuaded to stay by the Duc de Richelieu, which Saxe was grateful for, as the flight of the king at this point would have signalled defeat.[10] Louis was observed by Saxe 'nervously biting the *fleur de lilie* embroidered in the corner of his handkerchief'.[11]

The Dutch were preparing to attack again and Saxe stood up from his sedan chair, and in great pain mounted his horse to collect his cavalry for a final charge. Colonel Thomas Lally then implored him to send in the Irish Brigade to lead the attack. 'On what finer reserves could a general call in a moment of crisis than six battalions of the Wild Geese?'[12] Even Cumberland recalled in his memoirs: 'Marshal Saxe was now reduced to his last and principal effort to retrieve the honour of the day, and this was to bring up the Irish Brigade; a corps on whose courage and behaviour he entirely depended for a favourable decision of so great, so dubious, so well contested a battle.'[13]

The Irish infantry were kept in reserve behind the wood, shouting cries of 'huzzah!' as they formed into line. To get their blood up, Lally reminded them that France's enemies were also theirs and ordered them not to fire until their bayonets were at their stomachs. '*Cuimhnígí ar Luimneach Cuimhnígíis ar fheill na Sasananch!*' shouted Lally with drawn sword, 'Remember Limerick and Saxon perfidy!' The Maison du Roi, the Gendarmerie and light cavalry attacked the front of the column with the four cannon while the Swiss Guard attacked the Hanoverian left. The Irish Brigade led the charge on the British right, supported by the rump of the regiments of Normandie and Vaisseaux; the latter had suffered terribly in previous counter-attacks and only had one officer standing.[14]

Nearly 4,000 Irishmen advanced up the incline towards the British column. Bagpipers of the Irish Brigade played the Jacobite tune, 'The White Cockade' (both the bagpipes and 'The White Cockade' were banned in Ireland).[15] Victory now depended on the Irish and one can imagine how French hearts were lifted as they heard the skirl of the *píob mhór* or war pipes of the Irish Brigade resonate through the Belgian valley. The ordinary British soldier was well aware of the fearsome reputation of the Irish Brigade and of their wish to settle old scores. One can only imagine the terror when the fatigued British foot and guard regiments saw the red-coated Wild Geese advancing with fixed bayonets towards them, some shouting in Irish '*Cuimhnígí ar Luimneach*', 'Remember Limerick!' The high drama escalated as the Irish advanced, as an officer of the Coldstream Guards suddenly rushed out to the front of the Allied column and challenged an Irish officer, Captain Anthony McDonough from Co. Clare, to single combat with swords. The Irishman parried and smashed his adversary's sword arm and forced him to the ground, which invigorated the Irish further and a thousand huzzahing came from the back. The Irish received a British volley, which brought down the first line. They bayonet charged and penetrated into the right flank of the British column, and were ordered to withdraw, as otherwise they would have advanced too deep. The Irish second line then charged and drove the column back, inch by inch, and yard by yard.[16] The 'infernal column' broke into fragments, and what had been a sure defeat several minutes earlier was now a victory.

The Allies rallied the colours and retreated through the night to Ath, where Cumberland burst into tears at the defeat. Saxe ordered his light troops of mounted Grassins to pursue and harry the Allied rearguard. The Black Watch covered the Allied retreat and was afterwards singled out for special praise. Irishmen fought against Irishmen in the battle, as some Irish Catholics served on the British side despite the official Catholic ban on recruitment. A large Irish Protestant contingent formed the three squadrons of the Irish 6th (Inniskilling) Dragoons who were also present. After the battle, the Irish Brigade was dismayed to have engaged so many of their fellow countrymen, and to perk the men up, their bagpipers played 'Saint Patrick's Day in the Morning' amidst cheers from the Brigade, some shouting; 'Hurrah for old Ireland!'

The same day, King Louis and the Dauphin rode down to the Irish troops first and thanked them. Sergeant Wheelock of Bulkeley's was promoted by the king in the field to sous-lieutenant for capturing a British colour. Lord Clare was hit in the chest by two musket balls but his cuirass saved his life, as the balls bounced back off. Colonel Thomas Lally, who was wounded, and the commanding officer of Berwick's, Lieutenant Colonel Stapleton from Co. Limerick, were raised to brigadier generals. Many other officers were promoted or received pensions and gratuities, and were decorated with the coveted Cross of St Louis. The Irish Brigade spent the night in the middle of the battlefield amongst the dying and wounded.

Although the high casualties at the Battle of Malplaquet haunted Saxe, Fontenoy ranks among the most murderous of battles of the eighteenth century with nearly 15,000 killed. To this day, aerial photographs indicate the presence of mass graves. The ploughshare frequently turns up artefacts; a grave was recently uncovered which contained the remains of twelve British soldiers hastily buried after the battle. The Allies lost 7,545 officers and men and the French lost a similar number, but the Irish suffered higher losses in proportion to any other French unit and sacrificed themselves to compel an English defeat.[17] They lost one-quarter of their officers and a total of 656 men.[18] Irish losses were especially poignant, as many extended families served together; the nephews, sons and uncles of the MacCarthys, O'Reillys and Sweeneys all fell. When George II was informed of the English defeat, he reportedly cursed the Penal Laws that prevented him having Irish Catholics in his army.

In the following months, the French steadily removed the British army from Flanders, and Saxe's victory cut Britain off from her allies in the east. The Irish were rewarded further with captured British supplies taken at Gent. King Louis replaced Fitzjames's horses at his own expense, even though it was usual for the regiment to replace these losses themselves. Fontenoy was the only conclusive French land victory over a British commander since the fifteenth-century Hundred Years War. France was jubilant, and had a lucky escape. A French defeat would have curtailed Louis's reign by at least thirty years, and resulted in the British controlling a large portion of Northern France. Voltaire wrote jubilantly to Comte d'Argenson, 'It is three hundred years since a king of France has done anything as glorious, I am mad with joy.'[19] Saxe also provides us with an indication of French relief at the victory, finally defeating her old enemy:

> Voltaire, in particular, who never let slip an opportunity of associating his name with glory, attempted to express in his *Poeme de Fontenoy* the delirious joy all France felt in having at last, after centuries, beaten her hereditary foes. 21,000 copies of his dithyram were sold in a few days, everywhere there were fireworks, illuminations, *Te Deum*. The battle of Fontenoy, in a word, had a great renown; perhaps no military exploit has ever been so belauded.[20]

The Irish had old scores to settle and a victory over their oppressors was a huge achievement for the corps and for Ireland under bondage at home. 'The victory acquired a significance greater than its importance as a feat of arms from a defeated nation beaten down by discriminatory laws since the Treaty of Limerick.'[21] Fontenoy was the Brigade's highest battle honour and the pinnacle of Irish military prowess, and was the greatest Irish win over an English army (although under French command) since the Battle of the Yellow Ford in Co. Armagh in 1598.

There has always been controversy surrounding the part played by the Irish Brigade in the battle and there are a couple of reasons for this. This can be partly explained as Dillon's and Fitzjames's horse both took part in these ferocious counter-attacks prior to the main attack by the Irish Brigade en masse. Voltaire was also present at the battle but he downplayed the Irish charge, the famously proud Frenchman unwilling to admit that a foreign corps secured victory. Voltaire printed 21,000 copies of the battle stating that the Regiment of Normandie led the victory, ensuring that his version of events would dominate over the official version. The official French account which was printed in the Paris, London and Dublin papers stated otherwise: 'The six Irish regiments sustained by those of Normandie and Vaisseaux being thus drawn up, they marched to the enemy without firing, and broke them with their bayonets fixed to their pieces, while the Carbineers charged them in flank.'[22] Voltaire's version is also contested by Comte d'Argenson, who wrote in his memoirs: 'It is notorious how much the Irish Brigade contributed to the victory of the terrible English column, while Richellieu cannonaded it in front.'[23] Lowendahl, Saxe's second in command, wrote, 'whatever the Parisians may say, the victory is due to the Irish.'[24] The French commander, Marshal Saxe, who was on the elevated position at the Mont de Justice during the whole battle and was therefore able to see everything, wrote two days after the battle, 'The Irish Brigade, which was in front, behaved as bravely as possible.'[25]

However, other British historians have hardly mentioned the part played by the Irish at all. The British historian Lieutenant Colonel Arthur Burnes found 'no foundation for the legend that the Irish Brigade broke the English square and were mainly responsible for the French victory.'[26] *Chambers Encyclopedia* notes that 'A legend arose that the Irish Brigade saved the situation for France. This is incorrect; the credit is due to the regiment Normandie under Lowendahl.'[27] Prominent French historians refuted these assertions: 'our Irish troops were furious,' noted Jules Michelet, 'the Irish entered the English column first.' According to Jean Bois, 'the Irish charge was the decisive factor in the battle.'[28] The leading authority on the battle, the English historian Francis Skrine, also agrees that the Brigade turned the scale of battle: 'Among French infantry regiments, those of the Irish stood first. Their desperate valour was a factor of great importance in our disaster.'[29]

News of Irish bravery spread quickly throughout Europe. 'The Irish have done wonders,' King Auguste III of Poland was informed.[30] Letters written three days after the battle show the Irish community in Paris were joyful and proud of the Irish involvement but remained worried about the fate of friends and relatives. 'Shopkeepers and the lowest people in the street, who do not know there is an Ireland in the world tell one another that the affair went very bad until a regiment called *Irlandais* retrieved the day.'[31] Irish involvement in the battle was subsequently downplayed. With the demise of the Jacobite cause, the Irish lost political favour in France, especially with the death in 1761 of the influential Marshal of France, Charles O'Brien, the 6th Lord Clare. To post-Revolutionary historians, the Brigade was a foreign corps and was suspected of being particularly royalist.

It was regarded as an enemy of the Revolution, and many of its officers were guillotined. The battle itself had also lost renown in France, as Revolutionary France naturally tended to celebrate her victories after the fall of the monarchy, particularly during the Napoleonic period, at Jena and Austerlitz.

A second controversy surrounds the British regimental flags or colours taken in the battle.[32] Junior officers, escorted by two battle-hardened Colour Sergeants, carried silken colours measuring 6 foot square. Stands of colours provided the location of a regiment to a soldier in battle, and they were a rallying point if something went wrong or if he lost his bearings in the confusion of battle. For a regiment to lose its colours was a major disgrace, less so if the regiment was overwhelmed in a major defeat. In Waterloo, French soldiers virtually committed suicide in hopeless efforts to gain glory by taking British colours back to their lines as prizes. Captured colours adopted a quasi-religious significance where they were draped high in the vaults of churches. The Irish were the only ones to capture a British colour. In his official account of the battle, Cumberland reported to the British government that 'we lost no colours, standards, kettledrums …'[33] The historian Skrine was not convinced that colours were taken and returns a verdict of 'not proven' as he felt that it was not possible for the loss of colours to have been kept a secret for so long. However, the official French account of the battle that was reprinted in the *Gentlemen's' Magazine* in Dublin, and London, in July 1745 reported:

> The 2nd regiment of the English Guards [now the Coldstream Gaurds] who had Buckley's Irish regiment to deal with must be almost destroyed. The latter took from them a pair of colours and two pieces of cannon, with the horses belonging to them, which were before the battalions.[34]

However, the Coldstream Guards do not have any record of their loss and all other accounts mention only one flag being taken. Comte d'Argenson wrote to the French Queen 'that the Irish captured a flag'.[35] Sergeant Wheelock from Bulkeley's Regiment would not have been promoted by King Louis for taking a flag if it had been untrue. This promotion was significant as at the time it was uncommon to rise from the ranks into the officer class.[36] A letter from Downing Street, London, proves they were aware of colours taken, otherwise they would not have requested their recovery. After Napoleon's defeat at Waterloo, the British Secretary of State for War wrote to the Duke of Wellington, the British army commander in occupied France:

> I understand that there are at Paris-at the Ecole Militaire, if I am not mistaken, several English colours, particularly one belonging to the Coldstream regiment, taken at Fontenoy. I hope your grace will make enquiries about these trophies, and that you will take the proper measures for their restoration.[37]

Captain G. Bowles, following orders to retrieve these colours, reported 'we are proceeding on more liberal principles, and do not talk of requiring anything except some old colours now hung up at the Hotel des Invalides, which were, I believe, taken at the battle of Fontenoy.'[38] The historians O'Callaghan and Skrine were unaware of the whereabouts of the flags. Sir Charles Petrie finished his article on the battle, stating that what eventually happened to them would likely remain a mystery. Through the course of my research, I have found the famous Fontenoy flag and solved this 265-year-old mystery. The French writer, E.C. Freron, provided the only description of this flag in his 'Ode de la battaille de Fontenoy' published in the *Mercure de France* in July 1745. In the poem, Freron described the colour: '*nisi Dominus frustra*, the motto on the flag which was taken'. I have tracked this flag down in an illustrated MS in Paris containing watercolours of flags taken by the French from 1690 to 1745.[39] Included in this work is a flag taken in the Flanders campaign in 1745 with this same motto, '*nisi Dominus frustra*', identifying it as the Fontenoy flag wrestled by Sergeant Wheelock of Bulkeley's.[40]

This flag was not a colour from the Coldstream Regiment, but most likely from Sempill's Regiment (later to become the King's Own Scottish Borderers).[41] This regiment fought in the battle on the right alongside the Coldstream Guards, was attacked by the Irish Brigade and suffered heavy losses. Irish memories are long and they finally scored some retribution for Limerick and their forced exile, as Sempill's served in Ireland during the Jacobite War.[42] The British were not keen to admit the Irish took a flag as England was at that time under threat of invasion from France. They were fearful of a Stuart restoration and a Jacobite rising in Scotland loomed. Although England could not possibly cover up its defeat at Fontenoy, it may not have been willing to let it be known that they lost colours to the Irish Brigade – the Jacobite army in waiting. One wonders had the English lost a colour to a French regiment whether they would have been so secretive about its loss.

But what ultimately happened to this flag? Edward Fraser made a reference to this colour in *The War Drama of the Eagles*, apparently unaware of its controversy. During the Napoleonic Wars in 1814, as the Russian army closed in on Paris, the French took the most desperate measures to destroy enemy colours, kept as prizes and trophies of war. The French War Minister, Marshal Henri Clarke (born in France to Irish parents) ordered the governor of the old soldier's home of Les Invalides to oversee the mass burning of enemy colours taken over hundreds of years. It was common practice for colours to be destroyed, rather than to be taken by the enemy. Veterans scaled up ladders in the chapel of Les Invalides and stripped it of the flags, flinging them into the flames in the courtyard. Some 1,417 battle trophies were burned, some over 200 years old, taken at Steenkirk and Landen, and including a British naval ensign taken at Trafalgar. Regimental flags taken at Minorca and Gibraltar, together with most of the trophies won by Napoleon's Grande Armée, at Austerlitz, Jena and elsewhere were destroyed. Frederick the Great's sword and sash, together with British regimental colours taken by Washington at Yorktown, which were presented to France in gratitude for her contribution in the American War by Congress, were also tossed into the flames. Fraser continues: 'Other British battle-spoils, the trophies of France, which passed out of existence at the Invalides on that night, were these: a flag taken at Fontenoy by the Irish Brigade.'[43]

8

THE SECOND JACOBITE RISING (1745)

In 1744, King James II's grandson, the 24-year-old Prince Charles Edward Stuart (or 'Bonnie Prince Charlie' as he was fondly known) believed his time had finally come to restore the Stuart throne. In March that year, France planned an invasion of England shortly after declaring war in the War of the Austrian Succession. Charles was secretly summoned from his home in Rome to embark with the invasion fleet. 'Let what will happen, the stroke is struck,' Charles wrote to his father,' I have taken a strong resolution to conquer or to die, and stand my ground as long as I have a man remaining with me.'[1] A large-scale Franco-Jacobite army of 10,000 troops under Marshal de Saxe was assembled on the French coast to land near London along the Thames Estuary. At the same time Charles was to lead an expedition to the Jacobite stronghold in the Scottish Highlands, with half of the 3,000 troops drawn from the Irish Brigade of France. The mission was doomed from the very start. When Admiral de Roquefeuille's covering squadrons and the troop transports cleared port they were dispersed due to heavy storms with the loss of twelve ships, some of whom were lost with all hands. As a result, the French army was withdrawn from Dunkirk and the invasion was scrubbed. Charles urged the French to press ahead and attempt another invasion and even solicited a meeting with Louis XV, but the French king had by now lost all interest in the plan.

The following year, 1745, taking advantage of the British defeat at Fontenoy, and with French support lacking, Charles turned to the Irish community in France for help in organising a rising in Scotland. Anthony Walsh, the large-scale slave-owner and shipping magnate in Nantes, offered Charles the 18-gun *Doutelle*.[2] Dominic O'Heguerty and the Paris-based banker George Waters provided money and arms. Walter Rutledge from Dunkirk funded the old 64-gun battleship *Elizabeth*, which was heavily laden with field artillery, 1,500 firelocks, 1,800 broadswords and gunpowder. Around 100 troops from Clare's Regiment served onboard as marines, which they combined with a privateering mission.[3]

Officers in the Irish Brigade organised a French expeditionary force made up of 'pickets' (volunteers) from the Irish regiments of France to form a bridgehead for the main invasion. Charles set forth into the Channel, escorted by the *Elizabeth* and steered wide around the Irish coast towards the Western Scottish islands. The sea crossing was uneventful until they encountered the 58-gun HMS *Lion*, and in the sea-fight that followed, the *Elizabeth* and the *Lion* battered each other with raking broadsides, leading to both ships being crippled and returning to port. The *Doutelle* sailed on alone and luckily out-ran an English man-of-war, escaping due to her better sails and arriving safely on the little island of Erisca in the Scottish Outer Hebrides. As the boat anchored, an eagle hovered overhead, a good omen as one of Charles's party remarked: the king of the birds has come to welcome the king of Scotland. Charles's priority was to inform the powerful Highland chieftains of his arrival and he invited Macdonald of Sleat and Macdonald of Clanranald onboard as he sailed down the coast – but they believed that without French support the enterprise was doomed.

Towards the end of July 1745, Charles made landfall at Moidart with an odd mix of middle-aged supporters. These comprised the two Scotsmen – the banker Aeneas MacDonald and the aged Duke of Atholl – together with Colonel Francis Strickland, the sole Englishman. All the rest were Irish: Sir Thomas Sheridan was a veteran of the Boyne; Lieutenant Colonel Sir John MacDonald of Fitzjames' horse; an Irish Protestant clergyman called George Kelly; and lastly, Colonel Sir John O'Sullivan, Charles's closest friend. O'Sullivan came from the notable Gaelic aristocratic family of the O'Sullivan-Beares in Co. Kerry. He was

The Second Jacobite Rising (1745)

Officer of Clare's Regiment of France, 1772. (Courtesy of Het Legermuseum, Nationale Bibliotheek Van Nederland)

sent to France for his education and had recently served as aide-de-camp to Marshal de Maillebots in the Corsican campaign, and had acquired further experience in irregular warfare in Italy and Germany. O'Sullivan's military experience and knowledge of guerrilla warfare was to prove invaluable to the campaign.[4]

The *Doutelle* carried a cargo of a few thousand arms, ammunition and a stock of cognac. Charles dispatched his brig back with Walsh to France, with letters to his father and to the French court, informing them of his safe arrival. Anthony Walsh was one of Charles's most fervent supporters. He died in St Domingue (in modern-day Haiti) in 1758 and a testimony of his loyalty to Prince Charles was evidenced in his will: 'I give and bequeath to my son, my diamond, my gold sword and my snuff box with the portrait of Prince Edward [Prince Charles Edward], in order that he may always have the same longing and the same zeal that I have had to serve him effectually.'[5]

Charles argued with the Highland chiefs that conditions were perfect for a rising, pointing out that he needed the Highlanders to begin the war only before being seconded by French troops. The British defeat at Fontenoy was a good omen and in any case some of the newly formed unblooded Scottish regiments in the British army were no match for the Highlanders. One of the Highlanders rose and toasted the Prince in 'Erse' or Gaelic (the Highlanders' mother tongue) with *'Deoch slaint an Reogh!'*, which Charles understood to mean 'long live the King!' He adopted tartan dress and won support by wisely distributing his arms to the clans in person.[6] Charles had the charisma that his grandfather had lacked. He was an intelligent conversationalist, and together with his Continental education, personality, youth and his pleasing physical appearance won over many hearts. Three weeks after Charles landed, a Jacobite army of several thousand men was formed and the Stuart standard was raised in the picturesque village of Glenfinnan. The Duke of Perth and Lord George Murray were both appointed lieutenant generals and John O'Sullivan was appointed adjutant-general of the Jacobite army.

Whitehall viewed Charles's arrival as more of a local disturbance and thought it improbable that he would be joined 'by any considerable force from the Highlands'.[7] Sir John Cope, the British commander in Scotland, marched out of Stirling with 3,000 men to check the threat. The Jacobite army marched first to Perth and then to Edinburgh and took the city in a bloodless *coup de main*. The Chief of Lochiel rushed through one of the city's gates with a party of men, O'Sullivan gained entry through another, and shortly afterwards the city was in Jacobite hands, although the castle still held out. The following day the Royal Coronation began with much pomp and ceremony. Charles was then escorted in state to the palace of Hollyrood House, which was in the same condition as his grandfather James II left it fifty years previously. Great festivities took place, the famous blind Irish Harpist, Denis O'Hampsey, who was in Edinburgh at the time, played the Jacobite anthem that had also been played for Charles's grandfather when he arrived in Dublin: 'The King Shall Enjoy His Own Again.'

Charles languished for six weeks in Edinburgh before marching out with his 6,000-strong rag-tag army to much fanfare, with flags flying and bagpipes playing. The rebels' arsenal was bolstered with a thousand muskets taken from Edinburgh's magazine and they also received tents, which were not essential as many of the hardy Highlanders preferred to sleep in the open, drawing their highland plaid over their shoulder as a blanket. J.C. O'Callaghan called the mainly Catholic army a rural militia as they hadn't yet been reinforced by the Irish or Scottish regiments of France. It has gone down in folk memory that the Highlanders were mainly strong men in their prime, but when the chief called his clan out, the entire clan, both the very young and the very old, transformed itself into a regiment. 'They consist of an odd medley of grey beards and no beards,' described a spy sent from England, 'old men fit to drop into the grave, and young boys whose swords are near equal to their weight, and I really believe more than their weight. Four or five thousand may be very good determined men; but the rest are mean, dirty, who seem more anxious about plunder than their prince.'[8]

The Jacobites stumbled across Cope's army 7 miles outside Edinburgh at a place called Prestonpans. The Jacobites occupied the ridge and drew up their infantry in the centre, the dragoons and three artillery pieces in the wings. Both armies fielded were less than a mile apart and it was decided to attack at first light. The Jacobites advanced as the mist cleared the following dawn, with Charles shouting words of encouragement: 'Follow me gentlemen, and by the blessing of God, I will this day make you a free and happy people!' As the Highland bagpipers blew their signal, the clans attacked, raising their famous war cry, *'Claymore!'* (the Gaelic word for 'great sword'). The Highlanders rushed Cope's field artillery in the famous 'Highland Charge'. This was a yelled charge downhill that would provoke the enemy into firing. They would wait for the volley, duck, jump up, fire, and then throw their muskets away and (hopefully) smash through the enemy's lines with sheer brute force; although other Highland battle tactics were farcically amateurish. 'I galloped to the end of the village,' observed John MacDonald of Fitzjames' horse nervously, 'where I saw the Highlanders running in small groups in order to form up behind the enemy's left, I trembled as I watched this manoeuvre, which exposed the Highlanders to being destroyed on this plain before they had prepared to fight. Fortunately nobody attacked them.'[9] Cope's infantry gave out well-directed volleys and momentarily staggered the Highlanders' advances as they came in at close quarters, yelling their battle cries and within six minutes crashed through Cope's infantry in several places.

Like one of Homer's heroes or the Irish Achilles, Finn McCool, a legend arose that Charles could win a battle in minutes. Charles took the enemy colours and £2,500 in coin that was shared between the Highland chiefs, many of whom abandoned the army with their spoils. The Highlanders were simple, rural people and a story is told of one of them discarding a watch when it stopped, not knowing that it needed to be wound. Others found chocolate powder in Cope's carriage and used it as snuff.[10] Charles intended marching through England, confident that others would join him, but his aides advised against this until French reinforcements arrived. He was persuaded to march back to Edinburgh as they were expected to be joined by more clans due to their victory in Prestonpans. The clans marched with their spoils of war with a hundred bagpipes playing the now familiar Jacobite tune, 'The King Shall Enjoy His Own Again'.

Charles's threat was now taken a little more seriously by Whitehall, who called the militia out and recalled troops from Ireland and the Continent. Charles dispatched George Kelly to France with details of his victory and requesting urgent reinforcements. Charles's brother, Henry the Duke of York, was to lead the Irish Brigade, augmented by several French regiments for a landing in England.[11] In the end the French stalled as the invasion force was not given the go-ahead, and the opportunity of restoring Charles was lost. Several ships were sent to sustain Charles as Admiral Vernon commanded the English Channel Fleet so well that it was difficult for the larger French squadrons to leave harbour without being intercepted.

Three months after Charles landed in Scotland, several privateers slipped through the British blockade and anchored off the Scottish coast. With them came a number of Irish and French officers, including Colonel Brown from Berwick's Regiment and Captain MacGeoghegan, an artillery officer in Lally's Regiment and an Irish engineering officer called Grant, who would serve as the Jacobite's principal engineer. Two other ships carrying a volunteer composite battalion of the Irish and Scots regiments of France joined them. The Marquis d'Eguilles came ashore with the welcome news that a 10,000-strong invasion force was primed and ready in Dunkirk, including Lord Clare's Irish Brigade. Another ship carrying one squadron of Fitzjames' horse under Lieutenant Colonel Walter Stapleton from Limerick also managed to break through, along with a battalion of the blue-coated Royal Ecossais (Royal Scots), under the Scot Lieutenant Colonel John Drummond. These Irish and Scots regular troops marched to reinforce Lord Strathallan's Jacobite army at Perth. Other privateers were not so lucky: the Royal Navy captured the *Esperence* off the east coast of England, carrying twenty officers and eighty men of Dillon's, Bulkeley's and Lally's. The *Louis XV* was also taken with 18 officers and 158 men of Clare's, Berwick's, stands-of-arms, broadswords and horse furniture.

Spanish-based Jacobites funded four privateers for Charles's cause. But the mission was an unsuccessful one. The 16-gun *Corunno* carried sixty men and arrived safely in Scoland, but the *San Zirioco* was captured and taken back to Bristol. A third ship was wrecked off the Irish coast by heavy storms; the fourth, the *San Pedro*, was taken by an English privateer and brought into Cork as a prize amidst much excitement.[12] The *San Pedro* carried supplies and gold and a Catholic priest from Dublin and a cavalry captain of Irish parentage in the Spanish service.[13]

The Jacobite army had provisions for only four days when they marched south into England. As they crossed the English border, the Chief of Lochiel cut his hand while unsheathing his sword, which was seen by many of the superstitious Highlanders as a bad omen.

The weather was bad with sleet and snow and many deserted as they were unsuited to long marches. In November, Carlisle fell to the Jacobites and 300 Highlanders garrisoned the town under the command of Captain MacGeoghegan, who was described by Chevalier Johnstone, a Scottish officer in the Jacobite army, as 'an officer of talents and merit'. The Highland army hoped that English Jacobites would rise when they marched through northern England. Although Lancashire had been a Jacobite stronghold in 1715 they received little support there now. Racist English propaganda portrayed the Highlanders as 'brutal savages' and warned that no mercy could be expected from them. There was even a widely believed rumour that they ate young children.[14] They were also portrayed by the London newspapers as savages, having claws instead of hands.[15] The Highlanders trundled on south and arrived triumphantly the following month in Derby. There was a rush on the Bank of England when news reached London that the Jacobites were only four days' march away. There were rumours that the French had already landed in Kent and King George feared for his throne and was fitting out ships on the Thames to sail at short notice.

The Jacobites' enthusiasm, however, was short-lived as they learned of 30,000 government troops blocking their advance to London.[16] An Irish Protestant government spy called Dudley Bradstreet informed them, as a ruse, that 9,000 troops had also assembled 50 miles away in Northumberland.[17] A council of war was convened where Lord George and the other chiefs advised Charles to return to Scotland, arguing that the English Jacobites had not risen as expected and that the French too had not yet landed with support. Their small army of 5,000 was no match for 40,000 professional troops. They wanted to return to Scotland and join forces with Stapleton's regulars from the Irish Brigade and the Royal Scots, who together with Lord Strathalen's men at Perth numbered 4,000 men.[18] Even if they made it to London, their small force was not large enough to take the city or hold it for any length of time. The Irish officers backed Charles in going to London but the Highlanders pointed out that if they were captured they would be treated as prisoners of war, unlike the Highlanders who would be hanged as traitors. Charles argued that the French could yet land in Kent or Essex; fresh dispatches sent from Stapleton confirmed this.

The Second Jacobite Rising (1745)

There were many powerful Jacobites in London who were expected to rally to his cause. Providence had got them this far and although he was outnumbered he relied on defections from senior officers in the British army. Charles also knew that if news of a *volte-face* was received in France, the invasion would be stood down. Lord George advised Charles in the end that a tactical retreat was the best option. The rebel army was now on the back foot. Charles's mission 'would probably have been crowned with success' if he had pressed on as French troops were now battle-ready in Dunkirk, and had Charles arrived in London, the Franco-Jacobite invasion would have been given the all clear.[19]

Late at night in the middle of winter, the unbeaten Highland army retraced their steps and heavy footed it back on the long march back to Scotland. The rank and file felt bitter at retreating and 'losing all our glory', as one of them noted bitterly.[20] They had bested a professional British army at Prestonpans and marched through England in miserable winter weather only needlessly to retrace their steps. They arrived again in Manchester and instead of being welcomed they were attacked. While passing through the town of Wigan, O'Sullivan was mistaken as Charles, singled out and shot at, but his wound was not serious.

The Jacobite army entered Scotland by fording the river Esk and while riding through on horseback, Charles observed a man carried away in the stream. He quickly took hold of the man's hair and cried out for help in Gaelic: '*Cobhear! Cobhear!*', and the man was saved. With these acts of bravery and kindness, he endeared himself to his followers.

Towards the final days of 1745, they arrived in Penrith, and waited for Lord George's rear guard to arrive, which was running fifteen hours' march behind the van. Enemy cavalry was spotted just out of musket range on a nearby hill; drums and trumpets were heard as if an entire army was forming for battle just over the ridge. Colonel Brown of Lally's ran up with two companies to attack and was relieved to find two enemy squadrons who immediately dispersed. Cumberland had assembled drummers and trumpeters to give the impression that the whole British army had assembled there. If Charles's rearguard had avoided this confrontation Cumberland would have wedged between Charles army and destroyed it.

The original invasion plan involved sending a French invasion force to make a cross-Channel run under cover of moonlight. But with Charles's retreat to Scotland in early 1746, the Irish regiments were sent to Scotland to prolong the expedition, instead of being part of the main invasion force. In January 1746, Brigadier General Lally crossed over to Sussex on a fishing boat and rendezvoused with leading Jacobites and even managed to raise a red-coated Jacobite corps called the Prince Charles Volunteers. Lally thereafter went to London, a price was put on his head and he was pursued by the authorities but made it to Scotland and even landed in Ireland to muster support there and visited his ancestral home.

Carlisle was still held by Captain MacGeoghegan, as it was a strategically located prize, but it fell to Cumberland's army. The Kings Royal Irish Hussars of the British army also took part in the assault.[21] Two Irish Brigade officers called Narin and Gordon escaped from the besieged garrison and brought the news of the town's defeat. The Jacobite army entered Glasgow and rested there for several days before finally joining forces with the Irish and Scots regulars from France.[22]

Stapleton's Irish infantry marched with two artillery trains and placed Stirling Castle under siege. Irish pickets operated the siege, in preference to the Highlanders who were not experienced enough in this type of warfare. An inept French engineering officer called Mirabelle was in charge of constructing batteries and recklessly exposed the Irish pickets to sharpshooters lodged in the castle, resulting in heavy Irish losses. 'What a pity, that these brave men [the Irish] should have sacrificed, to no purpose, by the ignorance and folly of Mirabelle!' noted Chevalier Johnstone. General Hawley's 8,000 government troops had set off to march to the castle's relief. Hawley had a fearsome reputation and a hatred for the 'Highland rabble' as he called them, and had triangles for floggings, gibbets and executioners accompany his army.[23]

The Jacobites left a small body of troops to maintain the siege and marched out confidently to nearby Falkirk to confront Hawley's army. Lord George commanded the Jacobite right, and Drummond the left. Charles and the recently arrived companies of the Irish Brigade (350 men) and the Royal Scots (150 men) took post in the second line, as Charles had to give the honour of the first line to the Highlanders. Prior to the battle, Charles turned to Lally and said; 'Well, Lally, those English know you – they were at Fontenoy', Lally replying: 'Yes, your Royal Highness, but my officers and I would wish to be in the front line of battle in order to renew our acquaintance.'[24] Hawley's cavalry formed in front of two lines of infantry (along with the Irish 27th (Inniskilling's) Foot of the British army), and the militia formed the reserve. Hawley charged the Jacobite right, but the MacDonald's held off firing until 10 yards' distance and managed to break Hawley's charge. The MacDonald's advanced in triumph and reloaded their muskets, fired and threw them away, and lunged in with broadswords, scattering the enemy. When Charles appeared from the second line, Hawley's dragoons tried to snatch the Royal Standard as a prize but they were stopped in their tracks by the Irish pickets.[25] The Irish and Scots regulars advanced, which led to the enemy's centre giving way and Hawley retreating in steady order. This was the second humiliating defeat suffered by the government. The Jacobites didn't pursue the enemy as they had been in battle since early morning and were weary and soaked to the skin, where pools of water had turned to ice on the ground. The battle lasted twenty minutes; rebel losses were a mere 42 men against the enemy's 400.

Irish military expertise from the rear had to support the Highlanders in the front from disaster. The Irish pickets behaved with the 'most distinguished bravery and intrepidy at the battle of Falkirk,' observed Chevalier Johnstone, 'preserving always the best order, when the whole of the rest of our army was dispersed, and keeping the enemy in check by the bold countenance which they displayed.'[26] Lord George was criticised for being on foot fighting with his men instead of on horseback controlling events. He wanted to pursue the retreating troops into Falkirk 'but as the pipers had thrown their pipes to their boys, and joined the battle,' he explained, 'there was no means to summon the men back to the colours.'[27] The Jacobites sent a detachment of the Irish and Scots regiments into Falkirk and found the town abandoned, save for one government soldier, who lunged for Drummond and in the scuffle shot him in the arm.[28] The Highlanders, though, as was their usual *modus operandi*, returned to the mountains with their plunder, depriving the Jacobite army of several thousand men at a critical time in the campaign. The Jacobite army returned to the siege at Stirling Castle but had to abandon it and spiked their heavy artillery as Cumberland's 7,000 troops were pushing north and had joined up with Hawley's 3,000 troops. Cumberland later complained that he could get no intelligence on the rebels while in Scotland and reckoned himself 'more in an enemy's country than when he was warring with the French'.[29]

Ever since Lord George and the other Highland chiefs chose to retreat at Derby, Charles had lost confidence in them. He stopped convening councils of war and took advice only from Thomas Sheridan and the other Irish officers. The Jacobite high command now split between the Irish officers, who were the military commanders of the campaign and sided with Charles, and the Highlanders, who sided with Lord George. The Highlanders were jealous of Charles's relationship with the Irish officers and looked on them as mere adventurers wishing to progress their own careers in the French army, and not in Scotland's cause.[30] They had joined the campaign at their own expense and were close to mutiny when Charles proposed giving command of the newly formed Manchester regiment to Captain MacGeoghegan. Charles instead had to offer command to an English officer called Francis Townley.[31] Lord George and the Highland chiefs now presented Charles with a document stating that they were returning to the Highlands for the winter, but promised to return with 10,000 men in the spring. Charles was furious and sent Thomas Sheridan to speak with the chiefs, but they stood firm in their decision. Much to Charles's chagrin, the rebel army returned to the Highlands towards Inverness, which was still in government hands. Stapleton's Irish regulars besieged the town, which fell shortly afterwards. To add to his disappointment, Charles now received the news that the planned invasion from France had been abandoned.

In the spring of 1746, three ships carrying four squadrons of Fitzjames' horse sailed from Ostend and arrived in Aberdeen. The brig *Sophie* carried arms, money, and packloads of equipment, horse furniture and a squadron of 130 men under Captain Robert O'Shea. But the regiment's heavy chargers had sailed in another ship and had been captured at sea. Fitzjames' carried so much equipment ashore that ten carts and twenty packhorses were needed to transport it all.[32] Fitzjames' horse arrived with black trumpeters, who were symbols of regimental status at the time.[33] The troopers must have been a fine sight 'attired in red turned up with royal blue, tin buttons, placed in pairs, a black tri-corn hat, laced with silver, and beneath their coat, a breastplate of iron, painted black with yellow skin, buff breeches'.[34] As Fitzjames' were regular cavalry, they were given a higher priority on the army's limited resources and were mounted on old nags from Lord Pitsligo's and Kilmarnock's horse, who thereafter served as infantrymen.

The Irish regulars promptly reorganised the Jacobite army. Captain Francis Nugent was appointed as quartermaster and Major John Baggot of Fitzjames' was given command of a light cavalry troop of eighty mounts (thereafter known as Baggot's Hussars), who fought bravely in the campaign. The Scottish nobleman John Murray had raised this troop, but discipline had become so bad that it was thought a professional soldier was needed to keep it in line. Baggot from Limerick was clearly the man for the job as he was described as 'a very rough sort of man, and, so exceedingly well fitted to command the banditti of which his corps was composed, and to distress the country.'[35] The remaining troopers of Fitzjames were carried in the *Bourbon* and *Charité* but were intercepted by the Royal Navy.[36] The regiment's full complement of heavy cavalry horses were taken along with three squadrons of 36 officers and 359 troopers.[37] The Irish troopers were mainly battle-hardened men who had served in Italy and along the Rhine and their loss was a severe blow to the Jacobite's campaign. These men were brought to Hull and interrogated, as the British wanted to see exactly who these men were (especially after they had recently sustained a defeat to them at Fontenoy) and how they were recruited. A return of the prisoners showed the vast majority were Irish-born.[38] 'The men are all cloathed in red, and the officers have mostly gold-laced hats,' records a contemporary English letter describing their dapper appearance, 'To speak impartially, the officers are as proper men as ever I saw in my life, being most of them 5 foot 10 or 6 feet high, and between 40 and 50 years of age; and the common soldiers are very good-like men, and if they had landed, might have done a great deal of mischief.'[39]

The superiority of Britain's naval defences saved the country from invasion. Royal Navy patrols chased a privateer carrying the remaining troops of Lally's Regiment back to Dunkirk, although another ship broke through the blockade and landed in Scotland with money, supplies and troops from Berwick's Regiment. Whitehall ordered 4,000 troops to the south-east county of Kent to protect the coast from an invasion of Irish troops, as intelligence reported they had marched out from Dunkirk to Calais.[40] A chain of forts were built to keep the Highlanders in check, accessed by a military road between them after the 1715 Rising. Stapleton's 300 pickets marched from Inverness and destroyed Fort George and Fort Augustus by firing the magazine stores.[41] The Irish were also tasked with man-drawing the heavy field-artillery over 61 miles from Inverness to Fort William, in difficult mountainous terrain in the depths of winter. They were unable to take Fort William as it was too heavily defended, leaving Stapleton no other choice but to abandon the siege, spike his guns there and rejoin the main Jacobite army. Charles was now desperately low on funds and was forced to pay his men in oatmeal.[42]

In April, the brig *Prince Charles*, carrying gold and 150 troops from Berwick's under Captain Talbot, finally broke through the Channel blockade. She carried engineers and a number of Irish officers from Spain. After an intense sea-fight with the Royal Navy, she was run aground off the Scottish coast with forty killed in the mêlée. A total of twenty-one officers (of whom sixteen were Irish) and over 100 men were taken. This vessel was the last succour from France. J.C. O'Callaghan noted that if Charles's campaign failed, it was not from want of trying by the Irish military in France.

As Cumberland marched north, he had 9,000 foot and 1,200 horse, and sixteen artillery pieces at his disposal, supported by the Royal Navy anchored off the coast. His army was also reinforced by 5,000 Hessian troops who landed at Leith and who were to garrison southern Scotland. These auxiliaries were originally earmarked to be Dutch, but Captain MacGeoghegan protested in his capacity as an officer in the French army by sending a trumpeter with a letter to the Dutch commander that these be retired, as they had pledged in Flanders not to serve against France.[43] The odds were clearly stacked against the Jacobites. Charles's army of 5,000 men had just twelve artillery pieces, supported by just 150 Jacobite cavalry mounted on old nags. Things were not looking good for the Jacobites. Provisions were scarce and the army was already half starving, with even the officers being reduced to eating raw cabbages from farmers' fields.

Prior to the Battle of Culloden, Fitzjames' horse was used for patrolling and intelligence gathering.[44] The horses and men received little rest for three nights prior to the battle and were exhausted and unfit even for reconnaissance duties. Johnstone wrote that as they finally prepared to get some sleep he heard the trumpets and drum beats of Fitzjames' horse, calling the troopers to boot up and saddle as Cumberland's army was approaching only a few miles away.[45] Cumberland's army finally closed in on the Jacobites around Inverness. Fitzjames' horse and Baggot's Hussars together with twenty-five pickets from Bulkeley's and the Royal Scots were ordered to halt the enemy's advance. Fitzjames' formed in the wings as 200 enemy cavalry and loyal Campbell's confronted them, but they wisely retreated, fearing running headlong into Cumberland's main army beyond. The Irish regulars also exchanged volleys in skirmishes around Inverness with government troops on the bridge at Nairn. Hopelessly outnumbered, they prevented the enemy crossing the river Nairn.[46] O'Sullivan ordered pickets of Bulkeley's Regiment to position and burn two turf carts on the bridge and prevented Cumberland's pursuit.

Charles and his officers slept in Culloden House while his troops slept out on Culloden Moor. A plan was devised to surprise Cumberland's army, which was encamped a few miles away, arguing that as it was Cumberland's 25th birthday, 'they'll all be as drunk as beggars.'[47] The plan involved a 12-mile night march to surprise Cumberland's men while they slept. Lord George marched at the head of the column while Charles rode with Fitzjames' horse at the rear as it was feared that the noise of the horses would alert the enemy of their arrival.[48] When dawn broke they had only marched 6 miles and were only halfway. Some chiefs argued to attack anyway in daylight, that their broadswords would carry them through, but Lord George took the decision to return. O'Sullivan, a skilled tactician in irregular warfare, afterwards reproached Lord George Murray for not launching his surprise attack: 'We had nothing then for it, not ever can expect to conquer, without regular troops, but by surprise or attacking them before they prepared.'[49] The tired, sad and hungry army grudgingly retraced their steps to Culloden Moor.

The Highlanders were totally exhausted when they arrived back at Culloden. Some soldiers slept out in the heather, others left to forage for food. Officers, who were to convene and discuss tactics in Culloden House, instead snatched sleep anywhere they could. Food was so scarce that Charles himself could only obtain a little bread and whiskey. Most of the army had not eaten anything the previous day, and only one biscuit could be issued per man.[50] Lord George wanted the army to retreat to Nairn and take up position on high ground inaccessible to enemy cavalry, but Charles decided to make a stand at Culloden Moor on open, flat and marshy ground. The Marquis d'Eguilles, in his report to the French court, went down on his knees to Charles for him to delay the battle. Charles was not for turning. He had heeded to counsel advising him to retreat from Prestonpans and Derby, which had cost him dearly, and he now wanted to make a stand. Johnstone wrote that he 'could never comprehend why the Prince wished to attack the English army, so much superior in number to his own, with only a part of his men, in disorder, without waiting till the rest should come up, and without forming them in order of battle, to present a front of attack',[51] although O'Sullivan defended the choice to stand and fight, indicating they had no choice. Cumberland's vanguard had been biting at the heels of the Jacobite rearguard for the last two days, which was also affecting morale.

On 16 April 1746, Highland scouts spied Cumberland's army advancing only 4 miles away. The Highland bagpipers and drummers rallied the troops from their slumber, and it was clear that the night march had taken its toll and numbers had now depleted further.[52] O'Sullivan as adjutant-general drew up the army and planned the order of battle. The Highlanders were drawn up in two lines; the clans occupied the front under Lord George, and the Irish and Scots regulars took post in the second line. Behind them stood the 160-strong Jacobite cavalry under Lieutenant Colonel John McDonald, including Captain O'Shea's 75 mounts of Fitzjames', Charles's Escort Troop, Lord Elcho's, Baggot's Hussars and Lord Strathallen's horse. Jacobite artillery was positioned in front. The MacDonald clan was on the left, instead of the right like in Prestonpans and Falkirk, and felt their honour insulted. Robert de Bruce had given the MacDonalds the permanent honour of forming on the right wing for their actions in the Battle of Bannockburn in 1314.

This perceived slight would have major repercussions during the battle. O'Sullivan later accused Lord George of changing the McDonalds to the left.[53] The right flank was covered by some 6-feet high park walls towards Culloden House which the rebels failed to secure, and which cost them dearly as the enemy took up position there and fired deadly flanking fire on the Highland army.

Cumberland formed his army in three lines; dragoons in the left and cavalry on each wing, with artillery in front. Both armies cannonaded each other but the rebels came off worse with heavy losses. The poorly aimed Jacobite artillery was manned by inexperienced gunners who knocked out many of their own troops. Charles recklessly rode up and down the first line encouraging his men, providing a target for the enemy gunners, killing in his vicinity thirty-five troopers from Fitzjames and a similar number from the Life Guards. He was covered in earth thrown up by a cannon ball, had a horse shot under him. He was rehorsed and thereafter took post in the second line, just like at Falkirk. The Jacobite right wing charged with broadswords and was cut down by enemy musket fire, grapeshot and cannon, but still managed to break through Monro's and Barrel's foot regiments (who suffered the highest casualties on the government side). Lieutenant Colonel Rich of Barrel's foot was killed with a broadsword gash to his head, after his hand was chopped off in a vain attempt to save his colours, which were temporarily lost in the battle but were later recovered. In the face of an advancing Highland charge, Cumberland reinforced his second line by placing Sempill's and Bligh's regiments three-deep, the first line kneeling, the second stooping and the third standing and unleashed their deadly volleys which stopped hundreds of rebels in their tracks. Many were trampled on and the dead and dying were piled up three- and four-deep, Chief MacLachlann was killed and the wounded Lochiel was carried from the field. The MacDonald's clan on the left stood by and sulked, unwilling to fight, believing they were disgraced by being posted on the left instead of the right flank. The Duke of Perth took hold of the clan's colours and called them into action with the Highland attack-cry: '*Claymore!*' But even then, they would not move. The clan's chieftain, the Chief of Keppoch, ran forward with a pistol in one hand and a sword in the other before he was cut down by several shots but still the clan did not move, as the rebels' right and centre were routed. They stood by without striking a blow, kicking the dirt when they were within twenty paces of the enemy, although they had drawn their swords for attack.[54] Enemy cavalry advanced to the Jacobite left and nearly reached the MacDonalds when the Irish pickets unleashed a volley and pushed them back. The MacDonalds then fell in with the second line.

Cumberland's cavalry managed to open gaps in the rebels' rearguard, but Fitzjames' and Lord Elcho's troopers halted their advance. Charles reluctantly ordered a retreat and the Irish infantry and Fitzjames' horse covered the Highlanders' withdrawal from the battlefield and prevented a massacre.[55] This action was accomplished 'with a close and well directed fire' and cost half of the Irish casualties in the battle. The Irish infantry huddled behind stonewalls and volley fired the enemy as they advanced where Stapleton was mortally wounded. Cumberland's dragoons charged down and nearly encircled the Royal Scots, but the Irish drove them off and the Royal Scots fell in with the Irish. As Charles was gearing up to lead a last charge with the remaining Highlanders, O'Sullivan spied a troop of enemy cavalry advancing to cut off their retreat, and ordered Captain O'Shea of Fitzjames' to seize the Prince's horse bridle and lead him away to safety.[56] Charles left the battlefield in tears with his escort troop of Fitzjames' and Life Guards.

Charles crossed the river Nairn with two troops of cavalry and retreated towards Fort Augustus. The Irish and Scots regulars fell back towards Inverness. The fleeing rebels were pursued by Cumberland's dragoons, where no mercy was given. 'The wounded were put to the sword and others were shot on the spot. Houses were plundered, livestock were driven away, women and children were driven from their torched cabins and died of hunger and cold.'[57] A farm building with twenty wounded Highlanders was torched. In these atrocities, the Duke of Cumberland earned his sobriquet the 'Butcher of Culloden'. The mortally wounded Stapleton dispatched a letter of surrender and the Irish and Scots regulars turned themselves in. They were given parole in Inverness, respecting the Cartel of Frankfurt, whereby regular troops (irrespective of their countries of origin) were to be treated as prisoners of war. Fifty-one officers and 250 men from the Irish Brigade of France signed paroles of honour not to escape; those from the Royal Scots were not specified, but were thought to number around 150. After being interrogated, they were sent to England and were exchanged with British prisoners the following year. Cumberland took fourteen Jacobite flags and banners to Edinburgh where they were unceremoniously burnt.[58]

The government 'lost a mere fifty men, the Jacobite a thousand in the field and a thousand more as they fled – almost half their men. Culloden was the Highlanders' Kinsale, for it signed the death-warrant of their Gaelic culture.'[59] As many as 475 regular Irish troops and 225 regular Scottish troops in the French army fought there and 100 Irish and 50 Royal Scots lost their lives. The Highlanders paid a huge price for rallying to Charles's cause. The subsequent Disarming Act 1746 prohibited the carrying of arms and the wearing of highland dress. The Highland chiefs forfeited their lands, which were cleared of people and replaced with sheep. With opportunities lacking at home, many joined Highland regiments of the British army during the Seven Years War where they were seen as hardier than regular British troops and won many honours in the Americas.

Lord George and many of the Highland chiefs escaped to the Continent and raised regiments on the same footing as the Irish regiments and the Royal Scots of France. Charles escaped with Sheridan, O'Sullivan and others to Invergarry and the 70-year-old Sheridan escaped to France. O'Sullivan remained with Charles on the run for several weeks until he too made his way to France, as he was unable to keep pace with Charles. He later masterminded Charles's escape and boarded a cutter on the Scottish coast with Captain MacMahon and Captain Fitzgerald of the French Irish Brigade. On the Isle of Skye, Captain Felix O'Neill of Hibernia's Regiment of Spain was sent ashore dressed in Highland garb to locate the Prince but was captured.[60] O'Sullivan was forced to sail for France and luckily out-ran a Royal Navy patrol in the Channel, before crash landing on the Blankenberge sandbanks on the Flemish coast. He travelled directly to Paris to meet the French king and organised two ships to be fitted out to rescue Charles in Scotland.[61]

Charles's spent six months wandering ' in the heather', which became legend. He was 'hunted from mountain to island, and from island to mountain, pinched with famine, tossed by storms, and unsheltered by the rain'.[62] He had several hundred loyal supporters who, although many

David Morier, *Barrell's Regiment (4th Foot) at the Battle of Culloden*. (Courtesy of the Royal Collection, HM Queen Elizabeth II)

were desperately poor, did not turn him in even with a large bounty (£2 million in today's money) on his head. In September 1746, a rescue party led by Dubliner Colonel Richard Warren from Dillon's anchored in Lochnanuagh, accompanied by Thomas Sheridan, who came ashore with others to look for Charles.[63] After a sixteen-day search, they found Charles and brought him back safely to France.[64]

Ireland was always a troublesome colony but was strangely acquiescent during the '45. Deep resentment was festering among poorer Catholics who had much to gain with a Catholic Restoration. Charles had already turned back at Derby when news reached Ireland, and the ordinary people wore tartan plaid to show their support.[65] The invasion captured the imagination of the local Irish people and inspired the Irish-language Aisling vision poets (the Gaelic pamphleteers of their day), who depicted Ireland as a young damsel in distress, and sometimes as an old haggard woman, waiting to be rescued. The poets applied poetic code names to Charles, such as An Seabhac Siubhal (The Roving Falcon) and An Buachaill Ban (The Fair Lad) and the Blackbird, which still survives as a set dance today, two centuries later.[66]

An English agent reported in Munster that agricultural labourers were stealing sheep in anticipation of a change in the political status quo, one of whom defiantly told his wife 'he hoped to see the day he would not be obliged to slave for 5*d* a day.'[67] The Irish Catholics were literally living under the gun as fifty years of anti-Catholic Penal Laws left them 'unarmed, leaderless and demoralised'.[68] Inactivity can be partly explained by the militarisation of the Protestant community, who were the only group allowed to bear arms. The Crown maintained a standing army of 12,000 spread over 263 barracks throughout the country, supported by a well-armed 65,000-strong Irish Protestant militia.[69] The sons of influential Catholic gentry families 'who might have been leaders or agents in sedition' had been forced into military service on the Continent.[70]

There were Catholic families who could have provided leadership, but they were too few on the ground and were not prepared to rise with inadequate French support. They were trying to survive through some of the most difficult years of the Penal Laws and simply had too much to lose. The country lost leadership in the fall of the Gaelic order in the Elizabethan and Cromwellian conquests, in the 'Flight of the Earls' (1607) and later on in the 'Flight of the Wild Geese' (1691). This was in sharp contrast to the Scottish Highlanders who still retained their estates and had their chiefs to lead them.

During the crisis, a £50,000 reward was offered for the capture of 'the Pretender' – dead or alive.[71] The authorities were alarmed when two officers from Dillon's were seen in Galway and it was thought that the French Irish Brigade intended landing in Carrickfergus, in the north of Ireland.[72] When the Jacobite army crossed into England, there were fears that they would land on the County Down coast and the militia stationed 15,000 men there for two or three days.[73] There were also fears that the Jacobites were opening a second front in Connacht, as Thomas Lally landed there after the Battle of Falkirk. Comte d'Argenson and Marshal de Noailles proposed a landing to be made in Ireland, spearheaded by the Irish Brigade. The plan involved dispatching 2,000 men (then bottled up at the French port of Boulogne) to the west coast of Ireland to rally the Irish and to divert British troops there. But in the end, no landings were made, probably due to the vigilance of the English Channel Fleet. The Viceroy of Ireland Lord Chesterfield's non-alarmist approach restored calm to the kingdom.[74] He was well aware that Catholics were in no position to rise, as the relatively recent

1740 famine had wiped out one-quarter of the Catholic population. In the end, Chesterfield made it loud and clear: 'If the Irish behaved like faithful subjects, they would be treated as such. If they act in a different manner, I will be worse than Cromwell.'[75]

The Irish led Charles's campaign and behaved with consummate bravery, although historians have downplayed their involvement. There was intense rivalry between the Scottish and Irish officers, and by the time of Culloden, John O'Sullivan and Lord George were barely on speaking terms. Lord George published his version of events shortly afterwards and failed to recognise the Irish contribution in the rising. Johnstone's version is naturally biased towards the Scots although he commends the part played by the Irish Brigade. The Irish lacked a voice; O'Sullivan wrote an account on the orders of Charles's father, 'James III', which remained unpublished in the *Stuart Papers* until 1938.[76] His account is important as he presents a first-hand Irish account of Charles's campaign, including his time 'in the heather'. Volunteer detachments of the Irish Brigade and the Royal Scots only arrived in time for the battles of Falkirk and Culloden. If Charles had been provided with 3,000 regulars (ideally seasoned troops from the Irish Brigade) together with sufficient funds, those many thousands who held back and were waiting in the wings as Charles lacked French support would have joined him and a formidable force might have marched to London and triumphed.

9

THE DECLINE OF CHARLES EDWARD STUART

The failure of Charles's campaign practically put an end to any hope of a Stuart Restoration. The Jacobite cause, if not now entirely lost, was reduced to a sentiment with royal supporters drinking the Loyal Toast over a glass of water, to 'the King (over the water)' and dreaming of what might have been. Charles was hugely disappointed with the realisation that he might never claim his throne, a position he was groomed his whole life for. He found this hard to accept and acquired a habit of excessive drinking, which he learnt in Scotland when 'a dram of whiskey might sometimes supply the want of food and of rest.'[1] While the campaign was a disaster, it had at least restored Charles's reputation. He was admired upon his arrival back in Paris where he received the deference of King Louis and the French Court. He was even accorded a standing ovation when he appeared at the Paris opera, and was described by a contemporary as follows:

> Whenever the young Chevalier appeared in any of the public walks at Paris, all the company followed the path he took, as impelled by irresistible attraction. When he came to the theatres, the attention of the audience was fixed upon him, regardless of what was presented upon the stage; upon his entrance into a box, a general whisper in his favour ran from one side of the theatre to the other, and few of the fair

sex but let fall tears of pity and admiration; while he alone seemed to be above a sense of his misfortunes, and talked to the young nobility, with whom he was constantly surrounded, in the same easy, cheerful, and affable manner he had always done.[2]

Things deteriorated further for Charles, as several Protestant princes, including the King of Prussia, complained about the support France provided in his efforts to secure the throne. Charles became a political hot potato, as most of the French ministers were not prepared to offend their Continental allies and were more concerned with the progress of the war in Flanders. Charles's embitterment led to his alienation at court due to his, at times, outrageous behaviour, caused partly by his excessive drinking. He quarrelled with his officers and friends and even managed to antagonise the king and his ministers.[3] He became 'estranged from his father, whom indeed he never saw again and blamed Lord George Murray for the decision taken at Derby and still believing in near paronoid fashion that Murray had betrayed him'.[4] He rightly blamed his failure in the '45 on lackluster support from the French, who had used him for their own political purposes. Indeed an English spy reported at the time that the French government was 'using the Pretender and his partisans like marionettes, making them dance to any tune that suits its interests'.[5]

Under the terms of the peace treaty of Aix-la-Chapelle (1748), France was required to recognise the Hanoverian George II (at the expense of James III) as the rightful claimant to the English throne. They were also required to remove his son, Charles, from France. A proposal was made to set Charles up in Switzerland, where he could keep his title of the 'Prince of Wales' and maintain a company of guards, but Charles was unrepentant. He was *de jure* heir to the Kingdom of England, Scotland and Ireland as was his divine birthright and he had no intention of going to Switzerland with an empty title. He was ordered to leave Paris, refused, and against all his expectations was forcefully seized and thrown into prison in Valencienne. After a few days, he was sent to the frontier of Savoy and unceremoniously dumped across the border. He felt hugely humiliated and blamed King Louis personally for this ill-treatment of a fellow monarch, which he saw as a personal affront and an indication of

Louis's dislike of him. Charles moved to the papal city of Avignon in the south of France, accompanied by 200 of his supporters and entertained lavishly. The British government applied diplomatic pressure on France to remove him from there even though Avignon was a papal protectorate, as they still perceived him as a security risk and wanted him removed from France entirely. Comte d'Argenson feared that Charles's expulsion from France would lead to the withdrawal of the Irish Regiments of France, but this was never realised.[6]

A major disappointment came when Charles's right to the throne was no longer recognised by the Papacy. The House of Stuart maintained close ties with the Catholic Church, which initially recognised them as the rightful heirs to the British throne. The Papacy also authorised their right to nominate Irish Bishops. In 1685, James II's right to nominate bishops was extended to his son and between 1687 and 1765, of 120 appointees, all but five were appointed by the Stuarts. This was an important right which the Stuarts guarded closely as it legitimised them (especially in the eyes of Irish Catholics) and supported their claim to the throne. Charles's father (the 'old Pretender') had been recognised as King of England, Scotland and Ireland as 'James III and James VIII' *de jure* by the Papacy. In 1760, Pope Clement XIII removed James's name on all future briefs of appointments to the Irish bishops.[7] When James died, the Papacy refused to recognise Charles as 'Charles III' and the legitimate heir, 'ending the 75-year long status of Irish Catholicism as literally an established church in exile'.[8] However, the Papacy still continued to support the Stuarts financially. In 1719, Pope Clement XI provided a number of palaces in Rome to the Stuarts, the rent for which was paid by the Holy See until the last of the Stuarts resided there in 1807.[9]

In the 1750s, Charles travelled throughout Europe under the alias of John Douglas to keep his costs down (much to his father's disapproval) and sank into obscurity. He increasingly turned to drink to console himself for his frustration and disappointment. His heavy drinking remained a matter of concern to all of those around him and he drank regularly with his secretary and close friend George Kelly, the Irish Protestant minister who had accompanied him to Scotland. He lived the life of a typical aristocrat and filled his days hunting in the Ardennes

John Greenhill, *James II as the Duke of York*. Portrait of the deposed Catholic king, painted in the early 1660s when he was a young man. (Courtesy of Reunion des Musees Nationaux, Paris)

and dividing his time between secret lodgings in France, Belgium and Switzerland. He was an accomplished violinist, fencer and golfer and was reportedly the first person to play golf in Italy. In December 1748 he visited Avignon disguised in the scarlet uniform of an officer in Hibernia's Regiment of Spain, together with Sir Thomas Sheridan, who had also accompanied him to Scotland and another officer of Hibernia's.[10] Always conscious of security, he changed residences regularly to outsmart would be British assassins. In 1750 he travelled to England incognito with a view to organising another rising in the

Highlands but the plans never came to fruition. Ironically, in the same year he secretly converted to Protestantism, more for political expediency than for religious reasons, as it was generally thought that he was an agnostic. Charles returned to settle in Rome where his health began to decline. Charles was 40 years old in 1760 when he was closely observed by an English lady together with two Irishmen who were always in his company:

> The Pretender is naturally above the middle size but stoops excessively; he appears bloated and red in the face; his countenance heavy and sleepy, which is attributed to his having given into excess of drinking; but when a young man he must have been esteemed and handsome. His complexion is of the fair tint, his eyes blue, his hair light brown, and the contour of his face a long oval; he is by no means thin, has a scarlet laced with broad gold lace; he wears the blue ribband outside of his coat, from which depends a cameo, antique, as large as the palm of my hand; and he wears the same garter and motto as those of the noble order of St. George in England. Upon the whole, he had a melancholy, mortified appearance.[11]

His supporters discouraged him from seeing his mistress, Clemintina Walkinshaw, who bore him an illegitimate daughter, Charlotte, as they viewed her as an unsuitable match. They proposed he choose a wife with a view to producing a legitimate heir to perpetuate the Stuart line. But Charles had already proclaimed never to marry to beget royal beggars and obstinately replied, in true fashion, that 'he would not put away a cat to please these people!' His behaviour only served to alienate his supporters and some abandoned his cause altogether. In 1772 he stopped drinking for a while and married the Belgian-born Princess Louise of Stolberg-Gedern, but the marriage ended childless two years later and the union was an unhappy one, caused partly by Charles's renewed bouts of drinking.

Charles moved to Florence for a while before returning to Rome with his daughter Charlotte in 1785, and he died there three years later. As he lay dying, a piper played the Jacobite lament 'Lachaber No More' at his bedside. He was laid in state in Frascati Cathedral in Rome, dressed in royal robes, with a replica of the English crown on his head and was buried there before being moved later to St Peter's Basilica. The following year, his illegitimate daughter, Charlotte, died of a kidney complaint.[12] The deposed King James II, Charles' grandfather, who died in 1701, had been embalmed in the English Benedictine Chapel in Paris, in the expectation that he would be deposited in Westminster Abbey in London upon a Stuart Restoration, which of course was never realised. During the French Revolution, the *sans-culottes* raided the chapel and removed and tossed aside the 100-year-old, perfectly preserved embalmed body from the lead casket they wanted to use to make lead shot and the body thereafter disappeared forever.[13]

10

THE WANING JACOBITE CAUSE

In 1747, the murderous War of the Austrian Succession had been raging for seven long years and had engulfed most of Europe. The Irish Brigade of France rejoined Saxe's army from garrison duty along the French coast for the Low Countries campaign. The French fielded 120,000 men in Spanish Flanders and led a very successful campaign by capturing all the important fortifications there. Saxe (of Fontenoy fame) had skilfully foiled an attempt by Cumberland to take Antwerp, resulting in his army pulling out and marching south to the fortified city of Maastricht. Saxe pursued him there to nearby Lafelt, a village in modern-day Belgium. On a misty morning in July, hostilities opened with the pounding roar of the usual cannonade. The local people took refuge in a nearby church and were terrified by the thunderous noise of the heavy ordinance. The battle was characterised by large cavalry charges with as many as 15,000 horses taking part in four hours of viscous fighting. At one point in the battle, the Allies gained the upper hand as they holed up behind crumbling walls and deep ravines in Lafelt village. Saxe needed to dislodge them before they dug in too deep and so ordered a large French force to attack, but this was forced back by an Allied counter-charge. Cumberland even recalled in his memoirs that another wave comprising 'the best brigades, among whom were the Irish troops' were sent in.[1] The Irish, along with other French units, advanced to support the French regiments who had taken up position on the village outskirts. The Allies retreated but again counter-attacked and quickly recovered their lost ground. The Dutch cavalry advanced to secure victory but then they beat a hasty retreat, trampling their own infantry as they fled and forcing the Allies to abandon Lafelt. The battle finally turned when several Irish regiments, along with the regiments of Diesbach, Monnin and Betterns, while under heavy fire forced an opening in the Allied lines at a critical moment and secured victory. The Allies were forced to give way and retreated a few miles to Lanaken.

The Duke of Cumberland, George II's son, had a lucky escape. In the heat of battle he mistook the red-clothed Irish Brigade for his own troops. The London press reported how the Irish hacked their way through and lunged at the Allied commander in a near suicidal attack and very nearly took him prisoner. The capture of the king's son, the Duke of Cumberland and HRH The Prince of Wales, would have spelt ruin for the British and would have been a spectacular morale boost for the Irish, both at home and abroad:

> Irish, in the French service, who fought like devils that they neither gave nor took quarter, that, observing the Duke of Cumberland to be extremely active in the defence of that post, they were employed upon this attack at their own request that they, in a manner, cut down all before them, with a full resolution, if possible, to reach his Royal Highness; which they certainly would have done, had not Sir John Ligonier come up with a party of horse, and thereby saved the Duke, at the loss of his own liberty.[2]

The battle was a pyrrhic French victory due to the massive 10,000 casualties (along with 3,000 horses) on both sides. The Irish Brigade also suffered severely with over 1,400 killed or wounded, which were twice as many Irish losses as at Fontenoy. Clare's bore the brunt of the losses due to repeated assaults and close-hand fighting in and around the village. Colonel Edward Dillon was mortally wounded leading his regiment and Lieutenant Colonel Dominic Lynch died from wounds and was interred in the Irish College in Leuven, Belgium. Fitzjames' horse also suffered heavily as evidenced by the fierce hand-to-hand fighting. Most wounds were due to sabre gashes, compared with Fontenoy where wounds were mostly due to grapeshot and musketry. The vast majority of the Brigade's losses were Irish-born and some were very young; two 14-year-olds, Francois Hickey and Daniel Hagan, a sergeant's son attached to Clare's Regiment were both killed. King Louis generously rewarded the Irish for their bravery by showering them with promotions, decorations, and life pensions.[3] Charles O'Brien the 6th Lord Clare wrote an account of the battle to James:

> It is my duty to acquaint your Majesty that the Irish Brigade, which Lord Edward Fitzjames, Mr. Rooth and I commanded, had a great share in the battle that was fought near Maastricht the 2nd of the month. It was employed at the attack on the village of Larfeld [Lafelt] and had the good luck to carry it and remain in it, though many other brigades had been pushed out of it. We lost on this occasion Colonel Dillon, 25 officers, 70 wounded and 1,353 private men killed and wounded. We had to do with the English, Hanoverians and Hessian troops. I wish we had been more particularly employed or your Majesty's service and that this may conduce to your restoration, which is the only and hearty prayer of your faithful subjects but of none more than me.[4]

The Allies took seventeen and the French sixteen colours or standards; this was in contrast to Fontenoy where only one colour was taken. The wounded remained on the field for days before being transported to improvised hospitals. Thousands were buried in mass graves and even today the ploughshares continue to dig up bodies and artifacts, including many Celtic crosses worn by fallen Irish soldiers.[5] The French victory enabled them to take Maastricht the following year. The French Minister for War, Comte d'Argenson, wrote to Colonel Bulkeley commending Irish bravery in the battle:

> 'It is I rather, who am more justly indebted to you, for the distinguished manner in which the Irish Brigade, and your regiment in particular, charged the enemy; and, although the duties, confided to you at Ostend, did not allow of your being present at this engagement, you do not the less partake of the glory which your regiment has acquired, by these new proofs of its valour.'[6]

Dillon regimental flag, a beautiful contemporary hand-painted example made of silk. (Private collection, with kind permission of J. North)

The following year, 1748, Europe enjoyed a well-deserved period of peace with the Treaty of Aix-le-Chapelle. Eight years later, Europe and much of the world was once more plunged into war when the Seven Years War broke out between France, Russia, Sweden and Spain on one side and Britain, Prussia and Hanover on the other. The reasons for this war are unclear as W.M. Thackeray famously stated in *Barry Lyndon*, that it would take a greater philosopher and historian than he to explain its true causes.[7] One of its causes was that France and her allies wanted to challenge Prussia's growing militarism and power. The war was a major global conflict and was fought in the Americas, Germany, India and Africa, together with naval operations from the Indian Ocean to the Caribbean. In 1754, France wanted to protect her colonial interest in New France (Quebec) in the Americas and unseat the growing British influence in the region. A French expeditionary force sailed to Canada in May 1755 under an Irish admiral, John MacNamara, accompanied by two Irishmen, Captain Cannon of the frigate *La Valeur* and Captain Darragh of the frigate *L'Heureux*. The Marquis de Vaudreuil, the last governor of New France, requested an Irish battalion to join the expedition to attract deserters from the British, but only Irish officers were sent. 'Among the number of Battalions, that you will order over, I think it would be well to send over one Irish Battalion, the rather as it would possess all the necessary resources to recruit, itself.'[8] The French commander, General Louis-Joseph de Montcalm, came across a number of captured Irishmen among British prisoners of war and formed them into an Irish unit to join the Irish Brigade in France.[9] The British were sensitive to the presence of crack troops of the Irish Brigade in Canada. In August 1756, the British Commander, Major-General John Campbell, wrote to the Duke of Cumberland informing him of a battalion of the French Irish Brigade in Canada and the defection of Irish troops to it:

> The Enemy I am afraid are much stronger than You think, and all accounts agree that there is a Battalion of the Irish Brigade here; they Scattered letters all around here at Oswego, this last Spring, promising great rewards, to any soldier who would come over to them, which drew great numbers of the Irish Recruits, from the two regiments there, which are mostly Roman Catholicks [sic]; And I will be far from venturing to assure You, that there are no Roman Catholicks in the other regiments, tho' all possible care has been taken to prevent it, by Lieutenant Colonels Gage & Burtin, and I find, most of the deserters from them, are Irish.[10]

This composite Irish battalion was in fact raised from Irish deserters in the British army and was present when the French captured Fort Oswego. Before the fort fell, a French deserter was allowed to escape (as otherwise he would have been hanged) and 'saw the French from the opposite side of the harbour getting into boats, and among them some clothed with red faced with green, who belong to the Irish Brigade'.[11] The Irishmen's red jackets were recut from the British uniform with lapels and lace removed and green facings added to appear more Irish.[12] The following summer, the Irish formed part of the French garrison in Louisbourg, Nova Scotia, before it capitulated to General James Wolfe after a heavy naval bombardment. Sergeant Donald Macleod of the Royal Highlanders (the Black Watch) details an encounter with the Irish battalion before the town capitulated, and the heroic bravery of Lieutenant Colonel O'Donnell and his men:

> A few days after the siege of Louisbourg had begun, a party of the besieged had the courage to make a sally on the assailants. They were led on with great firmness and intrepidity by Lieutenant Colonel O'Donnell, an Irishman in the French service. This bold sortie made an impression that might have had led to dire consequences, had it not been counteracted and overcome by the spirit of the Royal Highlanders; a part of whom faced the Irish Brigade that had made the sortie, the rest threw themselves between them and the town and cut off their retreat. O'Donnell fighting vainly, was slain, but did not fall until his body was pierced through by several bayonets. His men were all killed or taken prisoner, or brought within the British lines.[13]

In the late summer of 1757, the Irish battalion took part in the British defeat at Fort William Henry in Albany, New York. The British surrender of the fort became one of the most notorious incidents of the war. As the 1,500 column of British troops and colonials marched out with their families they were set upon and nearly all scalped by a local Indian tribe although the French rushed to their defence.[14] By 1759, the British gained the upper hand in the war after General Wolfe's victory over Montcalm at the Siege of Quebec. This left Fort Chartres in Illinois as the last French stronghold in Canada. The town's governor was an Irishman called MacCarthy who held out after Montreal's capitulation for almost a year before surrendering, under orders of the French king, drawing to a close French power in Canada.[15] The Irish battalion raised was shipped to France and was incorporated into the Irish regiments of France.[16]

Meanwhile, the European theatre of the war was in full throes when the Irish Brigade of France joined the German campaign against Prussia. They were present in the crushing French defeat at Rossbach where they fought bravely under the eyes of the most famous soldier of all time, Prussia's Frederick the Great. He commended the steadiness of the red-clad Irish and Swiss regiments for their 'wall of red bricks' in standing firm and repelling wave after wave of enemy cavalry and infantry charges.[17] In 1759, Fitzjames' horse was nearly destroyed coming to the rescue of an Austrian cuirassier regiment that was attacked by Prussian cavalry. The following year, in 1758, the Irish infantry regiments of France were ordered to the coast of Brittany and repelled a small British coastal raid.

France, eager to break the stalemate in the war, now prepared a huge, three-pronged invasion of the British Isles. In 1759, a large-scale army numbering 17,000 men (including the Irish and Scots infantry regiments of France) was mobilised at Brest. Marshal Charles O'Brien the 6th Lord Clare was to lead an expedition to south-west Ireland. The king's brother, the Prince de Conti, was to lead the main invasion army in southern England and the Duc d'Aiguillon was to command a third force sent to Scotland to incite a rising there. The French Foreign Minister, the Duc de Choiseul, solicited a meeting with Charles in preparing the invasion, but Charles arrived drunk and was still blaming the French for his failed expedition in the '45 and for his forced removal from France. To make matters worse, he unreasonably made requests for 'reparations' from Louis XV and made it clear that he was determined not be used again like a 'scarecrow'. Charles made it clear that he was interested in leading an invasion on the condition it constituted a formidable force and not a small diversionary force like in the '45. Three years previously, he was asked to command an expedition against Mallorca and was also requested to lead an expeditionary force in America, but he always declined. He now rejected leading the expedition to Ireland where it was proposed that he would be maintained as King Charles III of the Kingdom of Ireland. Charles was adamant that the invasion had to be to England. It was his divine right to be the king of England, Scotland and Ireland or none at all.[18] Thereafter, he was written off by the French high command as a liability and he was dropped entirely from the mission. When the Jacobites in France learned of French commitment in launching an invasion they sprang into action and 'bombarded Choiseul with ideas about landings and "descents" in England and Scotland from Jacobites in the Church, the army, the navy, the East India Company and the masonic lodges'.[19]

However, British naval pre-eminence again saved the country from invasion. The twenty-one-ship French covering fleet under Admiral de Conflan left port to clear the Channel for the troop transports but was intercepted and defeated by the Royal Navy at Quiberon Bay. This resulted in all three invasion missions being cancelled. However, the famous French privateer Francois Thurot successfully charged through the British naval blockade at Dunkirk. Several British squadrons vigorously pursued his six ships but he luckily escaped. It is not known how many Irishmen served under him but a contemporary source mentions 'the principal pilot and best seaman on Thurot's ship to be an Irishman called Bates'.[20] It is thought that Thurot's grandfather was a Captain O'Farrell who left Limerick with the Irish army in 1691. Thurot was a notorious privateer who had taken sixty English ships the previous year. His mission had not been an easy one: his small fleet was scattered in a storm, two of his six ships were forced back to Dunkirk and he had to suppress a mutiny onboard. Half-starving, his sailors were sent ashore on the Scottish island of Islay to gather provisions and were observed by an islander gathering fresh vegetables to prevent scurvy:

> We may judge of the situation of this squadron from the conduct of these poor creatures, who had no longer touched dry land, than, with their bayonets, they fell to digging up herbs, and every green thing they met with. At length, they came to a field of potatoes, which they very eagerly dug; and, after shaking off the earth, and wiping them a little on their waistcoats, eat them up, raw as they were, with the greatest keenness![21]

Thurot knew he could not return to France empty-handed. French honour was at stake and he was determined to strike somewhere in the British Isles. In early 1759 he captured Carrickfergus Castle outside Belfast, as it was in poor condition and only lightly defended. He had even boldly considered sailing up through Belfast Lough and attacking Belfast with his four ships but wisely decided against it. Thurot remained in Carrickergus for a number of weeks and when he was loaded with supplies, he sailed back for France. The Viceroy in Dublin scrambled three British men-of-war in pursuit and intercepted him near the

Isle of Man. After several hours of close fighting, Thurot's ship was crippled and while urging his gunners to fire a broadside the famous privateer was shot in the chest and killed. Thurot's landing in Ireland was a great propaganda coup and it gave the Irish hope as his small force of four ships 'gained as much reputation as could be expected from a fleet'.[22] The 1759 invasion was Charles's last chance to claim the throne and the writing was on the wall for the Jacobites. The Gaelic poets drew comparisons between the invasion force of the Irish Brigade to the several thousand warriors of the Fianna, led by Finn McCool, who were maintained by the Irish monarchs in the third century 'to guard Erin against the Roman Legions' that had subjugated Britannia.[23]

With an invasion of the British Isles now shelved, the Irish infantry regiments were ordered from coastal defence duties along the French coast back to the German campaign. In 1761, supported by the newly formed Scottish d'Ogilvy Regiment of France, they fought the Allies at Marborg, Villinghausen, Soest and Unna. Fitzjames' horse's last hurrah was at the Battle of Wilhemstahl, when it was attacked on three sides and overrun in the village of Grebenstein losing '300 of their horses and their two standards'.[24] These two battle-flags were the only ones lost to the enemy in the Irish Brigade's history.[25] Poor old Fitzjames' was no more. Its predecessors, the Irish Jacobite cavalry, were the 'flower of the Irish army', who fought with valour in the Jacobite War. After Limerick's capitulation, they bravely served France for nearly seventy years. They quickly earned distinction in Luzzaro, Italy, in Speyer, Germany and in Ramillies, Oudenaarde and Malplaquet in Flanders. Fitzjames' survived severe losses at Fontenoy and Lafelt, and volunteer detachments served in Scotland, where many were captured at sea. Fitzjames' were the sole regular cavalry at Culloden and bravely covered the Highlanders' retreat from the battlefield. After suffering such heavy losses at Wilhemstahl, the regiment was officially deactivated in 1762. 'We cannot help, in this place, lamenting the fate of Fitzjame's horse,' observed an English account at the time, 'though in the service of our enemies, they proved themselves our brethren, though mislead. Is it not a great misfortune, that, through a false principle of policy, we suffer so many gallant men to enlist in our enemy's service?'[26] Another English account described their loss:

'I am sorry to say, that our nation has found from sad, almost fatal experience, the injury and prejudice we have suffered by it, (if losing battles may be so termed) through such unhappy men being employed in the armies of our enemies.'[27]

The Irish Jacobite Prime Minister of Spain, Richard (Ricardo) Wall was finally persuaded by the French Court in 1761 to join France in the Seven Years War against England. France argued that with the loss of Canada, this would cause a domino effect, putting the Spanish dominions of Louisiana and Mexico at risk from British domination. The following year, *The London Magazine* reported the deployment of the Irish infantry regiments of France from Germany to the French coast at Dunkirk, heightening fears of another Franco-Jacobite invasion of the British Isles.[28] But invasion never came and the Irish Brigade stood down as the Seven Years War drew to a close, with peace finally signed in 1763 with the Treaty of Paris.

11

Lieutenant General Thomas Lally's Expedition to India

Lieutenant General Count Thomas de Lally de Tollendal, an officer in the Irish Brigade of France, played a leading role in French imperialistic ambitions in India. In 1755 Thomas Lally (perhaps one of the staunchest of the Irish Jacobites) was summoned by Louis XV to Versailles to discuss the possibility of three schemes: an invasion of the British Isles with Prince Charles at its head, a challenge to British power on the Indian subcontinent, or an attack on the valuable thirteen British colonies in America. Lally advocated challenging British power in India. The British were longer established there and France was keen to open the door to East Asia by unseating British power in the region. In the seventeenth century, France had established the Compagnie des Indes (The French East India Company) to rival the longer established British East India Company. These two companies had their own well-armed semi-private armies and were established to develop colonial trade with the Indian subcontinent.

Thomas Lally came from an old Gaelic aristocratic family. He was the son of Sir Gerard Lally, an officer in Dillon's and his mother was Marie Anne de Bressac, a French noblewoman.[1] Young Thomas Lally accompanied Dillon's on exercises at the tender age of 7 years, so that 'he got used to the smell of gunpowder', in the words of his father. In 1734 at the Battle of Ettlingin, he saved his father's life by rushing to his assistance while under heavy enemy fire and removing him from danger. Thereafter his father always referred to his son as 'My Protector'. How many fathers could say that about their sons?

Thomas Lally had field command of the Irish at Fontenoy, and was wounded and promoted for his actions there. He was present at the hostilities at Barcelona, Lafelt, Bergen-op-Zoom and Maastricht and served in Scotland in the '45. In 1756, he was promoted to lieutenant general in the French army, while at the same time retaining the rank of colonel-proprietor of his own Regiment of Lally in the Irish Brigade. He was 'justly esteemed as the best soldier in all France', and was a well-respected military commander with the confidence of Marshal Saxe, who once declared 'we can sleep peacefully, for Lally is with the army.'[2] Lord Clare and the Duc de Fitzjames backed Lally's Indian appointment, although it was suggested that Lally's forces were inadequate for the task.[3] Comte d'Argenson, the French Minister for War, recognised that although Lally was an excellent soldier and a pugnacious hothead, his task in India required a more diplomatic approach, which he may have been unsuited to. 'I know Lally better than you do and he is my friend but he should be left with us in Europe,' explained d'Argenson. 'He is aflame with activity, he does not know what compromise is where a matter of discipline is in question; He has a horror of anything that is not straightforward and gives expression to his feelings in unforgettable terms.'[4]

Despite the surrounding uncertainty, Thomas Lally was given command of the French expedition and was presented with the Order of St Louis and made governor-general of India. In the spring of 1757, Admiral d'Ache's flotilla of three ships of the line; the 74-gun *Zodiac*, the *Bellequeux* of 70 guns and the *Superbe* of 64 guns, accompanied by a 50-gun frigate belonging to the *Compagnie*, were finally ready to sail for India. A war chest of six million livres was provided and the expedition comprised six battalions of 2,500 men. Thomas Lally's own red-coated regiment of the Irish Brigade provided 1,080 troops and was re-formed for the expedition, comprising two battalions of eighteen companies.[5] As the French expedition was leaving port, the *Bellequeux* and the *Zodiac* were disabled by a heavy squall which damaged their masts, forcing d'Ache's fleet to return to port for repairs. The *Bellequeux*, carrying two battalions and two million livres, was requisitioned for the French war effort in Canada. Lally strongly protested and made it clear that with his force depleted by one-third he could no longer guarantee the success of the mission.[6] The French expedition sailed anyway two months later, in May 1757, carrying four battalions, two of whom were from Lally's Regiment. This delay proved costly as while Lally's expedition was on the high seas, the British defeated the French at the Battle of Plassey, further compromising French control on the Indian sub-continent.

Less than a year later, in April 1758, Lally arrived in the south-east Indian French settlement of Pondicherry (the headquarters of the French East India Company). Lally not only had to re-establish French power in the region, but he also had to clean up corruption at the Compagnie, which was in financial dire straits. Lally had already made many enemies by exposing those in the French East India Company who had made vast fortunes through corruption.[7] He was also tasked with suppressing several mutinies, preventing desertions to the British, and at the same time, his force was being steadily decimated by tropical illnesses. Upon arrival in Pondicherry, Lally did not even wait for the customary *Te Deum* to celebrate his arrival but proceeded directly to invest British-controlled Fort David. Within six weeks, Fort David was secured and Lally went on to take Cuddalore and Devicotah and forced the British back from the coast to St George in Madras (in modern-day Chennai), the British East India stronghold.

By July of the following year, Lally wanted to besiege the town and required naval support, but Admiral d'Ache's damaged squadron sailed to Madagascar in the Indian Ocean for repairs, owing to an earlier scrap with the Royal Navy, despite protestations by Lally. His public condemnation of corrupt colonial officials also brought him into conflict with Comte de Bussy, the commander of the Compagnie, who was now also unwilling to assist him in the operation. Lally went ahead anyway and dug entrenchments outside Fort St George in Madras, and to add to his difficulties, 'Two hundred French soldiers deserted to the English and entered Fort George; they could be seen on the ramparts holding a bottle of wine in one hand and a purse of money in the other, urging their compatriots to imitate them.'[8] After two months, Madras was close to capitulation but Lally was forced to lift the siege when a Royal Navy squadron came to its relief. Lally was furious and was forced to jettison sorely needed artillery and ammunition and retreat to Pondicherry.

In January 1760, the British advanced towards the French-held town of Wandiwash, located halfway between British-controlled Madras and French-held Pondicherry. Colonel O'Kennedy of Lally's Regiment commanded the 168-man Franco-Irish garrison and held out against the British East India Company, who invested the town. The town capitulated the following month as it was low in morale, compounded by the fact that O'Kennedy's troops hadn't been paid in ten months. Lally set out with his army from Pondicherry determined to retake the town. He launched a night attack and scaled the fort, sword in hand, at the head of his own red-coated troops, while a marine detachment attacked the flank, but the attack failed and Wandiwash held out. Lally was then forced to dig entrenchments outside the town to starve the British garrison into submission.

When news reached the British camp that Wandiwash was being besieged, the East India Company's commander, Lieutenant Colonel Eyre Coote was rushed to its relief. Coote was the son of an Irish Protestant clergyman from Co. Limerick; the fate of the Indian subcontinent was decided by two men of Irish descent, one in French and the other in British service. Lally had crossed swords with Coote before in the Battle of Falkirk, in the Scottish '45. Coote had served as an officer in the 27th (Inniskilling's) Foot and had carried the King's colour and prevented its capture by escaping with it to Edinburgh.[9] Lally fielded 1,350 European troops; of whom 600 were from Lally's own regiment, together with 1,800 Indian sepoys. Coote's force comprised 1,700 Europeans and 3,500 sepoys. After a closely run battle of six hours the French were decisively defeated with 600 losses, the commander of the Compagnie, Comte de Bussy, was captured, along with Lieutenant Colonel Murphy and two captains and lieutenants of Lally's regiment.

The remnants of Lally's army withdrew again to Pondicherry, which was now the last French possession in India, pursued by Coote's army, and by the end of the month he was surrounded. Lally held out for Admiral d'Ache's squadron to return from the Indian Ocean as he had promised, but he waited in vain. Their supplies were depleted to the extent they survived by living on horses, dogs and rats. Lally's fate was sealed when a Royal Navy squadron moored off the coast and bombarded the French garrison and razed the town to the ground (the ruins of the fort and the settlement are still visible today). After an eight-month siege the besieged

Lieutenant General Thomas Lally's Expedition to India

Soldier of Lally's Regiment of France, 1761. (With kind permission of The Vinkhuizen Collection, New York Public Library)

garrison had no choice but to surrender. The campaign had taken its toll on the 59-year-old bedridden general, who had to be carried on a sedan chair. The Franco-Irish garrison were taken prisoner and transported to Bombay for repatriation to France, while Lally was transported to London. Lally's Regiment was disbanded shortly afterwards, Pondicherry's fall signalled the end of French power in India.

While Lally was incarcerated in London, he received news from France that he was being blamed for losing French control of India and was now publicly referred to as 'L'Irlandais'.[10] The French were furious they had lost their interest in the Indian sub-continent even as the army was still held in disgrace after losing Canada.[11] Many powerful people in France, including Voltaire, had invested and lost everything in the Compagnie and were now looking for a scapegoat. Lally was granted a parole of honour from the then British Prime Minister William Pitt and voluntarily returned to France, and perhaps naively expected to be exonerated of the charges due to the limited financial and military resources that had been at his disposal. He grossly underestimated public opinion and upon arrival in France he was impeached and a *lettre de cachet* committed him to the Bastille prison. He wrote to the Duc de Choiseul for support, unaware at the time that Choiseul had signed the same *letter de cachet* that incarcerated him two days before. Choiseul was one of the most powerful and influential advisors to King Louis XV and was even related to Admiral D'Ache, who had failed to support Lally.[12]

> My Lord – the rumours, which prevail in Paris, have brought me here. My enemies will never be able to terrify me, since I depend on my own innocence, and am sensible of your equity. The king is master of my liberty, but my honour is under the safeguard of the laws, of which he is the protector. I do not ask you, my Lord, who are my slanderers; I know them; but what their slanders are, that I may obviate them; and repel them with shame. I have brought here my head and my innocent, and shall continue here to wait your orders.[13]

While in prison, old wounds suffered at Maastricht reopened and his teeth were giving him trouble. Visitors also mentioned the deterioration of his physical and mental state.[14] Many Irish officers were compelled to keep their distance from him as they also feared for their own safety. Lally was eventually brought to trial and accused of the trumped-up charges of 'a betrayal of the interests of the King, of the State and the French East India Company; with the abuse of the high authority vested in him; with the unwarrantable exactions from the inhabitants of Pondicherry; and with the mismanagement of the public trust committed to his care.'[15]

He languished for four years in prison before being found guilty and sentenced to be beheaded. General Arthur Dillon and friends at court including the king's influential mistress, Madame de Pompadour, made representation for Lally's release to King Louis but to no avail. His execution was brought forward as it was feared that he would take his own life, and he travelled bound and gagged in a cart to prevent him from making a speech at the scaffold to the Place de la Concorde amidst much public excitement. The executioner botched the job, and swung too high, failing to take Lally's head off in one clean sweep, the blade instead coming down onto the unfortunate general's jawbone, requiring a second, fatal chop.[16]

Thomas Lally was an important public figure in France and his death was the news of the day for the French and British pamphleteers. He had hoped that his efforts in India would gain him a marshal's baton, but instead he was condemned for losing French possessions there, which cost him his life.[17] Ultimately, the jealousies and disloyalties of other officers, together with inadequate funds and limited naval support, prevented him securing India for France.[18]

The Lally case became a *cause célèbre* in France. The historian Frank McLynn has described Lally's treatment as the 'most hideous miscarriage of justice in French history'.[19] Lally wrote his memoirs in prison, vindicating himself of his actions, which he 'addressed to the Judges, in answer to the charges brought against him by the Attorney General of his Most Christian Majesty'. He made his son Trophime-Gerard Lally, then a 15-year-old schoolboy, promise to clear his father's name. He was assisted by officers of the Irish Brigade and by Voltaire, who pressured the authorities by dramatically describing Lally's treatment as an official murder carried out with a sword of justice. He also made ceaseless references to the Lally case as an example of official injustice. Twelve years later, in 1778, Louis XVI issued a royal decree declaring that the court in the Lally case acted without proper authority, and Lally's honours, titles and lands were restored to his son.[20] Voltaire on hearing the verdict, although near death,

Artist unknown, *Arthur, Comte du Dillon (1750-1794)*. The hapless general was guillotined during the French Revolution. (Courtesy of Réunion des Musées Nationaux, Paris)

wrote: 'the dying man revives on learning this great news. He embraces very tenderly M. de Lally. He sees that the King is the defender of Justice. He will die contented.'[21] In 1929, General Thomas Lally was finally, publicly exonerated and his name was restored to the army list. He is remembered today in Paris by having a street named in his honour – the *Rue Lally Tollendal* – located in the Polish quarter.

12

THE WAR OF AMERICAN INDEPENDENCE (1775–83)

The War of American Independence began between Great Britain and revolutionaries of the thirteen American colonies in 1775. There had been growing discontentment amongst the American colonists for a number of years due to a wide array of imperial fiscal controls imposed on the Thirteen Colonies. These protected trade to suit British interests, and other taxation measures imposed by the British only served to increase the colonists' anger and frustration. Matters came to a head in April 1775, when a British force clashed with the colonists on Lexington Green in Massachusetts. This incident left a number of Americans dead, which sparked the American struggle for Independence.

By the summer of 1776, a huge British Expeditionary Force comprising 300 ships and 30,000 troops was dispatched to crush the rebellion. The British were badly in need of manpower for the war and relaxed legislation preventing Irish Catholics from entering the army. This had the desired effect of recruiting thousands of Irishmen being sent to the America as part of the British Expeditionary Force. Of the forty-four battalions serving in America in 1776, sixteen were raised in Ireland.[1] In addition, George III had also entered into a number of treaties with German states, resulting in the British effort bolstered by a huge German contingent of 30,000 Hessian troops.[2]

Congress appointed the 43-year-old Virginian plantation owner George Washington as commander of the newly minted Continental army, which at the time was a poorly trained militia. Irish immigrants also provided thousands of foot soldiers and scores of officers for the Americans. Of the first nine companies raised in Pennsylvania, seven were made up of Irishmen, and the remaining two were German. The historian R.F. Foster has calculated that 250,000 Irish Presbyterians from Ulster (who were later known as Scots-Irish) and 100,000 Irish Catholics emigrated to the American colonies during the period.[3] These two Irish groups resented British domination in the Americas, which they compared to British tyranny back home in Ireland. A travelling English merchant recalled: 'Some 8,000 to 10,000 people were imported there from Ireland last year. These settlements are composed of an uncultivated banditti which lawless publications take great effect. Can the event [the rebellion] be any other in a few years to throw off their dependence? They are ripe for it.'[4]

It is thought that roughly one out of every four Continental soldiers was of Irish descent and formed 'the backbone of the lines of the middle states' of Pennsylvania and Maryland.[5] Three years into the war, the British commander General Henry Clinton reported that the Irish were 'our most serious antagonists'.[6] The Americans were in need of experienced commanders and Congress granted as many as 100 French officers commissions in the Continental army, including the Marquis de Lafayette and Comte Thomas Conway, who were seeking fame and fortune in the war. Kerry-born Thomas Conway became the highest ranked Irish officer in the Continental army in his time as inspector general.[7] He was later embroiled in a unsuccessful plot (which became known as the 'Conway cabal') to oust General Washington as commander-in-chief of the Continental army.[8]

During the American Civil War (1860–65), Irish immigrants who had already fought with gusto in the Union army formed an Irish brigade. They adopted the war cry 'Remember Fontenoy!' in homage to their predecessors who served in the French and Spanish armies. Their involvement in the Civil War has been well documented. One hundred years earlier, during the American Revolutionary War (1775–83), the Irish Brigades of France and Spain fought alongside the American

The War of American Independence (1775-83)

rebels but details about this are sparse. This is partly due to French regimental records disappearing during the turmoil of the French Revolution and American accounts tending to concentrate on American involvement only.[9]

General Washington was aware of the need to ally his cause with a European maritime power and found a willing ally in France. Prior to the American victory at Saratoga in 1777, the French clandestinely supplied the American rebels, but would not commit troops. This soon changed after the turning point at Saratoga when the Americans were confident of success and France threw in her lot behind them. In 1778, Benjamin Franklin signed an alliance treaty with France (and later on Spain) whereby she agreed to provide naval support and transport troops along the American eastern seaboard and in the islands of the West Indies. France was primarily concerned with reducing British power in North America and Spain's main focus was in regaining her territories of Gibraltar and Minorca, which she had recently lost in the Seven Years War.

French contribution to the American war effort was huge. She provided sixty-two ships, 47,000 troops and issued over 100,000 French-issue Charleville muskets to the rebels. This was in addition to a war chest of six million livres, excluding the cost of military hardware. The three remaining Irish regiments of Dillon's, Walsh's and Berwick's volunteered to serve in America as the Irish, noted General Arthur Dillon, 'always demanded the privilege of going first into battle against the English, everywhere the French were at war with them'.[10] The 1st battalion of Dillon's, numbering 1,400 men, left Brest for the West Indies in May 1779.[11] These were followed by a smaller detachment drawn from Walsh's shortly afterwards.[12] Berwick's 2nd battalion had left France the previous year and served as marines in the French fleet.[13] At this time, although the Irish regiments in France were still officered by Irishmen, there were few Irish foot soldiers serving in the ranks, as most of the ordinary soldiers were foreigners.[14]

The Spanish did not play a major part as she was still reorganising her army after the Seven Years War and confined operations to Europe and to South and Central America, where most of her interests lay. The Irish Regiment of Ultonia of Spain took part in the attack on the

British-held island of Minorca in 1781, and the Regiment of Hibernia's 22 officers and 588 men formed the second largest Spanish force that captured the British West Florida capital of Pensacola. Colonel Artura O'Neill of Hibernia's was then installed as governor.[15] Hibernia's suffered heavy losses when it took part in Field Marshal Alexander O'Reilly's Spanish attack in Algeria that ended in a military disaster. The following year, the Regiment of Irlanda served in the long-running Spanish Siege of Gibraltar.[16]

As France was again at war with Britain in the Americas, the French high command saw an opportunity to attack Britain closer to home by launching an invasion of Ireland. In the spring of 1778, Irish Brigade officers on leave in Rome wrote home that invasion plans were afoot.[17] There had also been a Franco-Spanish invasion attempt the following year, but as the ships' crews were decimated by illness, the mission was aborted. An invasion of Ireland was also a scheme close to the heart of high-ranking French officers. 'Ireland is a good deal tired of English tyranny', wrote the Marqus de Lafayette to General Washington. 'I, in confidence, tell you that the scheme of my heart would be to make her as free and independent as America.'[18] Irish exiles in Paris proposed to the French high command that the illegal Whiteboys (a militant group who used violent tactics to protect tenant farmers) could serve as light cavalry in an invasion. It was thought, rather optimistically, that 1,500 could be mobilised in Kilkenny within a few hours notice.[19]

Moreover, support from the Catholic gentry and the small but growing Catholic middle-class was not guaranteed. The once powerful gentry had delicately manoeuvred their families around the Penal Laws for nearly 100 years, and some had even become de facto part of the Establishment. The influential Catholic landowner Lord Kenmare had drummed up for new recruits for the British war effort. Catholic merchants in Cork had also addressed the Viceroy, proclaiming the city's loyalty to the Crown and warning France of 'its imaginary hope of assistance in Ireland from the former attachments of our predecessors'.[20] It was felt that the Catholic gentry were not prepared to risk losing whatever they had gained by siding with the rebels. The ordinary peasantry with nothing to lose were expected to rally to the French, who 'would deliver them from the tyranny under which they have existed for so long'.[21] However, in the end, the country did not rise up during the American War. General Washington wrote eloquently from Mount Vernon of his disappointment 'that they [the Irish] slumbered during the favourable moment none, I think, can deny, and favourable moments in war, as in love, once lost are seldom regained'.[22]

The Irish Brigade were always to spearhead an invasion of Ireland, and the decision to deploy them to the Americas and West Africa suggested that no invasion was to go ahead.[23] The Irish regiments had served so long in France that many officers had adopted a French outlook. Even Dillon's Regiment volunteered to go, though there were ongoing discussions with the Stuart court in Italy for an invasion of Ireland.[24] 'For many Irishmen in the French army, integration had reached the point where they were less concerned with liberating Ireland than with serving their adopted king and country.'[25] This was not strictly the case across the board, as some were more gung-ho: 'Would to God that we were at this moment 200,000 strong in Ireland,' wrote the young Lieutenant Richard O'Connell, 'I would kick the Members [of Parliament] and their Volunteers and their unions and their societies to the Devil; I would make the Rascally spawn of Damned Cromwell curse the hour of his Birth.'[26]

Meanwhile, the Thirteen Colonies began building up their own fleet and Congress sought the expertise of John Barry from Co. Wexford, who was appointed the first flag officer of the United States Navy.[27] Barry's ship (the *Alfred*) was commissioned by Benjamin Franklin as the first of eight to be fitted out to fly the thirteen stars and stripes flag as the first American fleet. Barry rose to the rank of commodore and captured the first British ship by an American cruiser in the war. Scotsman John Paul Jones captained the 40-gun American frigate *Bonhomme Richard* and brought the war into British waters by operating as a privateer, attacking shipping around the British Isles. He even boldly captured a British man-of-war in Belfast Lough.[28] In mid-1779 a number of Irish Brigade officers (James O'Kelly, Eugene MacCarthy and Edward Stack) were commissioned as marine lieutenants and served onboard the *Bonhomme*. They were joined by a 137-man volunteer detachment drawn from the Regiment of Walsh who were inducted into the newly formed American Continental Marines (the forerunner of the US Marine Corps).[29] The 40-gun *Bonhomme* fought a ferocious four-hour battle with HMS *Serapis* (50 guns) and the frigate *Countess* (20 guns) off the English coast at Flamborough Head in what became known as one of the most famous American naval engagements. James O'Kelly was killed in the mêlée and MacCarthy was injured, and Stack bravely commanded the main tops in the action, which cost over 170 lives. The *Bonhomme* was close to sinking when two other ships in Jones's squadron came to his assistance. Jones closed quarters, took command of the *Serapis* and escaped with the *Countess* as a prize to the Dutch coast. MacCarthy and Stack were promoted and were recommended by d'Estaing and Lafayette for the prestigious Order of the Cincinnati.[30] Their run of good luck ran out when they were arrested by the authorities after they pulled into Derrynane, in Co. Kerry recruiting for the American war effort.[31]

The West Indian islands of the Caribbean were the prizes in the war and the French Irish Brigade campaigned heavily there. The French focused on wrestling the lucrative sugar and rum trade from British hands. This trade in the period was immense 'with 246 ships fully laden with 97,317 casks of sugar and 16,712 casks of rum departing from the seven or eight Caribbean islands for England in the twelve months from March 1789 to March 1790'.[32] The West Indies were so important to Britain that she sent one-third of her army from the Thirteen Colonies to protect her interests. George III had once declared that he would rather risk an invasion of Britain than lose the West Indies, as without them he would be unable to finance the war. In the bitter fighting taking place in the Caribbean, the islands were taken and re-taken several times, French troops replaced British garrisons and the British in turn wrestled some of those islands back.

A French fleet of twenty-nine ships under Admiral d'Estaing anchored in Delaware on the eastern American seaboard in July 1779 and Dillon's Regiment boarded for a raid on British-held Grenada. The fleet anchored in the harbour, and a landing party disembarked and charged up to the island's summit to take the island's fort. General Arthur Dillon led the first column on an attack with 1,300 troops (half of whom were from Dillon's) while another kinsman, Edouard Dillon, commanded the second column.[33] Hospital Hill was a major strategic point for the battle and the Franco-Irish force still managed to take it despite being cannoned by a British man-of-war moored outside the bay. They lost 300 men and overpowered the 800-strong enemy garrison. The Irish took advantage of similarities between their red uniform and the British redcoats to launch their *coup de main*. 'The troops, who were in possession of the hill that commands the fort, were deceived by the French, who sent up the Irish Brigade in their service to make the first attack,' noted an English observer. 'It was then dark, and the Irish speaking the same language, were admitted into the entrenchments as friends, and they immediately overpowered our troops by numbers.'[34] The island's governor was an Irish Protestant called Lord MacCarthy from Co. Antrim who refused to agree terms. D'Estaing's troops decided to plunder the town until the Irish intervened. One English witness recalled: 'The French soldiers were indulged, it had been said, in the most unwarranted irregularities, and had they not been restrained by the Irish troops in the French service, would have proceeded to still greater.'[35]

The French commandeered thirty merchantmen, loaded with rum, and 26,000 hogsheads of sugar, valued at £520,000, which were to be shipped to England with the fleet that August. Dillon and his men would have received a part of this booty as the spoils of war. A Royal Navy squadron under Admiral John Byron was scrambled from nearby St Vincent to Grenada's relief. As his ships entered port, shore batteries opened up and crippled several of his ships, as he had been unaware the island had fallen into French hands. Byron limped to St Kitts for repairs, expecting to be pursued by d'Estaing to finish him off, but luckily for Byron, d'Estaing was ordered to attack British-held Savannah. The action that followed became the first French operation on the American mainland.

D'Estaing's thirty-four-ship fleet moored off the mouth of the Savannah River in late 1779 where the British had heavily fortified the town. D'Estaing was ill-prepared for a long drawn-out siege as he lacked supplies and his troops were dressed in flimsy uniforms inadequate for the season.[36] He landed 6,000 French troops, along with 500 from the Irish Brigade and joined forces with 545 native troops from Haiti and 2,000 men from the Continental Army and the Charleston Militia.[37] British forces under General Prevost's command numbered 7,000, of whom 3,055 were regulars, along with 4,000 native troops.

The Franco-Americans planned to attack at nightfall on the weakest part of the town (known as Spring Hill), when an attack signal was to be sounded, but it was drowned out by the skirl of the bagpipes from the Black Watch who played to rally the troops.[38] The Franco-Americans succeeded in entering the British fort where Colonel Browne of Dillon's (aide-de-camp to Admiral d'Estaing) was killed trying to plant the French flag on the parapet, but were eventually forced to retreat as the British counter-attacked.[39] An American officer reported: 'The loss of both armies in killed and wounded amounted to 637 French and 457 Americans, the Irish Brigade in the French service, and our 2nd Regiment, particularly distinguished themselves and suffered most.'[40] British casualties were light but Dillon's suffered sixty-three killed and eighty-four wounded. D'Estaing was injured in the attack and Count Arthur Dillon was given overall command, and he, along with Lieutenant Colonel Lynch of Walsh's and six other French officers, were commended for bravery. There were no reported casualties from Walsh's, save for a Captain D'Arcy who died of fever prior to the assault.[41] The French were forced to raise the siege, and d'Estaing sailed from Savannah, taking advantage of a break in the weather. Comte d'Estaing was commended by the Americans for his part in the siege 'by bravely putting himself at the head of his troops, and leading them to the attack'.[42]

In mid-1781, the next French target was the Caribbean island of Tobago, where the Irish Brigade's 700 troops overpowered the British garrison. This event went down in folk memory back in Ireland as a Gaelic drinking song, celebrating the island's capture by the Irish troops. Dillon's also besieged British-held St Kitts, where British troops fought skirmishes with the Irish Brigade and succeeded in driving them back, but the island eventually fell under French control after a month-long siege. Dillon's then garrisoned the island before the regiment's 600 troops were sent to garrison Haiti, where Count Arthur Dillon was appointed governor. The British afterwards commended him for his good governance of the island. The British now feared that their most lucrative sugar island of Jamaica would also fall to the French. The following year, a company of Walsh's took part in recapturing the largest French slave-trading colony in British-held Senegal and garrisoned Martinique the following year. Walsh's and Dillon's also served as marines in three naval battles under Comte de Guichen against a Royal Navy squadron under Admiral Rodney.[43] The French attack on Saint Eustatius – defended by the British 13th and 15th Regiments of Foot – was also spearheaded by the Irish Brigade. General de Bouillé detailed the events leading up to the attack:

> Having learned that the garrison of the island guarded it very badly, that the governor was in the greatest security; and knowing besides of a place of debarkation that was not guarded, I thought, I could, by arriving in the night with 1,200 men, carry that important island. In consequence I left Martinico on the 15th with three frigates, and four armed cutters, that carried the troops, composed of a battalion of Auxerrois, and one of Dillon and Walsh, of the same number, and of 300 grenadiers and chauffeurs of different corps. I caused it to be reported, that I was going to meet our naval forces; and I weathered Martinico, where after a thousand obstacles from winds and currents, I could not get up until the 22nd; and the 25th I arrived in sight of St. Eustache. The debarkation took place the same night. The light vessels and the sloop were to catch anchor and the frigates to remain under sail, at hand to send the troops on shore; but our pilots were mistaken, and the boat which was Count Dillon's was the only one that could affect the debarkation.[44]

However, 400 men from the Irish Brigade (along with another French unit) disembarked safely in long boats, despite the heavy sea swells. Several other launches were dashed across the rocks and many were drowned.[45] The Irish troops were ordered to take the barracks and marched for 6 miles with their arms shouldered. They were met by some of the islanders and passed themselves off as British soldiers in their red coats and entered the barracks where some of the soldiers were on parade. 'Dillon and his men, under the advantage of the red uniform, were allowed to proceed, when a loud shout, a point-blank volley bringing several to the ground, and a close, with fixed bayonets, had naturally such an effect on men so assailed, as rendered resistance impossible.'[46] The island's governor, Colonel Cockburn, was seized on horseback by Captain O'Connor of Walsh's, and Colonel Thomas

Fitzmaurice from Co. Kerry was appointed governor in his place. The Irish took 840 men prisoner and 350 Irish Catholics among them defected to the Irish Brigade.

In July 1780, the American war effort was bolstered with the arrival of Comte de Rochambeau's twelve ships transporting the French army's 12,000 troops to Rhode Island, Newport. This was the most significant French contribution in the entire war. The following summer, General Washington requested Comte de Grasse's fleet to sail from the West Indies to blockade Yorktown harbour in Virginia to pin down the British there. Washington and Rochambeau's army force-marched 700 miles from New York to confront General Cornwallis in Yorktown. The Americans' 11,000 regulars and militia were supported by 9,000 French troops under Rochambeau, and by de Grasse's twenty-nine ships, a detachment of Walsh's serving seaboard as marines. British forces at Yorktown comprised the elite of the English army and numbered 9,000 men.[47] In September 1781, French engineers prepared to invest Yorktown, and following an intense bombardment, the British garrison surrendered. This was the largest British defeat until the fall of Singapore in 1942. Legend has it that Cornwallis was so shocked that he requested his army musicians play 'The World Has Turned Upside Down' while his army marched, as directed by the Articles of Capitulation, 'with shouldered arms, colors cased and drums beating' before being ordered to 'ground their arms'.

French naval victories under Comte de Grasse at Chesapeake contributed to the British surrender at Yorktown by preventing the Royal Navy from resupplying or evacuating their forces. These sea-fights were the largest French naval victories of the eighteenth century. It is doubtful if the Americans would have won the war without French support as American success was also due to naval success in the West Indies in the previous three years.[48] John DeCourcy Ireland has researched Irish involvement in the French fleet, and it is thought that around 120 men of Irish origin served from ships commanders to chaplains to cabin boys. These numbers exclude the Irish Brigade who served as marines.

A legend arose that a battalion of Dillon's Regiment served at Yorktown[49] but Dillon's isn't listed among the regiments present at the Battle of Yorktown and French archives have no record of it arriving from

The War of American Independence (1775-83)

the West Indies. This legend probably arose as a twelve-man corporal's guard from Dillon's served there attached to Lauzun's Legion and fought in the minor stages of the battle at Gloucester outside Yorktown.[50] It was not unusual that this detachment served alongside Lauzun's, as three family members served in Lauzun's: the 16-year-old Lieutenant Francois (Frank) Dillon; the 19-year-old Gauillaine (Billy) Dillon; and the 26-year-old Colonel Robert Dillon, the second in command.[51]

Only three officers from Dillon's Regiment served at Yorktown: Colonel Arthur Dillon; Colonel Barthemy Dillon and Lieutenant Colonel James O'Moran, although many Irishmen served in other French units.[52] Lauzun's Legion was raised for French Colonial Service and comprised foreign volunteers of the marine. They sailed to America with Rochambeau's Corps and were a tough unit: 20 per cent of its officers were involved in duels while in the Americas, including the regiment's second colonel, the hothead *furur Hibernicus* and serial dueller Robert Dillon. He was even forced to leave France due to a duel he fought there against a gendarme which cost him two sabre wounds; he was shipped to America under arrest for punishment and to care for his wounds.[53] Robert Dillon had recently served in West African Senegal with a company of Walsh's and had recaptured the French slave-trading colony from the British.[54] Lauzun's officers reinforced the American militia at Gloucester and routed Colonel Tarleton's British cavalry, who had charged across the York River, looking to break out of Yorktown. Lauzun's supported the militia towards Gloucester 'while one company of the Legion dragoons, under Robert Dillon, and a small but excellent corps of militia grenadiers, took the York Road'.[55] Robert Dillon later commanded Lauzun's and was rewarded for bravery by being appointed a Knight of St Louis 'for his good behaviour during the siege of Yorktown'.[56]

Many Irish officers served in Lauzun's, who, although they were not members of the Irish Brigade, rose to high rank in the French army.[57] Colonel Robert Dillon and Captain Dominic Sheldon became lieutenant generals; Isodore Lynch, aide-de-camp, died a major-general; Charles Kilmaine, who was a sub-lieutenant in Lauzun's, rose to command the French army in Italy; Lieutenant Billy Dillon (one of only two French officers wounded at Gloucester in the encounter with Tarleton) rose to become a general, but would not survive the French Revolution. He would be guillotined along with his brother Arthur Dillon.[58]

The Irish fought bravely in the war. Washington wrote to Congress the day Yorktown fell: 'I wish it was in my power to express to Congress how much I feel myself indebted to the Count de Grasse and the officers of the fleet under his command.'[59] Washington's capture of Yorktown effectively ended the war. Towards the end of 1782, Berwick's 2nd battalion garrisoned Martinique, before hostilities ceased and the three Irish regiments in the French army were sent back to France the following year. Irish Brigade losses are not known, but we can only assume that they were high, between battle casualties and death through disease. The war followed a familiar theme: Irishmen fighting against Irishmen: the Irish in the French army fought alongside Irishmen in the Continental army against their compatriots in the British army. They were far away from home and far removed from Ireland's cause. A case was recorded of two Irish Maguire brothers who fought on opposite sides and were reunited after the Battle of Saratoga. One brother emigrated to the Americas years before and joined the Continental army; his brother joined the British army.[60]

Peace was eventually found with the Treaty of Paris whereby Britain lost many of its gains from the Seven Years War. The treaty recognised the former Thirteen Colonies as the United States of America, and she acquired a territory exceeding her sanguine hopes. The year 1783 concluded the war of Revolutionary America. In six short years, France herself would be plunged into the chaos and social upheaval of her own revolution, which would have major ramifications for the Irish community living in France.

13

THE FRENCH REVOLUTION (1789)

French involvement in the American War, coupled with disastrous expansionist policies in India, nearly bankrupted the French treasury. Her large standing armies were funded by raising taxes from the nobility and the clergy, which exacerbated tensions between Church and State. Poverty was rife throughout France and, during the harsh winter of 1788, food shortages even threatened famine and triggered food riots. There was discontent among the bourgeoisie (the growing number of merchants, civil servants and bankers) who benefited from trade with France and her colonies. They had always used their wealth to buy their way into the nobility and the State earned revenue from the sale of noble titles. The established nobility resented this and limited the bourgeoise's social mobility by restricting their sale. Disaffection also existed in the army, which was beset with poor pay and limited promotion opportunities. The status quo was also challenged by writers such as Rousseau and Voltaire who were affected by the ideas of the Enlightenment, which questioned established thinking such as the doctrine of the 'divine right of kings' and the rejection of all ideas that could not be rationally justified.

In May 1789, a General Estate was convened representing the nobility, the clergy and the bourgeoisie. Its aim was to find solutions to the country's financial problems. The Estate failed to come to an agreement and was eventually replaced by the National Assembly, which paved the way to Revolution. On 14 July, the Parisians stormed the State prison of the Bastille, which had always symbolised the king's absolute power. Richard Hayes recorded that this event has an interestingly Irish connection, as Dublin-born Chevalier James F.X. Whyte was one of seven prisoners held there that day. In 1782, while serving as a captain in Lally's Regiment, he suffered a mental breakdown and was incarcerated in the Bastille. Upon his release, he was paraded through the Parisian streets as an unlikely hero of the Revolution. Abbé MacMahon from Co. Galway was one of two chaplains at the Bastille, and Joseph Kavanagh planned and led the assault on the prison.[1]

The French Revolution was partly inspired by the doctrines and intrigues of freemasonry. The Irish military diaspora may have played a very small part in spurring the French Revolution as they brought freemasonry to France: in 1661, the Royal Regiment of Foot (later known as the Regiment of Walsh) constituted the first freemason's lodge there, which was called the Lodge de Parfaite Equalite. All the Irish regiments had their own military lodges, which were an integral part of regimental life. Their popularity spread rapidly in the French army as there were seventy-six military lodges warranted by the Grand Order of France throughout the French regiments by 1787. Many French revolutionary leaders including Robespierre, Marat, Lafayette, Danton, Mirabeau and Voltaire practised the craft.[2] It was thought that Napoleon Bonaparte and his brothers were also freemasons. The American War of Independence provided further evidence that revolutionary ideas were linked with masonry, as several signees of the American Declaration of Independence, including Benjamin Franklin and John Hancock, and of the US Constitution, including George Washington, were freemasons. The Irish political writer Jonathan Swift (reputedly a closet Jacobite) also practised the craft.

The practice of freemasonry was a pleasant relaxation that relieved some of the tedium of military life, and broke down some of the barriers and snobbery amongst the aristocratic officers of the day. It was not uncommon for officers to be invited in as visitors to other lodges even while 'on parole' as prisoners of war in England or when stationed in various towns throughout France. In 1764, while Dillon's was stationed in Carcassonne, eighteen officers, including the regiment's colonel-proprietor Theobald Dillon, were admitted as temporary members into the town's lodge.[3] Irish Jacobite exiles in France constituted the first *native* French lodge in 1726, as pro-Jacobite lodges in the British Isles were suppressed and driven underground.[4] 'James III' and his son Charles Edward Stuart were also freemasons. There is evidence to suggest there were efforts to create a new influence within masonry (with Jesuit participation) known as Stuart Masonry, centring on the Stuart family as a political means to restore them to the throne.[5]

The French Revolution disrupted trade and the flow of student priests and cadets between Ireland and France. The Irish Colleges in France and Belgium were suppressed and their superiors arrested, including all the Capuchins from the Irish monastery in Bar-sur-Aube.[6] As it was no longer possible to send student priests abroad, the Catholic bishops of Ireland petitioned Parliament for their own clerical training college. The British were aware that revolutionary principles were fast gaining ground in Ireland and were keen to appease Irish demands. This led to 'An Act for the better education of persons professing the Popish or Roman Catholic religion', which established Maynooth College in 1795.

Soldiers returning from the American War were also exposed to revolutionary ideas and helped fan the flames that would ignite France. The foreign regiments in the French army were considered especially pro-Royalist: foreign regiments threw a cordon around Versailles to protect the Royal Court after the French Guards fraternised with the mob and refused to do their duty. The Swiss Guards protected the royal household, before being cut down by the mob that seized the royal family. General Count Daniel O'Connell (the Liberator's uncle and namesake) was colonel commandant of a German Regiment in the French army and a key commander around Paris at this time. O'Connell had a long and distinguished military career and rose to the rank of general in the French army. Born in Derrynane, Co. Kerry, he left for France at the age of 14 years before joining Clare's Regiment. He was appointed a Knight of St Louis and served as a military engineer in Gibraltar, where he was severely wounded when it was besieged by the British in 1782.[7]

The newly formed National Assembly intended to reorganise the army, and embarked on other reforms, such as ending the nobility's monopoly to senior military rank. These measures, while welcomed by the rank and file, only alienated the officer cadre. The foreign regiments were viewed with suspicion, and as the Irish regiments enjoyed a semi-independent status they were particularly distrusted. In a debate on the army's re-organisation in the National Assembly, the Marquis de Thiboutant declared he saw no reason for preserving the Irish regiments, as they had ceased to be Irish.[8] Count Arthur Dillon (then an Assembly deputy) was furious and challenged this assertion in a long Memoire, which he placed before the Assembly. Dillon asserted that all officers in the Irish regiments were Irishmen or sons of Irishmen. He argued that although for various reasons, there had been difficulties recruiting Irishmen for the rank and file, the recruitment of Irish officers into the Irish Brigade had been uninterrupted for nearly 100 years since their arrival in France.[9]

> As long as there was a hope of replacing the House of Stuart on the Throne, a continuous emigration of Irishmen to France took place. They came in large numbers and enrolled themselves under the flag of the King who they regarded as the defender of their religion and as their lawful sovereign … when various treaties confirmed the possession of the throne of Great Britain to the throne of the House of Hanover, a decree was passed in 1736 condemning, under the penalty of death these same emigrations of Irishmen. Since that reign, the Irish regiments were unable to obtain other soldiers except those who, at tremendous risks, came in numbers to join … and, as regards those officers born in France who are in Irish regiments there are none save the sons and kinsmen of former officers of the regiments.[10]

Arthur Dillon also argued that the term 'foreign troops' did not apply to the Brigade, 'as more than hundred years previously Louis XIV conferred French citizenry to the Irish, who were to be treated as his own subjects enjoying the same rights as native Frenchmen'.[11] Many Irishmen had deserted the British army to join Irish regiments in France, and Dillon argued that during the American War more than 350 Irish Catholics captured in the West Indies enlisted in the Irish Brigade, where the greater part of them still remained. He concluded that the Irish always 'demanded the privilege to march in front rank against the English in whatever country France was at war'. Edward Fitzjames, the 5th Duke of

Fitzjames, also petitioned Louis XVI to have the Brigade continued as a distinctive unit.

The king could do nothing, however, as he had now lost all his influence with the Assembly. Dillon in a last-ditch effort even frantically tried to transfer the Irish regiments from France to Spain, but without success. In July 1791, the Assembly decreed the abolition of all the foreign regiments in France (with the exception of the Swiss). Accordingly, the Irish regiments lost their distinctive red uniforms and higher pay and were absorbed into the regular French army on an equal footing. Prior to disbandment, the Brigade mustered 4,500 men, spread over two battalions each of Berwick's, Dillon's and Walsh's. After the changes, their regimental colours were laid up and burned as per protocol and Dillon's was re-designated the 87th, Walsh's the 92nd and Berwick's the 88th Régiment d'Infanterie. Arthur Dillon, as colonel-proprietor of the regiment, was compensated with £12,000.[12] The colonel-proprietors of Walsh's and Berwick's would have received similar compensation. Although the Irish regiments lost their Irish name and were absorbed into the regular French army, they were still regarded as 'Irish regiments'.[13]

Three Irish battalions were posted to the French West Indies in 1791. A prominent colonial planter in Haiti called Count Victor O'Gorman from Co. Clare instigated sending the Irish regiments there to protect French interests on the island.[14] But the Irish were unable to quell a large-scale slave revolt on the island. When a British force raided the island, 180 men of the 87th (Dillon's) under Major Denis O'Farrell who garrisoned the island defected, as morale was low. Colonel Oliver Harty from County Limerick of the 88th (Berwick's) was sent to restore order and bring the island back into line. Harty commanded 2,000 regular troops and successfully drove 3,000 rebels from their encampments into the mountainous region of Les Plantons.[15]

The 43-year-old Dublin-born Count Theobald Dillon, a former officer in Dillon's Regiment, was promoted to Général de Brigade in the Revolutionary army. In 1792 while France was at war with Austria and Prussia, Dillon led 4,000 men across the border into Austrian-controlled Belgium. He was under orders not to engage the Austrian troops as the recently reorganised Revolutionary army was untested in battle. While approaching the border, Dillon suspected that a large Austrian army had assembled nearby and ordered his cavalry to advance to screen his retreating manoeuvre from the enemy. The French cavalry suspected their aristocratic officers of conspiring with the Austrians, turned and fled in wild disorder, informing their comrades behind them that they were betrayed. Dillon was seized and denounced as a foreign aristocrat. As Dillon's carriage entered Lille it was accosted by a mob 'a shot rang out and the gallant Irishman rolled over dead in his carriage. His body was dragged out, trampled on, and bayonets driven through it.'[16] The same evening his body was thrown into a fire, which caused indignation right across France. His murderers were later pursued, apprehended and executed; the unfortunate Theobald Dillon himself was later exonerated of any charge of disloyalty.

Dillon's murder led many to question their loyalty to the new Revolutionary army. The Irish Brigade in France split between royalist followers of the exiled king, and republicans faithful to the Revolution. Officers were required to take a new military oath to the National Assembly which gave rise to many resignations in the Irish regiments, as it did amongst the French army generally.[17] Richard Hayes claimed that the majority of Irish officers chose to remain in France and fight in the Revolutionary army. In 1791, a testimony of how far the Irish had progressed into the senior ranks was apparent, as there were at least ten Irish-born generals in the Revolutionary army (not including generals of Irish parentage): Generals Theobald Dillon, Arthur Dillon, James O'Moran, Thomas Ward, Thomas Keating, Isodore Lynch, John O'Neill, Charles Kilmaine, Thomas O'Meara and Oliver Harty. Napoleon honoured Generals Arthur Dillon Bourke, D'Alton, Kilmaine and his Minister for War, Henry Clarke, by having their names engraved on the Arc de Triomphe in Paris. In 1793, an examination of the muster rolls of the former Irish regiments indicated the vast majority of officers were still Irish.[18]

In 1792, Chevalier Trant and Captain James Rice were two royalist Irish officers who planned to rescue Marie-Antoinette and bring her to Ireland. They had organised sets of horses to race the French queen from Paris to the French coast, where a boat was waiting. It was proposed to take Marie-Antoinette to Rice's house in Dingle, Co. Kerry. The plan never materialised however, as the queen was unwilling to leave France. Other royalist officers felt duty-bound to serve the king and joined the émigré army at Koblenz, Germany, to fight Revolutionary France with foreign assistance.[19] Edouard 'le beau' Dillon was a favourite of the French queen and restored the royalist Regiment of Dillon.[20] In April, a royalist Irish Brigade was formed comprising the regiments of Dillon, Walsh and Berwick and were described as being 'in excellent order and quite ready to take the field'.[21] The Irish officers were presented to the king's brother, the comte de Provence (the future Louis XVIII) and assured him of their loyalty. This royalist Irish Brigade was attached to the Austro-Prussian army in the Revolutionary Wars fighting against France. However, by 1792, following a short unsuccessful campaign, the royalists and France's foreign allies were unable to defeat the French Revolutionary army and retreated eastwards along the Rhine. The royalist émigré army and the Irish Brigade were then stood down. In 1792, the future Louis XVIII recognised Irish loyalty on their disbandment, with a new standard – a *drapeau d'adieu* or farewell banner. On the flag was an Irish harp, embroidered with shamrocks and *fleurs-de-lis* and it was accompanied by the following address:

> Gentlemen – We acknowledge the inappreciable services that France has received from the Irish Brigade, in the course of the last 100 year; services that we shall never forget, though under an impossibility of requiting them. Receive this standard as a pledge to our remembrance, a monument of our admiration, and of our respect; and, in future, generous Irishmen, this shall be the motto of your spotless flag: 1692–1792 '*Semper et Ubique Fidelis*' [Always and Everywhere Faithful][22]

Many royalist officers returned to Ireland to retire, others emigrated to Italy. Some joined the Spanish and Austrian armies, which both had particular appeal as they already had well-established Irish military communities. 'The more Irish officers in the Austrian service the better,' declared the Austrian Emperor Francis I. 'An Irish coward is an uncommon character; and what the natives of Ireland even dislike from principle, they generally perform through a desire of glory.'[23] During the Revolutionary and Napoleonic periods as many as 200 Irish officers were serving in the Austrian army.[24] In the 1750s, the Austrian army swarmed 'with the offspring of the best Roman Catholic families of that kingdom [of Ireland] – high spirited, intrepid, nervous youth – retaining a hankering desire after their country'.[25]

France and England were again at war in 1793 and an unlikely event occurred, as 'by a strange and most pathetic turn, the exiled descendants of the Irish Jacobites found a refuge under the English flag'.[26] The then British Prime Minister William Pitt invited a number of royalist Irish officers to London with a view to forming an Irish Brigade in the British army to continue the fight against Revolutionary France and restore the Bourbons. This 'Irish Catholic Brigade' was to comprise six regiments: The Duke of Fitzjames and Count O'Connell; Henry Dillon and Viscount Walsh; Count Walsh and Count Thomas Conway were given colonies of the new regiments. They were all capable and distinguished men. The regiments were fitted out in red tunics, faced in light blue for O'Connell's and yellow for Dillon's. As surviving evidence no longer exists, it is thought that the other regiments maintained the same facings as the *ancien régime* Irish Brigade.

In late 1794, the Irish Catholic Brigade in Dublin was given licence to drum up for local recruits but instead found the country 'seething with disaffection and revolutionary ideas'.[27] The Irish people were trying to remove the shackles of a British monarch, and failed to fathom a pro-Royalist Irish Brigade who wished to see the return of a French one. Henry Grattan exclaimed in horror in the Irish Parliament at the British being 'prepared to arm a brigade of 6,000 Catholics under Catholic and French officers'. The *ancien régime* Irish Brigade of France had always been the *bête noire* of the Irish Protestant Ascendency and now they were to fight for the British! The original plan was to raise six regiments, but opposition was so great that they were unable to muster the requisite troops. A decision was made to amalgamate the weakest regiments with the strongest ones; the 3rd Regiment of Berwick was to be abolished, and the Duke of Fitzjames complained bitterly that this was not the agreement made in London.

These descendants of once illustrious Irish families who were forced to leave Ireland 100 years previously found themselves strangely out of step among their own people. The officers who joined this Irish Catholic Brigade from France were not treated very well, which Wolfe Tone recounted to the delight of his French revolutionary counterparts.

They had to accept the King's pardon for treason for serving in the French army. Tone related how the État-Major was to attend mass in Dublin on Christmas Day in full uniform, but had to give it up for fear of being accosted by the mob.[28] Several officers were reduced to poverty, Fitzjames having to advance his own money to sustain them. Things were to go from bad to worse; Fitzjames felt honour bound to challenge Lord Blayney to a duel in the Phoenix Park, Dublin. Blayney said something derogatory about the Franco-Irish officers in the Irish House of Commons, which Fitzjames considered an insult. In the duel that followed, Fitzjames escaped with a slight injury – a ball grazed his side and another went through Blayney's hat.[29]

Fitzjames was evidently a man of action with a penchant for duelling, in common with many other Irish officers. *The Gentleman's Magazine* had reported a few years previously in 1783 how Mareshal DeCoigny had insulted Fitzjames – a challenge was instantly given and accepted, and within a half an hour DeCoigny lay dead, Fitzjames having run him through with his sword. Another incident related was between Fitzjames and Lord Tyrconnell, who commanded a cavalry troop in Fitzjames' horse and in a case of eighteenth-century 'road-rage' ran his carriage violently against Fitzjames's on the famous *Pont Neuf* in Paris to provoke him into a fight. Like a scene out of Alexander Dumas's novel *The Three Musketeers*, both men sprang from their carriages with swords in hand, to the astonishment of the local Parisians traversing the bridge going about their daily business. It was alleged they could not be persuaded to stop fighting before both men were severely wounded. The cause of the quarrel was that Fitzjames had given a commission to the young son of a woman who had nursed a family member. The other officers in the regiment were furious and would have nothing to do with him, Tyrconnell had said that he did not blame the young man concerned but had called Fitzjames himself to account.[30]

This 'Irish Catholic Brigade' in the British army was expected to be deployed in the European theatre to fight against Revolutionary France. Instead, they were posted far away to the West Indies and to Nova Scotia in Canada, as it was feared they would turn if they served in Europe. The Brigade came to an inglorious end, as four battalions were decimated by tropical disease while serving in Jamaica and Haiti, which necessitated their disbandment in 1798. Dillon's Regiment of Foot in the British army, under Edouard '*le beau*' Dillon as colonel-in-chief, comprised mainly foreigners, and continued to serve in Egypt, Malta and Spain during the Peninsular War, until it too was finally disbanded in 1814.[31]

La Terreur, 'The 'Reign of Terror' was a violent time in France, when twenty or thirty people a day were driven through Paris to 'kiss the blade'. It occurred between 1793 and 1794 and was presided over by Maximilien Robespierre. He was the most influential figure of the Revolution and it was thought that he was of Irish origin. The French historian Jules Michelet suggested that his family left Limerick with the Wild Geese in 1691.[32] The 'Terror' was not confined to Paris but extended through the French provinces. In November 1793, 1,800 people were tied up and thrown into the Loire River. In Lyon, the guillotine proving too slow and thousands were instead executed by grapeshot beside previously dug mass graves.[33] Events occurring here can be compared to events in Ireland during the 1798 Rising – the same resentments and the same mob rule. In 1798, Protestants were burnt alive in a locked barn at Scullabogue House, and others were piked in the stomachs and tossed over the bridge into the river Slaney in Co. Wexford.

The Irish in France would not escape the 'Terror'. The simple fact of being a foreigner could mean a death sentence. As Ireland was a British dominion, this made the Irish in France *de jure* British subjects, placing them particularly at risk of being accused of spying. The Revolutionary forces had always distrusted foreigners, especially after the wholesale emigration of foreign army officers in 1791. There was also widespread distrust of those foreign officers who remained in the army.[34] Richard Hayes contended that a couple of dozen Irishmen were put to death and many were arrested during the period. Dubliner General Charles Kilmaine and General Thomas Keating from Co. Limerick, together with Roscommen-men Colonel Thomas MacDermott and General James O'Moran were arrested. Kilmaine was imprisoned for thirteen months, contracted dysentery, and was finally released but his health never recovered. Major-General Oliver Harty from Co. Limerick, although considered a champion of the Revolution, was suspended from the army and imprisoned for over two months before being

Engraving by Pierre Charles Coqueret, *Portrait du General Charles Jennings Kilmaine (1751-1799), Francais d'origine Irlandaise*. (With kind permission of Réunion des Musées Nationaux, Paris)

reinstated. Other officers were not so lucky; Lieutenant General James O'Moran, who was wounded at Savannah during the American War, was accused of receiving English gold.[35] He was confident of being exonerated due to his distinguished military service and declared 'forty-one years of irreproachable service, marked by severe battle wounds, should establish my character.'[36] But even an exemplary military record could not save him, and he together with Dubliner Brigadier General Thomas Ward 'kissed the blade' along with his Irish servant John Malone. General Arthur Dillon who had distinguished himself at Grenada, St Eustatius and Savannah and at Valmy during the French Revolutionary Wars also 'got the chop'. As commander of the Armée du Nord he was accused of plotting against Revolutionary France by conspiring with the German Prince of Hesse (who was at war with France) and promising him an unmolested retreat through French territory. The story goes that as he was brought to be guillotined, a lady before him shuddered and turned to him, and said, 'Oh, Mr de Dillon, will you go first?' Dillon replied, possibly apocryphally, 'Anything to please a lady.'

When the Bourbons were restored in 1814, the possibility of forming a new Irish Brigade was raised before Louis XVIII but never materialised. The Irish officers suspected the British of applying diplomatic pressure on the new king against any new formation of an Irish corps. With the departure of the Irish Brigade in France, the baton was passed to the Irish republican organisation – the Society of the United Irishmen – who solicited French support for an invasion of Ireland.

14

THE UNITED IRISHMEN AND FRANCE

The year 1791 saw the formation of the Society of United Irishmen in a Belfast tavern with the aim of establishing Ireland as an independent republic with religious freedom for all. When war broke out between France and England in 1794, the organisation was deemed a security risk by the British government and went underground. Theobald Wolfe Tone, a Dublin-born Protestant lawyer, fled to France where he lobbied for French support for an invasion of Ireland. Wolfe Tone came from a mixed Catholic and Protestant background. His father was a Protestant coachbuilder and his mother came from a Catholic merchant family but she converted to Protestantism in 1771 after Theobald was born.[1]

There was a growing Francophile intelligencia in Ireland and the country warmly embraced the idealistic revolutionary ideas of liberty, equality and fraternity and was crying out for reform. Even after a 700-year connection with England, Ireland was as disaffected as a newly conquered province. The Catholics wanted equality, the Protestants parliamentary reform, and the country was a prime target for revolution to flourish. Under a suppressive system of government, the country was already rich in revolutionary thought and principles, and was a time bomb waiting to explode. There was an emerging culture of Protestant or colonial nationalism, facilitated by the receding Stuart threat, and the perception that the international influence of the Papacy was in decline.[2]

A new generation of Irish Protestants was coming forward, who were less sectarian than their forefathers. There was renewed interest and appreciation by Protestant academia in Trinity College Dublin in Ireland's rich ancient history, in Celtic mysticism, and in the Irish language and culture. James Macpherson's Ossian epics in the 1760s, which were based on ancient Irish mythology, were well received and widely appreciated. Previous to this, it had been perceived that Gaelic was a 'barbaric tongue', but this viewpoint was now being revised. The Protestant Ascendency recognised that 'the image of pre-conquest Ireland as a complex and advanced society challenged the establishment's view that civilisation only came to Ireland with the Normans. It also reinforced the patriots' contention that the country would profit if it was liberated from its political subordination to Great Britain.'[3]

The British army's establishment in Ireland had been reduced as troops were transferred to the Americas. The Volunteers were a part-time defence force and were formed to fill the void and protect the country from French invasion. The Volunteer Movement was mainly made up of Protestants who wanted reform and some supported the French Revolution, although the movement split over granting rights to Catholics. They brought the gun into Irish politics with public shows of strength in College Green, Dublin, firing a *feu-de-joie* around King William's statue on his birthday on 4 November 1779.[4] Partly due to public posturing and sabre rattling by the Volunteers, the British were forced to appease Irish demands by granting a degree of political autonomy from London. Henry Grattan's 'Patriot Party' had achieved limited home rule which produced the Constitution of 1782 and established Grattan's Parliament. With the cessation of the American War and the threat of revolution passing, the British government cracked down and disbanded the Volunteers in 1793 and replaced them with the Militia, who were more loyal. Some disenfranchised Volunteers joined the United Irishmen, such as the colourful Napper Tandy and Archibald Rohan Hamilton. Grattan's failure to reform and to deliver even a small measure of Catholic emancipation – including his failure to admit the Catholic gentry into the Irish Parliament – had disillusioned many. The disaffected moved away from constitutional reform to armed rebellion, with foreign assistance from France.

Wolfe Tone reasoned that if France sent a considerable force to Ireland, she could break the connection with England. This would lead to the unification of Catholics, Dissenters and Protestants.[5] When hostilities ceased, a new National Convention would separate Church from State and proclaim religious freedom for all. All property belonging to Englishmen in Ireland would be re-confiscated. These were the schemes and hopes for Ireland of the United Irishmen. Tone lobbied Irish generals in the French army and, in particular, General Clarke and General Kilmaine, who were the most influential and charismatic Irish generals in the Revolutionary and Napoleonic periods, and both focused their energies on Ireland's liberation.

General Charles Kilmaine's father was a doctor who left Galway in 1738 with his wife and settled in the south of France. His mother wished her son to be born in her native land, and when pregnant returned to Ireland where young Charles was born in Temple Bar, Dublin. Relatives there reared him until his father brought him to France when he was 11 years old. He joined the French Irish Brigade and commanded two cavalry regiments in the Revolutionary army. General Demouriez had called him 'le brave Kilmaine' (from the ancient family barony in Kilmaine, Co. Mayo), a name by which he was afterwards known, for saving the day at the Battle of Jemappes. Kilmaine was 'a superb cavalry officer' and was well known for both his extreme personal reserve and his military prowess. He had a brilliant military career, which began as a lieutenant in Lauzun's Legion during in the American War. He was a veteran of nine campaigns and forty-six battles and was imprisoned during the 'Reign of Terror' as a foreign aristocrat – an enemy of the Revolution – but was eventually restored to the army. He later commanded Armée d'Nord and the left wing of the Armée d'Angleterre (the army for invasion of the British Isles) in 1798. Napoleon reputedly remarked that he was the only senior officer he had complete confidence in. He distinguished himself under Napoleon in the Italian campaign and as commander of Armée d'Italie.

General Henri Clarke was an officer who had close links with the Irish Brigade. Born in France to Irish parents, his father was an officer in Dillon's (where Clarke himself served for a time) and his mother's father and her three brothers served in Clare's. Clarke appears to have been airbrushed out of history to a degree. He was created the Duc de Feltre by Napoleon for orchestrating the defence of Walcheren Island in Holland, thereby thwarting a British invasion in 1809. He was an able, astute diplomat and had brokered the peace treaty of Campo Formio. He served as Napoleon's most famous Minister of War from 1807 to 1814, when he developed the ministry into an efficient military–civil administrative structure and he was central to the creation of the Grande Armée. Clarke was on horseback beside Napoleon at Waterloo and was later made a Marshal of France. He had once suggested to the republican Tone – to his horror – that a descendent of the Stuarts could lead the rebellion in Ireland. He had also correctly argued to Tone that to succeed in Ireland clerical support was required, which Tone also rejected.

Anglophobia was widespread in Revolutionary France at the time. In 1793 the Directory (the executive power of the French government) seriously contemplated an invasion of Ireland. Tone opposed a French plan for landing a devastating force known as the Légion Noire in Ireland. This corps was so called as their uniforms consisted of captured British uniforms, recut into light infantry style and dyed to a very dark brown. This Légion was to be raised from criminals, deserters, royalist prisoners and unsavoury characters. After reviewing these troops, Tone referred to them as 'sad blackguards', and although he had reservations about unleashing them in Ireland, he reluctantly supported a French scheme for landing them in England and commissioning them to burn Bristol. 'The truth is, I hate the very name of England,' Tone wrote coldly. 'I hated her before my exile, and I will hate her always.'[6]

'To detach Ireland from England is to reduce England to a second rate power, and take from it much of its maritime superiority,' described one of the French war ministers. 'There is little point on elaborating on the advantage to France that Irish independence would bring.'[7] France also felt duty-bound to export the principles and universal rights of the French Revolution to the oppressed people of Ireland. In December 1796, the Expédition d'Irlande finally sailed from Brest late in the season, under the acclaimed General Lazare Hoche. The fleet comprised seventeen ships of the line and fourteen frigates and carried 15,000 French Revolutionary troops along with arms and ammunition. The expedition was originally planned to depart in September but was poorly organised and suffered delays due to desertions. The delay was also attributed to the French high command requisitioning resources and focusing instead on the campaign in Italy. General Hoche had been so disillusioned that he wrote to the Directory in Paris recommending the mission be abandoned altogether as he feared difficulties in making a landing on the rough Atlantic coast of Ireland in winter. The Directory agreed and wrote back to Brest, ordering the invasion to be stood down. However, the order arrived too late as the fleet had already left port.

Wolfe Tone was given the rank of adjutant-general in the expedition, where he served onboard the *Indomptable*.[8] Major-General Oliver Harty commanded a foreign brigade made up of newly formed, under-strength regiments of Lee and O'Meara.[9] Other senior Irish officers present were Général de Brigade Richard O'Shea and Lieutenant Colonel Andrew McDonagh. Richard Hayes found it nearly inconceivable that the former Irish Brigade regiments of the 87th, 88th and 92nd Régiment d'Infanterie (who were still officered by Irishmen or sons of Irishmen) did not embark with the expedition. The Irish regiments in France had for 100 years actively sought any opportunity to spearhead an invasion of Ireland. Now that the opportunity had finally arisen, they were sidelined. But a newly activated Irish corps called the 'Légion Irlandaise' sailed, but they did not register more than one weak battalion. They were officered by Irishmen or men of Irish descent dressed in red with facings in bright green. Their red uniforms probably came from the Irish Brigade who had been disbanded after the Revolution.[10] This new Irish unit was largely comprised of captured Irish sailors from the Royal Navy, as the French were eager to be rid of prisoners that were difficult to exchange and Tone was commissioned to offer them liberty if they joined his cause. A favourite tactic of his was to ply the prisoners with brandy; the recruiters would warn them of the ills of a French prison and then would animate them with tales of glory and of their plans for the liberation of 'old Ireland'. When their blood was up, Tone would then enter the room and raise them more, which resulted in the vast majority joining him. He was hopeful that other Irish sailors would defect to the French, as he was aware that a number of mutinies had recently occurred in the Royal Navy. The crews of several ships under Admiral Jarvis's command hoisted the Red Flag of international revolt off the Spanish coast in 1796, where Irish sailors were reportedly at the forefront of the agitation.

The French fleet moored off Bantry Bay, in the south-west coast of Ireland, without encountering any British men-of-war. Fifteen ships approached Bantry Bay with nineteen vessels lagging behind, just out of sight. General Hoche's ship got separated from the others en route and eventually returned to France. There was a difficulty in that the invasion was such a closely guarded secret within the Ministry of War that the United Irishmen and their supporters did not know when the French were coming or where they would land. They had even suspected they would land in Ulster, in the north of the country.

This was the second major force dispatched to Ireland since the Spanish Armada. During the Jacobite War, in 1689, the French navy had landed there with supplies of arms. The French were now within 'a cannon shot' of the Irish coast with 15,000 men.[11] They were six days in Bantry Bay, within 500 yards of the shore but due to the weather the fleet was dispersed four times and they were unable to land.[12] Hoche's reservation about conducting a winter landing in the Atlantic Ocean were well founded, it seemed.

They planned to disembark at Bantry Bay and launch a landward descent onto Cork city, in preference to making a seaward attack, as gun batteries there protected Cork harbour. The British army in Ireland was caught completely off guard. 'We had two days after they were at anchor in Bantry Bay, from Cork to Bantry less than 3,000 men, two pieces of artillery, and no magazine of any kind, no firings, no hospital, no provisions, etc.,' reported an English account. The commander of the British army in Cork, Lieutenant General Hew Dalrymple, wrote at the time that they were hopelessly unprepared, and even with 8,000 troops in Cork would not have confronted the French: 'our numbers will probably fall so short of the enemy, that a diversion is all to be expected.'[13]

The Protestant Kingdom of Ireland had a lucky escape – bad weather or 'protestant winds' again dictated the course of Irish history. On 22 December 1796, a storm blew up, with sleet and snow, which threw the whole mission into confusion. This resulted in nineteen ships being blown away from the bay and disappearing from sight and losing communication with each other. A French ship was damaged and a party boarded a long boat to get it towed, but the launch was blown ashore and taken as a prize.[14] The French had now to decide whether to return to France or attempt a landing with their depleted forces. They were also still unable to establish contact with the United Irishmen on the coast. The remaining fleet of seven ships could land 7,000 troops, but required a 45-mile forced march to reach Kinsale and Cork and lacked horses to move heavy artillery over a mountainous terrain in winter. Cork had a good harbour and was a major victualling depot for the Royal Navy, and would have provided the French with a good base, less than two days' sail from France. Major-General Oliver Harty (as the most senior officer present) convened an impromptu council of war aboard the *Indomptible*, together with Wolfe Tone and other officers. The decision was taken not to land at Bantry, but on a more favourable section further up the coast towards Cork. Harty narrowly escaped drowning when returning from his launch to his own ship. The French fleet was further exposed to gales and dense fog and in the end was forced to abandon the landing altogether.

The remaining ships made their way back to Brest on 29 December, evading the Royal Navy on their return journey. Only one ship, *La Ville L'Orient*, was captured and escorted to Kinsale, with 400 fully equipped troops, together with mortars, cannon, powder, muskets and clothing onboard.[15] Although the French were unable to land in Ireland, they succeeded in landing 1,400 troops from the Legion Noire in Wales. This unit was commanded by Irish-American William Tate, who together with other Irish officers, launched a coastal raid near Fishguard in Wales but swiftly returned to their ships when a large British force came to the town's relief.

'England has not had such an escape since the Spanish Armada,' Tone wrote bitterly of the failed mission, 'and that expedition, like ours, was defeated by the weather; the elements fight against us, and courage is of no avail.'[16] Hoche's expedition, like Thurot's landing in Carrickfergus in 1759, proved again that it was possible to evade the Royal Navy and invade the British Isles. The connection between England and Ireland had never been under so much threat as in the last weeks of 1796. If it had not been for the weather, 15,000 French troops would have landed and taken Cork and following rebellion in Ulster and in other provinces, Ireland might have temporarily separated from the British Empire.[17]

It is difficult to gauge the level of support for the French among the Irish population, outside of the United Irishmen and their supporters. The Viceroy John Pratt reported shortly after the French left the bay that the Kingdom of Ireland remained loyal during the threat. As the British army marched south from Dublin, 'the roads, which in some parts, had been rendered impassable by the snow, were cleared by the peasantry. The poor people often shared their potatoes with them, and dressed their meat, without demanding payment.' Among 'prominent examples of individual loyalty' was the address from the pulpit to the parishioners of Cork by the Catholic Bishop of Cork, Dr Moylan, who appealed for calm. Many of the local Catholic gentry remained loyal to the Crown, including the Catholic landowner, Lord Kenmare who 'spared no expense in giving assistance to the commanding officer in his neighbourhood, and took into his demesne a great quantity of cattle which had been driven from the coast' to prevent them falling into French hands. 'In short,' continued the Viceroy, 'the general disposition of the people through the South and West was so prevalent, that had the enemy landed, their hope of assistance from the inhabitants would have been totally disappointed.'[18] This account is, however, hard to put into context. Richard Hayes, writing in the 1930s, related an account given by an aged local resident, whose grandfather witnessed the French troops in 1798 marching at night through the countryside as a child. The local people lit straw to show them the road, and gave them milk and bread, and the French soldiers cut off some of their buttons from their tunics with their bayonets and gave them to the local children as keepsakes.[19]

The following year, Napoleon as commander of the Armée d'Angleterre inspected the French ports for another invasion, but reported back to Paris of the infeasibility of the expedition, owing partly to the strength of the English Channel Fleet: 'To carry out an invasion of England without command of the sea is as difficult and daring a project as has ever been undertaken. It could only be done by a surprise crossing

– either by eluding the fleet that is blockading Brest and Texel, or by landing in small boats, during the night, after a 7 or 8 hours passage, at some point in the counties of Kent or Sussex.'[20]

Thereafter French attention turned to Egypt, made more appealing as French intelligence was aware of the Royal Navy's absence in the Mediterranean. Ireland was put on the back burner and the bulk of the French army was removed from the French coast and was sent to the campaign in Egypt. Napoleon appointed Dubliner General Charles Kilmaine as commander of the remaining French divisions of the Armée d'Angleterre stationed in Brittany and Normandy.[21] The British press at the time scurrilously reported the continued threat mustered there as being led by 'Paddy Kilmaine and his gang'. Hoche was assigned to Germany and Tone (devastated at such a missed opportunity) accompanied him.[22] France had hoped that success in Egypt would destabilise British influence and provide a link to India. After some initial successes there, plans for the region were ultimately destroyed by Admiral Nelson's victory over the French fleet in the Battle of the Nile. The Irish cause received another blow upon the death of General Hoche in Germany. 'He had thoroughly made [Ireland's] cause his own,' wrote John Mitchel, 'convinced that to strike England in Ireland is the surest and easiest way to destroy her power.'[23] Napoleon had later declared while exiled on St Helena, that if Hoche had lived another year he was sure he would have been successful in Ireland, to counteract French disasters in Egypt.[24]

After the unsuccessful 1796 invasion, the duly alarmed British government imposed martial law and suspended habeas corpus to restore calm to the kingdom. In early 1798, *The Gentleman's Magazine* reported that hit squads operating 'under the commands from the [United Irishmen] Committee rooms in Dublin' were targeting British army officers and members of the local Yeomanry in Dublin, Kildare and Cork. In a number of incidents reported: a British army colonel was shot dead in Dublin; and a member of the local Protestant gentry, a tithe collector to the Established Protestant Church and a soldier were shot dead in Cork. Major Allen from the 14th Dragoons, whilst riding along the Grand Canal in Co. Kildare, was shot and wounded in the neck by a would-be assassin from the opposite canal bank. The government clamped down; in March virtually the entire Leinster Committee was arrested including the brothers John and Henry Sheares, who were promptly tried, hanged, drawn and quartered. Lord Edward Fitzgerald escaped but was later arrested and mortally wounded. Tone, recently returned to France from Germany, received rumours that a powder magazine in Belfast had been broken into, an arsenal in Dublin had been seized and 15,000 arms had been smuggled into the country. He also learned that insurrection had already broken out in Ireland and knew he had to get French help fast.

In May 1798, the Irish Rebellion broke out in Counties Dublin, Wicklow and Mayo and shortly afterwards the rebels seized Ballymena in Co. Antrim. As so many United Irishmen leaders were arrested, the rebellion lost purpose and largely became a peasant revolt, the void in leadership filled by several priests. The rebels proclaimed the Irish Republic and unfurled their green flags emblazoned with a harp and the words 'Erin go Brath' ('Ireland Forever'). They were outgunned and outnumbered, their main weapon being the pike made by local blacksmiths. This was ideal for repealing a cavalry charge but no match against modern musketry or grapeshot. 'Nothing of course could be better in its way than the pike at close quarters,' an anonymous rebel recalled. 'No cavalry could stand the pike, for when the horse got a prod he reared and the rider was either thrown out of the saddle or could not use his sword, so we had him at our mercy.' The pike was later adopted as the symbol of the United Irishmen. A local Protestant landlord and United Irishman Bagenal Harvey was appointed commander-in-chief of the rebel army, who were shortly afterwards defeated in the bloody Battle of New Ross, with over 3,000 rebels, who were known as croppies, being killed.[25] Harvey later relinquished his command as he was disgusted at the massacre of loyal Protestants at Scullabogue House. The following month, the rising was finally snuffed out at Vinegar Hill in Enniscorthy, leading to the rebel stronghold of Wexford town falling to crown forces the next day.

In August 1798, (two months after the Rising was suppressed) General Humbert's French Expeditionary Force of 1,099 men landed from three frigates at Killala, Co. Mayo. Humbert's army was designed to rally the Irish but they arrived too late. His small force was to form a bridgehead for the 7,000 French troops that were to join the expedition (Humbert thought this larger force had already left port and were on their way) but they never materialised. The French brought 6,000 spare muskets and uniforms for the Irish, who were organised into a locally raised 500-strong legion, dressed in green uniforms.[26] The red-coated Légion Irlandaise did not sail with Humbert, but other Irishmen did. Colonel Jean Sarrazin (Humbert's second in command) wrote in his diary that around forty Irishmen accompanied the expedition to provide a cadre for locally raised Irish volunteers. These Irishmen were not dressed in the red coats of the Légion Irlandaise but in the brown coats of the Legion Noire.[27] Among the Irishmen present were Bartholomew Teeling and Wolfe Tone's brother, Matthew, and two former Irish Brigade officers, John Hayes and William Barker. Humbert also appointed James O'Dowd, a veteran in the Austrian army who had retired to his native Co. Mayo, as an officer.[28] James O'Dowd and Matthew Tone were hanged for treason after the rising. Hayes was executed on Wexford Bridge for complicity in the rebellion.[29]

The French had landed in Connacht (the poorest province in Ireland) and were appalled at the poverty and living conditions of the local people. They were also unimpressed with the quality of the rebels, many of whom, unaccustomed to the rigours of military life, continued to come and go throughout the campaign.[30] A French officer remarked of the rebels that he would gladly keep one third and have the rest shot.[31]

Moreover, there were other issues why the campaign failed. Communication was difficult, as many French officers could not speak English. Henry O'Keon from Ballina, Co. Mayo accompanied the French expedition as translator. Language difficulties between the Irish and their French allies were nothing new, having also caused difficulties during the Jacobite War in 1690. Humbert appointed local man James McDonnell, a fluent French speaker, and George Blake from Co. Galway as officers.[32] McDonnell managed to escape to Paris after the Rebellion and joined Napoleon's Irish Legion; Blake was not so lucky as he was later hanged. Matthew Bellew, a former colonel in the Austrian army who retired to Ireland after being injured in the siege of Belgrade in 1789, offered his services to the cause and was commissioned to lead the insurgents. He too was hanged.[33]

Humbert's band of 1,099 joined up with 5,000 rebels and defeated a British force under General Lake at Castlebar, subsequently known as the 'Castlebar Races' for the speed of the British retreat. Colonel Sarrazin single-handedly captured the King's colour from the enemy. After a number of small battles at Castlebar, Ballina and Colooney, the Franco-Irish army were overwhelmed and decisively defeated in early September at Ballinamuck in Co. Longford. Humbert was forced to make a stand there as General Lake's and General Cornwallis's 30,000 army blocked the road to Dublin.[34] Humbert dispatched a brief report back to the Directory in Paris: 'after having made the arms of the French Republic triumph during my stay in Ireland, I have been obliged to submit to a superior force of 30,000 troops.'[35] The French rank and file were escorted to Carrick-on-Shannon and the officers were brought to Dublin and signed paroles of honour not to escape and were wined and dined and put up in the best hotels. They were feted by Dublin society from the balconies of their hotel fronting the fine Georgian squares of Dublin, and were eventually exchanged for English prisoners of war, and repatriated back to France together with the rank and file.

The Armagh Militia captured a colour of the 2nd battalion of the French 70th Demi-Brigade after the battle, one of the very few enemy flags captured anywhere in the British Isles.[36] General Lake's cavalry ploughed into the rebels after the French surrendered. Many fled into the bog, which was inaccessible to cavalry.[37] The Armagh Militia pursued the fleeing rebels for several miles on foot, and without firing a shot they lunged in with bayonets until 'the country was covered for miles around with their slain,' witnessed a militia member.[38] The Irish Yeomanry was a voluntary, part-time local defence force, described by Grattan as 'an Ascendancy army' and became infamous for their cruelty in the treatment of the defeated rebels. Houses were burnt and plundered, 500 rebels were massacred at the battlefield site, 53 were hanged the day after the battle, and 143 were executed in Ballinamuck before the army departed.[39] They also massacred a 500-man battalion of the Longford militiamen who had joined the rebels. The Yeomanry engaged in other atrocities such as torture, public flogging and hangings, half-hanging and pitch capping – in which the rebel had a cap filled with boiling tar forced onto his head and lit.

Nine days after Humbert's surrender, Napper Tandy, together with General Blackwell, sailed from Dunkirk and landed on Rathlin Island off the Donegal coast with 270 French troops, stands-of-arms and ammunition. After hearing that the rebellion had been quashed, Tandy departed back to the Continent and captured a British ship along the way as a prize.[40] Tandy and Blackhall were later captured and were brought to Dublin and condemned to death, but Napoleon intervened on their behalf and instead they were imprisoned in Kilmainham Gaol before expatriation to France.

The following month, Wolfe Tone again moored off the Irish coast with a French squadron in Donegal and 3,000 troops under General Jean Hardy. He attempted to make landfall at Lough Swilly but was intercepted by a larger Royal Navy squadron. In the action that followed, Tone fought bravely, commanding a gun battery, but was eventually forced to surrender. He travelled under the alias of Adjutant-General James Smith and was brought to Dublin where he was identified by an ex-fellow student of Trinity College and put on trial for treason. 'The British connection, in his opinion, was the bane of his country's prosperity,' the *Dublin Journal* reported, 'and it was his objective to destroy this connection, and in the event of his exertions he succeeded in raising three millions of his countrymen to a sense of their national debasement.' Tone was found guilty of treason and was sentenced to be hanged. General Kilmaine, who befriended Tone – they being two fellow Dubliners in exile – requested the French government intervene on Tone's behalf and to hold British prisoners of equal rank to Tone for his safety, but his appeal was strangely ignored.[41] Tone had requested to be shot like a soldier and not hanged as a traitor; he beat the hangman's noose by slitting his own throat and dying from his wounds a few days later. His family were refused all access to see him.[42]

The Act of Union, which came into law on 1 January 1801, joined Ireland to the United Kingdom of Great Britain and Ireland. The Act was a direct result of the rebellion, although the British had recognised that Ireland was slowly, legislatively, moving away from Britain. She would have liked to have reined Ireland into a union earlier, but was fearful of encountering too much opposition. The British were concerned that if Catholic emancipation was granted in Ireland, she may in time create a Catholic parliament, which would break away from Britain and then ally herself with France. Britain feared being placed between the 'blades of the scissors', a phrase cleverly adopted by General O'Connell in describing a connection between France and Ireland.[43] So the Act of Union was passed by the Irish and British Parliaments, with much opposition in Ireland. It was a desperate situation, with Grattan himself (although being unwell) arriving in College Green, Dublin, by sedan chair at 5 a.m. amidst much excitement, when the session was still in progress. He was dressed in his old Volunteer uniform and, while seated, delivered a two-hour anti-Union tirade, ending his speech with 'I will remain anchored here with fidelity to the fortunes of my country faithful to her freedom, faithful to her fall.' These were the last words spoken by Grattan in the Irish House of Commons. Even Grattan could do nothing. The Irish Parliament treasonously voted itself out of existence by 158 votes to 115. Votes were publicly sold, with money and titles offered to swing it. The bill was read while troops from the Royal (now Collins) Barracks were drawn up under the Ionic colonnades of the Irish Parliament in College Green ready to sweep the streets of any unrest at a moment's notice. The Act solved none of Ireland's problems and thwarted reform and Catholic emancipation for many years, due to entrenched vested interests and religious bigotry.

With the demise of the Irish Parliament, its 300 members with their families and servants left the city for London, and Ireland declined and 'dropped out of international politics, forgot her European relations and sank into second rate isolation and provincialism, behind the first rate isolation and provincialism of Britain'.[44] The Georgian period was a golden age in Irish history when the Protestant-dominated city of Dublin emerged as a modern, bustling metropolis and became the second largest city in the British Empire after London. A speculative property boom, funded by widows' inheritances, fuelled major construction projects. In 1757, the Wide Streets Commission replaced the narrow medieval streets with wide modern boulevards. Acres of grand Georgian squares and many landmark public buildings were built. The Grand Canal Dock was opened (which was then the largest in the world) and the Custom House, the Grand and the Royal canals were also built. Key civil institutions were founded, such as the Rotunda Lying-in Hospital, the Royal Dublin Society and the Royal Irish Academy for the Sciences. In 1742, the inaugural performance of Handel's *Messiah* took place in Dublin and in 1759 Arthur Guinness founded his famous brewery. After the Union, the speculative boom ended and the economy collapsed. In the 1780s, a fashionable mansion in Fitzwilliam Square that had fetched £8,000 was valued at just £2,500 and by the Famine in the 1840s was valued at just £500.[45] By the early 1900s, the slums in Dublin were the worst in Europe. Many of the grand old mansions became tenements with up to ten families living in one house, exploited by greedy landlords.

The 1798 rebellion cost 30,000 Irish lives, most of whom were noncombatants. The Rising was always going to be an unequal contest; the rebels lacked uniforms, equipment, training and modern weaponry while the British held almost all the heavy ordnance. The French arrived too late and the Irish rose too early. The end was inevitable. One can draw many parallels with the Scottish Rising of 1745; Cumberland butchering the rebels after Culloden and Lake doing likewise after Ballinamuck. However, unlike the '45', Irish officers in the French army were not accorded prisoner-of-war status, despite formal protestations by Humbert. British army generals were severely criticised after the rebellion. Dublin Castle failed the loyalists; British intelligence and the Royal Navy had let them down, and only the local militia and yeomanry had protected them. The British laid the blame for the insurrection as much on the efforts of the rebels as on the misrule of the country by the Protestant Ascendancy. Previous to the French landing, Ireland was always seen as a boring posting and was shunned by the best British generals, but now it was recognised that it could be the Italy of the west, where 'reputation, honour and glory could be won.'[46] After the Rising, the authorities increased fortifications by erecting around fifty Martello towers and gun batteries around the Irish coast. A new military road and barracks were constructed in Co. Wicklow. Many ports such as

Cork harbour were fortified in response to the continued French threat. The rebels under James Corcoran and Michael Dwyer continued the war and waged a guerrilla campaign in Wicklow (which was to be the last stronghold of the rebellion), finally surrendering in February 1804 after the defeat of Robert Emmett's rebellion in 1803.[47]

15

NAPOLEON'S IRISH LEGION (1803–15)

The Treaty of Amiens in 1802 temporarily secured peace between France and England, but they were at war again within a year. The French Revolution had purged both the Armée Royale and the Marine Royale by condemning and putting to death many capable and experienced officers, while thousands more were forced into exile. The Revolutionary army and navy were formed in their place. The difficulties facing the reorganised navy were well illustrated in July 1795, when a French squadron of 12,000 men left the French port of Brest; two-thirds comprised unblooded new levees who had never been to sea before.[1] Revolutionary France recognised that for any invasion of the British Isles, it was not necessary to have superiority at sea; they just required control of the Channel for a limited period of time. The ability to keep the English guessing the exact location of the landing was more important than controlling the Channel.[2] It was not surprising that Britain, as an island nation, was the pre-eminent naval power, as France shared land borders with other potentially hostile countries and accordingly had to divide her military resources to protect her frontiers on multiple fronts.

A large-scale French invasion of 'Perfidious Albion' was again seriously considered in 1803. 'The Channel is a mere ditch,' wrote Napoleon confidently, 'and it will be crossed as soon as someone has the courage to attempt it.'[3] The Irish community in France received a fresh exodus of Irishmen who fled Ireland after the recent failed rising, men such as William Lawless, Thomas Emmet (brother of Robert), Miles Byrne and Dr MacNevin. Miles Byrne, a Wexford farmer, had fought in the '98 and continued the struggle with Michael Dwyer into the Wicklow Mountains. He finally fled to France after Emmet's failed 1803 rebellion. Byrne wrote his *Memoirs*, which provide us with excellent, generally accurate, first-hand source material for the regiment.[4] Many United Irishmen were earning a living by teaching English in Paris. Some were lawyers and medical doctors and most emanated 'from the upper strata of Irish society'.[5] Those Irish exiles took advantage of the renewed hostilities between France and Britain, and lobbied the French government for military support in Ireland. Whatever the arguments put forward favouring an invasion of Ireland, the French were lackluster: Ireland was always to be a sideshow to the main military operations on the Continent as French policy again intended diverting British troops and resources from the war there.

Former Irish Brigade officers General Alexandre D'Alton (aide-de-camp to the Minister of War, Marshal Louis Berthier) and General Oliver Harty explored the possibility of establishing a new Irish corps amongst these exiles in Paris.[6] In August 1803, based on D'Alton's and Harty's recommendations, Napoleon issued a decree for the formation of the light infantry La Légion Irlandaise. Dubliner Adjutant-General Bernard MacSheedy was tasked with the formation and subsequent command of the Irish unit. One wonders if MacSheedy was the best choice. Wolfe Tone described him as a 'sad blockhead' in his *Memoirs*, but nevertheless, MacSheedy was an experienced infantry officer who had joined the French army directly from the Irish College in Paris and had recently served in the French expedition to Egypt in 1798.

The new Irish unit was officered by a mixture of officers from the old Irish Brigade under the *ancien régime* and former United Irishmen. Captain Dillon and Lieutenant O'Moran (the sons of Irish generals murdered during the Revolution) also joined the Irish Regiment. The London Coffee House in the Rue Jacob in Paris was a favourite haunt of the exiled Irishmen, who kept themselves abreast of developments at home by reading the anti-British, English-language newspaper the *Argus*, which was published by Irish refugees in Paris.[7] General Humbert's small invasion force which landed in Ireland in 1798 gave the Irish hope, and many joined the corps to continue the struggle; Edward Masterson wrote to General D'Alton, requesting to join the Legion 'to revenge the injuries of my long-shackled nation', and others wanted to join 'to seek the independence of that place which gave him birth'.[8] Former United Irishmen were particularly welcome into the corps as they had military experience organising insurrection in Ireland. The historian John Gallagher concluded that more than half of these men were in their thirties and less than half were proficient in French, which no doubt would cause difficulties between the Legion and the French high command.

The Legion comprised one battalion of eight *chasseur* (hunter) light infantry companies, and a company of chosen men or elite *caribiniers* – subsequently replaced with a company of *voltigeurs* or riflemen. This battalion was later increased to four battalions and a regimental depot or headquarters. The Legion served in Germany, Flanders, Spain, Portugal and in Central Europe and underwent many changes in its relatively short history. In 1808 its name was changed to the Regiment Irlandais; when the foreign regiments were reorganised in 1811 it changed again to the 3eme Regiment Etranger to the disappointment of some officers, who claimed that the removal of 'Irlandais' reduced them to mercenaries.[9] However, General Henri Clarke, who helped to establish the corps, ensured the regiment kept 'Irlandais' in parenthesis. In 1815, prior to its disbandment, it was re-designated the 7eme Regiment Etranger, leaving out the word 'Irlandais', which was said to please the British.[10] The Chief Secretary of Ireland, Lord Castlereagh, had objected to the word 'Irlandais' in the regiment's name and any to re-organisation of the Irish Brigade. Castlereagh had played a leading role in suppressing the 1798 Irish rebellion and had focused his energies on the pursuit of the rebel leaders. Many officers resented losing its Irish name; however, throughout the regiment's history, it would always be referred to as the 'Irish Battalion' or the 'Irish Regiment', even with its name change, even though commands were given in French, unlike in the old Irish Brigade where commands were in English.

Napoleon adopted the Imperial Eagle to disassociate himself from the monarchy and to emulate ancient Rome. The Eagle symbolised Napoleonic France and became a prime enemy target on the battlefield, even more so than colours or standards, and accordingly was guarded by two grizzly battle-hardened NCOs. Originally both battalions of the French line regiments received an Eagle, but this was restricted to one per regiment due to so many being taken by the enemy. The Irish were one of the few foreign regiment (of around twenty foreign regiments) in the French army entrusted with the Imperial Eagle, no doubt due to the reputation of its predecessor, the grand old Irish Brigade. The Legion was dressed in bright emerald green coats, with yellow facings, instead of the traditional red coats of the old Irish Brigade. The uniforms of the foreign regiments were made very showy to attract recruits, which in turn attracted the opposite sex. The Irish apparently used them to their full advantage. One Frenchman described this band of exiles: 'in their handsome green uniforms they made a large number of female conquests, especially among cooks.'[11] In May 1804, the newly formed unit was given the honour of sending two officers, the Presbyterian Captain John Tennant from Co. Antrim and Captain William Corbett from Co. Cork, to attend Napoleon's coronation as Emperor in Notre Dame, Paris. The Irish received their Regimental Colour of a gold harp in each corner, with a tricolour on a green background, with the motto: *'Le Premier Consul Aux Irlandos Unis'* ('The First Consul to United Ireland' – Napoleon's title before proclaimed emperor), while the other side had the motto *'Liberte des Consciences/Independance de L'Irlando'* ('Freedom of Conscience/Independence of Ireland'). A French eyewitness described the Irish proudly receiving their Imperial Eagles on the parade ground of the Champs de Mars, Paris:

> There was, in addition to the sailors, an Eagle deputation the strange appearance of which attracted special curiously and interest that afternoon. Everybody gazed in wonder at a group of strapping looking foreigners of all ages who marched along by themselves, got up as light infantrymen with green tufted shakos and bright green uniforms. They belonged to the Emperor's newest creations: and were the Eagle escort of Napoleon's 'Irish Legion'. They had come to the Field of Mars to receive the only Eagle that Napoleon ever gave to a foreign regiment in his service, with a flag specially designed for them of 'Irish green', as it was described, of silk, fringed with gold cord, inscribed on one side with gold in letters; *'Napoleon, Empereur de Francais, a la Legion Irlandais'* and bearing on the other, a gold harp, uncrowned with the words; *'L'Independance d'Irlande'*.[12]

In the winter of 1803, the Legion was stationed in Morlaix, Brittany, as that was the proposed embarkation point for the expedition to Ireland. Some officers undertook to march the fifteen days from Paris to the coast, to be better prepared for the upcoming campaigning. Officers with sufficient funds chose to take the mail-coach down. The Legion was essentially an officers' unit and contained few rank and file. By late 1804, they comprised sixty-six officers with only twenty-two privates and NCOs.[13] General Oliver Harty took an active part in organising and training the Irishmen in his time as the Legion's inspector general, and the best French army instructors were sent to drill them.[14]

The Irish remained in Brittany for three years until 1806 awaiting invasion plans of the British Isles and were primarily involved in coastal defence, although an important security function was an uninteresting duty. Celtic Brittany has many cultural similarities with Ireland and the Irish would have felt at home there. Some officers spent their evenings hiring horses and riding to nearby Brest. Here they dined with their compatriot Captain John Murphy and boarded some of the ships of the line at anchor there which were earmarked for the Irish invasion. Captain Murphy from Rush, Co. Dublin captained a trading vessel when the French arrived in Killala in 1798, and was asked by the French General Humbert to carry dispatches of his safe arrival in Ireland back to France. Murphy was rewarded with the captaincy of a frigate and was given the plum job of head pilot of the fleet at Brest and remained in France.

Napoleon planned an invasion of Ireland principally using Irish soldiers. The Legion was to be officered by Irishmen or sons of Irishmen only. It was envisaged that their ranks would be swelled with Irish volunteers upon landing in Ireland, before being seconded by French troops. The Irish population would further perceive the invasion force as an army of liberation and Napoleon could deploy his own troops elsewhere. Napoleon replaced the Stuarts as the object of Irish Catholic fantasies as he was seen as a saviour from British oppression, in contrast to much of Continental Europe and particularly Britain where he was vilified. Irish balladeers assigned him the code name of 'The Green Linnet' and wrote songs and set-dances sympathising with his exploits such as 'The Plains of Waterloo', 'Napoleon Crossing the Rhine', 'Madame Buonaparte', 'Napoleon's Farewell to Paris' and the 'Salamanca Reel.'[15]

The Legion was not actively recruiting but was permitted to recruit from captured prisoners of war. As the British army was not serving on the Continent at the time, the Legion could only recruit from Irish sailors in the Royal Navy or from deserters of the 18th Royal Irish Regiment of Foot (nicknamed 'Paddy's Blackguards') who were stationed in the Channel Islands.[16] Eight Irish soldiers deserted and rowed across in an open boat from the British garrison in Jersey. They were sent to General Oliver Harty and they told him that all of the other Irish soldiers would be only too keen to join the Legion when the opportunity to do so arose. Joining the Irish Legion for a prisoner of war was the obvious choice for many, as Irishmen 'believed that it was better to live as a soldier in a French uniform than to rot as a prisoner in an English uniform'.[17] Discipline in the French army was also less severe than in the Royal Navy, where deck floggings in the form of the cat-o'-nine-tails were part and parcel of service, and the food was a lot better. Many deserted at the first opportunity. Sailors were by no means ideal recruits as they lacked essential infantry training and when the Legion was later ordered to Germany the 800-mile march from the French coast to the Rhine resulted in many desertions. Later on in 1811, Napoleon ordered the dismissal of English and Scottish ex-prisoners from the Legion's ranks because of high desertion rates and because he believed they constituted a security threat.[18]

The Legion was also beset by infighting that seriously affected morale. As early as 1804, it was recognised that the Irish Regiment's 'principal weakness were its internal rivalries, poor discipline, and chaotic administration'.[19] One can imagine the boredom in the sleepy, rainy, towns of western Brittany, without much to do. Arthur O'Connor and Thomas Emmet had history between them that started in Ireland and this fighting continued in the Legion. MacSheehy was appalled to learn that O'Connor was to command the Legion when it landed in Ireland, believing he owed his high rank to political intrigue only.[20] O'Connor may have been militarily inexperienced but he transformed the United Irishmen prior to the 1798 Rising. The French had confidence in him and he had displayed diplomatic skills as the chief negotiator in gaining French support for the 1796 invasion of Ireland.[21]

The Irish were required to take an oath of allegiance to Emperor Napoleon. This caused a major rift in the Legion as many felt this oath compromised their loyalty and allegiance to Ireland. Some officers refused to sign and a fistfight broke out on the parade ground between Captain Thomas Corbett and Captain John Sweeney that ended in a duel with Corbett being shot dead. The whole incident had a disastrous effect on the corps and in the subsequent inquiry Colonel MacSheedy lost command and left the corps.[22] MacSheedy later became aide-de-camp to Napoleon, beside whom he was killed by a cannon ball in 1807 at the Battle of Eylau in eastern Prussia.

The French high command realised something needed to be done to reform the Legion, to bring it back into line, and appointed Italian-born Colonel Antoine Petrezzoli as battalion commander. The well-experienced infantry officer had the difficult task of managing these hotheaded revolutionaries. The Irish officers partly resented the fact that he and the other Polish and Prussian officers were not one of their own. Captain Markey went so far to boast that if an angel descended from heaven and if the angel was not Irish, he would take no orders from him.[23] Miles Byrne recounted an incident in which a small party of English sailors launched a coastal raid in Concarneau a short distance away. A French detachment was sent to repel them and the English quickly re-embarked. The Irish officers were furious they had not been ordered to engage the old enemy and afterwards laid down their swords in defiance. Petrezzoli later dismissed eight officers for insubordination and others for causing trouble in the corps.[24]

Napoleon directed that commissions for the Irish officers were to be on the same footing as French officers, due to the dangers of captured Irish officers being hanged as traitors. He was aware that many Irish officers were hanged in the '98 and had personally intervened on Napper Tandy's behalf when Tandy was sentenced to death. He also knew that although Wolfe Tone was commissioned as an adjutant-general, he had cheated the hangman's noose by slitting his own throat. In January 1804 Napoleon ordered 'that every Irishmen sailing with the French army, and taking part in the expedition, will be given a French commission; if he is captured, and treated otherwise than as a prisoner-of-war, reprisals will be practised on English prisoners'.[25]

In 1805, France assembled a huge flotilla in Boulogne on the French coast, comprising 200 flat-bottomed craft to convey 100,000 troops over the Channel to invade England and finally end the war. General Augereau commanded 20,000 French troops, including 4,000 troops of the Irish Legion assembled further down the coast in Brittany for a landing to be made at Lough Swilly in north-west Ireland. General Augereau had time for the Irish and was keen to see the unit succeed, as he himself started his career within the Irish Brigade. The Legion's ranks were swelled for the planned invasion, comprising vagabonds, renegades and thieves, and the Irish officers were said to be unhappy at leading such a motley crew into their own country.[26] Napoleon dispatched a decoy fleet to the West Indies to draw off the Royal Navy who were blockading the Channel. With the invasion force now battle ready, Napoleon wrote confidently to Admiral Villeneuve from the embarkation point at Boulogne in August 1805, 'I hope you have arrived at Brest, Start, without losing a moment, and sail up the Channel with all the ships you have. England is ours; we are all ready; every man is on boards. Appear for 24 hours, and the thing is done.'[27]

However, all hopes were dashed due to the disastrous Franco-Spanish defeat by Admiral Nelson at the Battle of Trafalgar, which scuppered the planned invasion. It is thought that one-third of Nelson's sailors at the battle were Irishmen, but it is not known how many Irishmen or their descendants served in the Franco-Spanish fleet. John DeCourcy Ireland has identified Enrique MacDonnell, who captained the 100-gun *Roya*, one of the few Spanish ships that managed to escape to nearby Cadiz. Two days after the battle, he launched an attack with two other ships against a larger British squadron, but was captured. After he was exchanged with other British prisoners, he was promoted to the rank of commodore for his actions.[28]

After the fiasco at Trafalgar, the Legion remained on coastal defence in Brittany and French attention was diverted east. Napoleon defeated the Austro-Russians in December 1805 in the famous Battle of Austerlitz, which is widely viewed as the beginning of the 'glory years' of the French Empire. Trafalgar was also a turning point in the fate of the Legion's officers, as many had joined with the specific purpose of liberating Ireland from British rule. Now with the proposed invasion abandoned, these men who were not professional soldiers were deployed to fight France's interests elsewhere. Some had put lucrative careers on hold, others were medical doctors, and many had no interest in embarking on a professional military career in France.

The Irish would have to wait another few years before an invasion of Ireland was again entertained. Napoleon later on dispatched a Legion officer to Dublin 'to investigate the likely reaction to a French descent of Ireland'.[29] He also wrote to his Minister of War, General Henri Clarke, with a view to organising another invasion of Ireland, but nothing came of the plan in the end.

> I want at you to send for O'Connor and the other Irishmen in Paris, and to see if you can revive a party in Ireland. At the present moment I have 25 war-ships off the Scheldt and 9 in the Texel. I am very much inclined to send an expedition of 3,000 men and 4,000 horses to Ireland in October; if I can be sure of finding support there … I will agree to any terms the Irish like. It is a matter of immense importance. I want to have a plan, and to know what I can expect from it, within a fortnight.[30]

The Legion's discipline continued to deteriorate even under Petrezzoli's firm hand, such that several officers felt compelled to write to Napoleon to complain. Napoleon responded in October 1806 by sending the eighty-strong Legion to fight in the German campaign in Mainz (then called Malence). This came as a relief to many as they escaped the bickering and boredom of four years of coastal defence duties in Brittany and they would now finally see some action. Married officers departed in coaches with their wives and children, whilst others departed on foot. As they marched in their bright green uniforms through the small French towns, they were favourably compared by the local inhabitants to the Irish Brigade and were welcomed with exclamations that the Irish were France's faithful allies. While passing through Verdun, they were aware of the presence of British prisoners of war. They proudly marched through the town, chests out and shoulders back, with their Imperial Eagle uncovered and their green flags unfurled, inscribed with '*L'independance d'Irlande*', and the Legion band loudly belting out the marching tune 'Saint Patrick's Day in the Morning' to the astonishment of the British prisoners of war who were billeted there.

When the Legion arrived in Mainz, they were reinforced with 1,500 Poles from the Prussian army who had volunteered after the Prussian defeat at the Battle of Jena along the Rhine. Around 200 Irishmen who had been pressed into the Prussian army joined them, many of whom were now fluent in German; the British government had sold these men after the '98 to labour in Prussian salt mines. Marshal Kellerman, the hero of the French victories at Marengo and Valmy, ordered these new recruits to be resupplied and kitted out in the Legion's green uniform, which was completed within a couple of days. Kellerman also complimented the Irish that their bravery was proverbial, as he recalled he began his career as a cadet in the Irish Brigade.[31] With so many Poles joining, the character of the Legion changed; the rank and file comprising mainly foreigners, officered by Irishmen. This led to language difficulties with recruits who could speak neither English nor French. Many understood German military commands and had been trained in Prussian manoeuvres only. Time was needed for them to learn French military tactics and the Legion was accordingly not battle-ready for the Grand Army's Russian campaign.[32] The Legion therefore spent the remainder of their time in Germany in routine garrison duty and retraining their new recruits. On the plus side, Byrne wrote that the quality of the food improved as they were happily sustained with Polish food, which consisted of mixing potatoes with fried bacon made into a soupy broth. The Legion recruited a near 7-foot-tall drum major at Mainz to march at the head of the Legion band. He must have been a formidable sight as the uniforms of the drum major were well known to be the most flamboyant in the French army.

The Legion's attention now focused on the war in Flanders where the 1st battalion would receive their baptism of fire. The 1st Irish battalion in Germany, commanded by William Lawless, was ordered to march to Antwerp to defend Flushing (known in Dutch as Vlissingen). In 1809, the British had assembled a huge combined army and naval force of 70,000, known as the 'Grand Expedition', with which they intended to destroy the French naval fleet at Antwerp and Flushing. Napoleon had invested heavily in Antwerp for the repair and harbouring of his fleet, which was then a major shipbuilding port for the French navy. The British hoped that success here would divert French forces and assist her Austrian ally, who was struggling in Central Europe.[33] It has been suggested that Napoleon ordered his unblooded Irish troops to Antwerp as he considered they were only strong enough for garrison duties and he wanted to deploy his more experienced troops elsewhere. He would, however, shortly revise his opinion of his Irish legionnaires.

Gun batteries at Walcheren Island protected Antwerp, where malaria was rampant. In July, British troops under General Dundas along with the 88th Foot (Connaught Rangers) disembarked on the island. The French garrison of 4,500 was forced to give way and fell back to the fortified town of Flushing, where the Irish contingent of 480 men lost half their strength, fighting a rearguard action over several days. The following month, Flushing was eventually reduced after heavy British bombardment, and the French garrison, including the entire 1st Irish battalion, was taken prisoner and sent to England where it remained until the end of the war. The Irish were treated in every respect as French officers, as Napoleon had demanded, no doubt from the fear of reprisals on the part of the French government.[34] A British officer present observed the surrender of Flushing, which was led by the Irish Legion and their band, followed by the French garrison. After the Irish Legion brass band came

> the Colonel commander of the Irish Brigade, with his adjutant, both of them stout looking men, the Colonel dressed in a plain green coat, with gilt buttons and gold facings, with a handsome French *chaco*. He was followed by his men in strong sections, followed by their officers, all of whom wore the moustache ... their pantaloons were tight to the leg, and short white gaiters covered the feet. Some of the officers in their movements appeared to imagine themselves at a dance, as they swung along on the light fantastic with first the right shoulder forward, and then the left, with a short catch in their march, keeping time to the music.[35]

Although the French garrison surrendered, a small party of Irishmen saved the Eagle and evaded capture by crossing the river Scheldt and going into hiding. They included the injured Commandant Lawless, who had been struck by a musket ball that had entered below his right eye and lodged below his ear; Captains McCann and O'Reilly, who saved the Regimental Eagle; Captain Dowdall, who would die of his wounds two days later; and Captain Barker, an ex-officer of Walsh's. Lawless and others escaped in a small open boat but were forced to return to enemy-occupied Flushing. They took refuge in a doctor's house and crossed the river Scheldt four days later. They escaped through enemy patrols after spending the night in a storage hole, covered by ropes.

As Lawless was the highest-ranking officer to have escaped, he was sent to Paris to present the Eagle to Napoleon personally, and there he and O'Reilly were promoted and awarded the Legion of Honour. This honour was France's highest military decoration, which Napoleon introduced as the successor of the Order of St Louis.[36] Lawless was later ordered to write an eight-page account of the fall of Flushing at the request of the Minister for War while convalescing from his wounds.[37] With the capture of the 1st Irish battalion at Flushing, 'the Legion lost its most significant Irish element and never again would the Irish account for more than about 10 per cent of the rank and file.'[38] Thereafter, Hungarians, Poles and Prussians constituted the largest numbers of rank and file, officered by Irishmen. In February 1812, the remaining Irish battalions returned to their new regimental depot in Holland and were re-formed and rebuilt. This resulted in a new 4th Irish battalion formed with the rump of the 1st battalion that had escaped capture at Flushing.

In 1807, the Peninsular War (1807–14) broke out between France on one side and the Allies comprising Spain, Britain and Portugal on the other. The war was fought on the Iberian Peninsula; Napoleon invaded Spain and Portugal and placed his brother, Joseph, on the Spanish throne. Britain responded by sending a large expeditionary force to Spain to support their Spanish allies in ousting the French. The Irish Legion served a four-year tour of duty there. In late 1807 the newly formed 2nd Irish battalion, commanded by Captain Louis de Lacy, was ordered to Spain and was attached to the French army who were ordered to Madrid.[39] The Irish were one of the first troops called to restore order when Spanish nationalists rebelled in the rising known as 'The Second of May', which killed around 1,500 people.[40] That day was considered to be the opening shot of the Spanish War of Independence against the French. De Lacy had difficulties fighting against his own countrymen and disguised as a woman defected to the Spanish, where he received a commission as a Spanish colonel, which was a serious blow to Legion morale. In 1812 he rose to brigadier general and commanded a 10,000-strong Galician army, and he played an active role driving the French out of Spain.[41]

Map of the Iberian Peninsula.

Two months after De Lacy's defection, the Legion's 2nd battalion was reinforced with 600 men under Commandant Fitzhenry, who led the Irish contingent in Spain. They arrived in Burgos and engaged in routine patrolling and in humdrum garrison duties. They were also tasked with escorting the mail coaches from France to Madrid while under regular guerrilla attack. They took part in dangerous counter-insurgency activities, such as hunting Spanish nationalists in the mountainous terrain around Castille and the Asturias. It was a task the former United Irishmen didn't relish as they sympathised with the guerrillas as patriots and drew analogies with their own experiences hunted by the British in the Wicklow Mountains in the recent Irish risings.

Napoleon inspected a Legion advanced post on the road near Burgos, and pulled up his horse, as their distinctive green uniforms had impressed him. He enquired from Sergeant Mooney what regiment he belonged to. Miles Byrne recalls that thereafter Mooney and his twelve merry men got great mileage from this and never passed up an opportunity in mentioning that they had been inspected by the very Emperor himself. Mooney and his men must have made a good impression as they were chosen to provide an escort guard for Napoleon and he later issued a decree increasing the regiment's strength. While serving in northern Spain in 1809, the Legion was disappointed not to have engaged a British army under General John Moore. Some of the officers had fought against Moore in Ireland in the '98 and were eager to settle the score, this time on equal terms.

The Legion's 2nd battalion celebrated St Patrick's Day in Burgos with other Irish officers and sons of Irishmen in the French service. The officers gave copious amounts of wine to their men, who celebrated riotously and sacked the Spanish town, before armed troops intervened and locked many of them up in the town's prison to cool off.[42] Opposing them was the Hibernia Regiment of Spain who were also celebrating St Patrick's Day. The Irish in France had, since leaving Limerick in 1691, always fought together with their compatriots in Spain, but this time they were fighting on opposite sides. It is not known if Napoleon's Legion fought against the Irish Brigade of Spain in the war, as Spain and England were allies against France. However, it is thought that Napoleon's Legion faced the Irlanda Regiment of Spain when Wellington pulled back to Torres Vedres in 1810 and during the siege of Badojaz two years later.[43]

The Irish Brigade of Spain played a prominent role in the war, most notably during its heroic defence of Gerona. In June 1808, a French army commanded by General Duhesme besieged the town, which was a strategic entrance into north-east Spain. The Spanish garrison at Gerona comprised 400 men from Ultonia's, commanded by Colonel Anthony O'Kelly from Co. Roscommon. The French failed to take the town and withdrew after an eight-month siege. The Spanish garrison was then reinforced with an additional 400 men from Ultonia's, together with 102 grenadiers from Hibernia's under Colonel Juan Sherlock. The Irish were accompanied on campaign by their families, as was customary in that time. Lucy Fitzgerald, the wife of a captain in Ultonia's, obtained permission from the Spanish high command to form a women's unit made up of soldiers' wives to care for the wounded and to supply ammunition. This unit became known as the Company of St Barbara.

A French army of 33,000 men under the famous Lieutenant General Saint-Cyr was sent to besiege the town again. The town's commander, Colonel O'Kelly, was ordered to surrender as otherwise no mercy would be given. He refused. After a two-month siege, the town's walls and fortifications were destroyed by French artillery and the town was forced to capitulate. French casualties were as high as 15,000, with many lost to disease.[44] The Irish distinguished themselves along with the local townspeople, who suffered severely. The Irish lost over half their strength numbering 600 men and women, including Colonel O'Kelly and Lucy Fitzgerald, who died alongside her husband. When a new battalion was formed to replace their losses, Ultonia's was permitted by King Ferdinand of Spain to put the words '*Distinguidos de Ultonia*' ('Distinguished Ultonia') on their colours, in recognition of their heroic defence of the town.[45]

In 1809, the Legion's 3rd battalion was formed and ordered to Spain, commanded by Lieutenant Colonel Mahony who was controversially appointed by General Clarke over the more experienced Hugh Ware, a '98 rebel leader from Co. Wicklow. Mahony had, according to Byrne, 'nothing to recommend him to hold a rank in an Irish regiment in the French service'. The 3rd Irish battalion joined forces with the 2nd battalion in April 1810 and placed the Spanish town of Astorga under siege, since it was used by the Allies as a supply base for the war in Spain. The Legion was joined in this assault by the former Irish regiments of the French Irish Brigade (Berwick's and Walsh's, re-designated as the 88th and 92nd infantry regiments), many of whose officers, as Byrne recalled, were still Irishmen or the sons of Irishmen. The French entrenched for three weeks in front of the town and suffered heavy casualties before the Irish formed part of the assault battalion that lifted the siege. A body of advance troops, led by the 'forelorn hope' – comprising an Irish elite company of *voltigeurs* under Dubliner Captain John Allen (a '98 veteran), dashed 200 yards under a hail of grapeshot and close-range musket fire and stormed a breach made in the wall. The Irish were then given the honour of being the first troops to march triumphantly through the city's gate. For their death-defying action in storming the breach, three Irishmen received Legions of Honour for bravery: Lieutenant Perry for carrying a ladder to the breach, Captain Allen and a drummer of Allen's company, who despite having two legs blown off, continued to beat the charge.[46]

After the fall of Astorga, the Irish Legion were detailed with escorting the 5,000-strong captured Spanish garrison on their 90-mile march to Valladolid. The Legion were also given charge of a number of Spanish prisoners of war, including a Major Dorran from the Irish Brigade of Spain, whose uncle, Miles, Byrne knew in Francis Street, Dublin. Dorran later made a break of it and escaped on the road to Burgos (Byrne does not mention if he assisted him in this enterprise).

The Irish Legion was later decimated by disease. Its strength was reduced from 1,500 to 350 men. The following summer, the 2nd and 3rd Irish battalions were present in the Siege of Almeida. Captain Hugh Ware was promoted to colonel there and Miles Byrne related the action:

> a battalion d'élite, or chosen troops of the Irish regiment, was assembled to act at the advanced posts during the siege, and Captain Ware of the grenadiers of the 2nd battalion of the Irish was named by the Duke of Abrantes to command it. In an attack made on a division of advanced posts by General Sainte-Croix, and his brigade of cavalry, seconded by Captain Ware, the English were driven back under the walls of Almerida and the Fort of Conception.[47]

The French then blew up the town's magazine and the town capitulated, which forced the Duke of Wellington's Allied army to retreat from Spain and fall back into Portugal.

The Anglo-Irish Major-General Sir Arthur Wellesley, the Duke of Wellington was born in Dublin in 1769. A brigadier-general in the Spanish army called Joseph O'Lawlor from Co. Laois was attached to Wellington's general staff. He was mentioned in Wellington's dispatches to the Spanish minister of war as 'an officer of great merit, who has served most meritously throughout the entire war', and Wellington recommended him for promotion.[48]

In September 1810, Wellington decided to make a stand against the advancing French and occupied a high ridge above the town of Bussaco. Before the battle, the Legion's officers reminded their men to recollect Irish valour at Fontenoy and the wrongs done to Ireland. The French attacked five successive times at a cost of 4,500 men but failed to dislodge Wellington. The 88th (Connaught Rangers) Foot (raised primarily from recruits from the west of Ireland) fought with valour at this engagement. Several Connaught companies, together with another unit, charged and overthrew three French regiments, including the Irish Legion, and drove them back down the mountain. Dublin-born William Grattan wrote an account of the Connaught Rangers' adventures in the war and noted after the action that they came across several wounded men of the Irish Legion but 'could not discover one Irishman amongst them'.[49] One can imagine the scene of the 88th Connaughts and Napoleon's Irish Legion both playing the same regimental Irish airs of 'St Patrick's Day' to rally their men before the attack but from opposite sides! This exhilarating Irish air was guaranteed to get men's blood up. In 1810, when a British force attacked the French in Tarifa, Colonel Gough of the 87th (Royal Irish Fusiliers) Foot 'bade his band play up *St. Patrick's Day* and the men were so inspirited that it was scarcely impossible to restrain them from pursuing the fugitive right up to their very trenches.'[50]

For every Irishman who wore a French uniform in the Napoleonic period there were ten who wore a British one. Irishmen fighting on opposite sides has always been a cause of bitterness and this was evidenced during the Peninsular War. In 1811 an Irish officer, Chef d'escadron O'Flyn serving in a French regiment led a sortie against a British force near Salamanca in north-western Spain but all his men were killed and he alone was captured. An Irish private called Fitzpatrick serving in a British dragoon regiment pistolled O'Flyn on the spot because, as his commanding officer recorded in his diary, 'the fellow said he was an Irishman which the dragoon could not hear and permit him to escape alive.'[51]

Wellington was forced to pull back from Busaco towards Lisbon and took up position around the heavy fortifications of Torres Vedras, which he had secretly built the previous year to protect Lisbon. The French and the 3rd Irish battalion pursued him and encamped for several months within cannon shot. The Allies dug in deep and were well supplied from the coast by the Royal Navy. This was in contrast to the French who were short of provisions, as Spanish guerrillas had disrupted French supply lines. Disease claimed many lives, compounded by the coldest winter Portugal had seen in years. Desertions also weakened French forces. The 3rd Irish battalion sustained appalling losses as a result and was sent back to its depot in Germany and deactivated. The rump of the 3rd battalion was transferred into the 2nd Irish battalion.

Napoleon's Minister of War, General Henri Clarke, had always taken a personal interest in the Legion and had furthered the careers of many Irishmen within its ranks, although Clarke himself was accused of undue interference in the corps. After he secured a captaincy in the Legion for a Scottish acquaintance with little military experience, Miles Byrne vented his spleen at him for 'depriving those brave young officers of the advancement they were so well entitled to, and appointing men to situations who had no claims as Irish patriots, showed that the Duke of Feltre cared little about the independence of Ireland'.[52] Clarke also placed a relative of his, Colonel Daniel O'Meara, into the position held in the 2nd Irish battalion by Colonel Fitzhenry, who was forced to accept a subordinate rank. General Jumet later dismissed O'Meara as commander for incompetence and Fitzhenry was reinstated.

Although Fitzhenry was reinstated, the whole affair may have soured him as shortly afterwards he was captured by Spanish guerrillas, requested a pardon from the British, which he arranged through the Irish College in Salamanca, and resigned his commission. He requested permission to return to Ireland and was one of the few Legion officers who ever managed to return home. Later, in December 1811, a court martial was convened against Fitzhenry, *in absentia*, where he was accused of providing French military intelligence to Wellington, but he was acquitted. Fitzhenry later wrote defending himself: 'my only offence to Napoleon consisted of a desire to die in Ireland.'[53] Nevertheless, Fitzhenry's dishonour disgraced the battalion and his departure caused more shame than Lacy's defection. In December 1811, due to Fitzhenry's defection and having lost so many men due to desertions, the 2nd Irish battalion was recalled to France and disbanded. It was a sad end to the Legion's four-year campaign in the war.

The Irish Legion had lost two of its four battalions to the war in Spain, but was re-formed and brought up to establishment by recruiting 1,500 Germans and other foreigners who had been serving in foreign regiments in the Dutch army. After serving in the campaigns in Germany, Spain, Portugal and Flanders, the Legion was assigned to Central Europe, where France was at war with Russia and Prussia. General Desbureaux, the Minister for War, inspected the Legion at their headquarters at Landau (located close to the Franco-German border) and voiced concerns at the high number of Germans within its ranks. He advocated a push to recruit young Irishmen instead and proposed creating a separate German regiment, but this never materialised. The desertion of German enlistees became such a serious issue that Lawless imposed harsh disciplinary measures to counteract it. He also moved the regimental depot away from Landau, which was located in a German-speaking area of France, where it was easy for recruits to slip across the border back into their own areas.

The Irish luckily missed Napoleon's disastrous Russian campaign in 1812. When news of the catastrophic retreat from Moscow became known, Colonel Lawless wrote to General Clarke requesting permission to join the Grande Armée. This resulted in Clarke ordering two newly formed Irish battalions (2,000 strong) east to join the Grande Armée's Vth Corps in Magdeburg, Germany, the following year. Thereafter they were dispatched to Seehauzen on the river Elbe and saw action against the Prussians. They engaged irregular Russian cavalry, known as Cossacks, who had retreated from the town of Celle in Saxony and set fire to the wooden bridges there. The Legion vigorously pursued them through the flames before they were recalled back to French lines.[54] They guarded the river Elbe crossing and formed part of the contingent that captured Wurzen and rebuilt the bridges that were destroyed by the enemy. In May, the Legion saw action at the Battle of Reichenbach where their riflemen, while positioned in hollow squares, were continuously employed in driving off wave after wave of Cossack cavalry charges.[55] One of Napoleon's most famous generals who was also present at this action, Marshal Michel Ney, reprimanded Sergeant Costello for not falling back immediately when the trumpet was sounded to retreat. Costello said that a Cossack had fired twice at him and that he wanted to kill the fellow before quitting the field, 'And did you kill him?' asked the marshal who was pleased, 'I hope so,' replied Costello, 'for I saw him fall from his horse.'[56] Napoleon had been impressed by how well the Irish fought and rewarded six Irish officers with the Legion of Honour at the battle; Commandants Tennant and Ware, Captains Myles Byrne, Saint-Leger and Parrot, and Lieutenant Osmond.

The Legion also took part in the French victory in the battle at Bautzen and succeeded in driving the enemy back several miles. As a reward, Captain Allen's company of *voltigeurs* were given the honour of placing sentinels at Napoleon's lodgings in Lignitz, Poland, before his Imperial Guard, in their characteristic bearskin hats, relieved them.[57] Towards the end of May, the French army attacked the enemy's rear-guard near Leipzig. A Legion officer called Lieutenant Osmond, then serving as aide-de-camp to General Martial Vachot, alighted from his horse and was first to wade through the river whilst under enemy fire to encourage the men to follow. Afterwards Osmond was the talk of the army for this act of bravery and was recommended for advancement.[58] Opposing the French there was Major-General Joseph O'Rourke, the son of Leitrim-born General Cornelius O'Rourke. Joseph O'Rourke commanded the Russian Imperial cavalry. The previous year, in 1812, he led the vanguard of the Western Army and played a leading role in driving Napoleon out of Russia.[59]

The Irish continued their difficult 1813 campaign in Poland, forming part of Jacques MacDonald's Division and 'spearheaded a counter-attack across the river Bober and took the strategic Goldberg Hill'.[60] In August, the Legion fought at the Battle of Lowenberg where they bore 'almost the entire brunt of the action falling upon them'.[61] They were honoured when General Vachot chose to stand in the Irish square rather than the two other squares formed by other regiments. The Irish squares were blasted by Russian grapeshot and cannon balls, which carried off whole ranks before the order to retreat was given. They halted and volte faced, firing every two minutes until they reached the safety of the wood, before French artillery drove the enemy back. Lieutenant Saint-Leger was credited with saving the French General Vachot's life; while retreating near a farmyard they were pursued by enemy cavalry.

Saint-Leger threw the general over a wall and then quickly followed and both escaped injury. The Irish lost 400 of their bravest soldiers there and the battle represented the Legion's most costly engagement.[62] It was reportedly a very bloody action, with bodies heaped on top of each other with their faces shot off. Commandant Tennant was literally cut in two by a cannon ball; Captain Evans, Lieutenant Osmond and McAuley were also killed; Sergeant Costello had an arm blown off; and Commandant Hugh Ware received three grapeshot wounds and had a horse shot from under him. A few days later, Napoleon personally commanded the French army in the Second Battle of Lowenberg. The Irish were ordered to cross the River Bober and attack the enemy when Lawless again had a second horse shot from under his feet:

> The Irish regiment had to pass through a mill, which stood in the centre of the river, the bridges having been destroyed the day before; the town was bombarded by the enemy's batteries. Under this tremendous fire, Colonel Lawless passed at the head of his regiment, and saluted the Emperor, who was on horseback in the street leading to the river where the regiment had to pass. The Emperor was surrounded by his staff officers, the King of Naples (Murat), etc. Colonel Lawless seeing the grenadiers and the most part of the regiment had got through the mill, immediately rode through the river and placed himself at the head of his regiment to attack the enemy; he had hardly advanced a few steps, when his leg was carried off by a cannon ball from the enemy's battery, which was placed on an eminence to defend the passage of the river.[63]

Lawless was carried off the field and Napoleon sent his chief surgeon to amputate. It would have been a procedure Lawless would have been all too familiar with as a former Professor of Anatomy at the College of Surgeons in Dublin. This ended Lawless's career and he was sent back to France to recuperate. A total of eleven Irish officers were awarded the Legion of Honour for bravery there. As a result of the French commander Marshal MacDonald's defeat at Katzbach in Poland, the Irish Legion formed part of the French rearguard. They were pinned down with their backs to the Bober River and surrounded by a combined Russo-Prussian army of 30,000. The enemy launched a massive frontal attack and thousands of horses and men were drowned as they were forced into the river; 1,400 men of the Irish Legion were either killed or taken prisoner.[64] Just 150 Frenchmen escaped, including 'eight officers and thirty men of the Irish Regiment with commandant Ware and the ensign who saved the Eagle of the regiment, had the good fortune to get out of the bed of the river, but had to wade through a sheet of water which covered the other side for more than a half mile under the fire of the enemy.'[65]

The Irish suffered appallingly in the Central European campaign. Out of the 2,000 men who marched out to join the Grand Armée eight months earlier, only 117 managed to make it back safely to their regimental headquarters. Once back at their depot they were re-formed into one battalion from the under-strength 3rd and 4th battalions, together with recruits from other deactivated regiments.

In January 1814, British troops occupied the village of Merksem, close to Antwerp where Major Hugh Ware led a combined Franco-Irish force of 1,000 men, who successfully recaptured the village.[66] The Legion also secured the access roads towards Antwerp by laying down trees to impede cavalry advances. They later formed the largest component of the garrison sent to defend Antwerp, mustering 85 officers and 396 men, when it was besieged by an Anglo-Swedish force.[67] Irish casualties are unknown but the Legion's Captain Ryan was shot and wounded while launching a sortie in Antwerp's *grote markt* (square).[68] Lieutenant Saint-Leger was entrusted by General Carnoy to communicate with the enemy, due no doubt to his fluent English, and the governor of Antwerp afterwards recommended him for advancement. The Anglo-Swedish force failed to take Antwerp, which was too well defended, but the siege lifted when Napoleon was forced to abdicate later that year.

After Napoleon's removal from power in May 1814, the Legion marched south from Antwerp to their new regimental depot in Montreuil-Sur-Mer, near Boulogne. They were ordered to destroy their Imperial Eagle but instead hid it in the regiment's military chest. The Irish, in common with other units of the French army, were divided between their loyalty to Napoleon and to the Bourbon monarchs.

They 'hedged their bets' by pledging loyalty to the Bourbons whilst at the same time hiding Napoleon's cherished Eagle in anticipation of his return. In February 1815, the Irish publicly declared their support for Napoleon when he escaped from Elba and they remained on coastal defence duties during Napoleon's 'Hundred Days' campaign. Napoleon was keen to maintain the Irish identity of the Legion and ordered all non-Irish personnel to other units. As a result of so many experienced foreigners leaving, the regiment was under-strength and not battle-ready to take part in the Battle of Waterloo.[69]

After Napoleon's defeat at Waterloo, the Legion was blockaded by Allied forces in Montreuil before it finally surrendered, burning its colours to prevent them being taken by the enemy. When Napoleon was removed from France, King Louis XVIII was returning from his exile in England and a royalist officer asked if the Legion was loyal to the new king. Colonel Ware replied 'Colonel, give your orders and they will be executed. If the king wants an escort to the frontiers he may rely on the regiment doing its duty. But we Irish patriots will never go to the enemy's camp, to fight against France, our adopted country.'[70]

When Louis XVIII was reinstated, the Legion was disbanded by a royal decree in September 1815 along with all the other foreign regiments in the French army, ending a 125-year tradition of Irish military service to France. This was despite protestations by Colonel Mahony who pleaded for the return of the Irish Brigade, with its distinctive red uniform and its motto *'Semper et Ubique Fideles'* ('Always and Forever Faithful').[71] Upon the Legion's disbandment, all remaining flags and regimental property were destroyed along with the Regimental Eagle. The rank and file was sent to the 4th Royal Foreign Regiment (the forerunner of the French Foreign Legion) based in Toulon, although there is no record of any Irish officer transferring there. Irish service on the Continent had always been a political thorn in the British side, and the Irish officers, like their forefathers in the Irish Brigade again suspected that the British had pressured the French for their disbandment. They were now concerned that they would press them further to have the Irish expelled from France entirely. True to form, the Irish officers were initially allowed to remain on half-pay and reside in any French town, but they were then ordered to leave France. The Irish-cadre officer class was lost to France forever, although a few managed to remain to serve in other French regiments. The Irish regiments in Spanish service were deactivated several years later in 1818, invoking a clause from when the regiments were first raised that they were to be deactivated if they no longer had a large Irish contingent.[72]

16

Conclusion

The Wild Geese were renowned for their fidelity and valour throughout Europe, where they flourished in the armies of France, Spain and Austria. In the mid-eighteenth century, Dublin became the second city of the British Empire, in the Protestant-dominated Kingdom of Ireland, but it has been argued that the real Ireland was to be found on the Continent. Paris had a considerable second- and third-generation Irish population and 'became the capital city of Catholic Ireland's hopes and aspirations, as Dublin was the capital city of its fears and laws'.[1] The Jacobite cause was the cause for Irish freedom in the eighteenth century. By the 1750s, seven banking houses in Paris were Irish owned and many used their wealth and influence for Jacobite political purposes. Bonnie Prince Charlie's Jacobite Rising in the '45 would not have happened without Irish support:

> It was planned, promoted, financed and directed by Irishmen. The officers of the Irish Brigade contributed generously. Prince Charles procured 180,000 livres from Irish bankers in Paris. One Irishman fitted out a privateer with eighteen guns. The expedition was commanded by Colonel Sir John O'Sullivan. A detachment from the Irish Brigade, drawn from its six regiments, fought alongside the clansmen.[2]

There was scarcely a battle between 1690 and the Treaty of Aix-le-Chapelle in 1748 in which Irish troops did not take part. They shared French disasters at Blenheim, Ramillie, Oudenaarde and Malplaquet and fought at Luzzara, Cassano and Spiers. They also had success at Barcelona, Cremona, Fontenoy and Lafelt. Charles Forman, the eighteenth-century English pamphleteer, praised Irish service in France:

> It may be said to their eternal honour that from the time they entered the service of France to this hour they have never made the least false step, or have had the least blot on their reputation, and what is more, I defy the most malicious and prejudiced man to name the place where the Irish misbehaved themselves either at home or abroad since they became disciplined men. Had they done so in the French service Europe would have known about it, for, believe me, France is not a country for cowards to gain renown in.[3]

Many Catholic families provided unbroken service to the armies of Europe, such as the Dillons who were one of the most illustrious Irish families in France. They supported James II during the Jacobite War and fled to France with the Wild Geese, and by so doing, forfeited their ancestral lands in Meath and Roscommon. The family provided over seventy family members to the French Irish Brigade, many of whom attained high rank. Both Dillons were killed leading their regiments in Fontenoy and Lafelt. 'This honest and brave officer whom I esteemed and loved,' referred Louis XV to the loss of Colonel James Dillon at Fontenoy, 'I know he has a brother who is an ecclesiastic, give him the first vacant benefice, if he is worthy, as I believe him to be.'[4] His brother Richard was Archbishop of Narbonne and was an influential figure in the French Church. General Arthur Dillon was also an active figure in France in the last quarter of the eighteenth century and the cause of Irish freedom was always close to his heart. In 1792, he spoke at a meeting in Paris of the enslaved condition of Ireland and expressed his hope that 'the time was near when he would give his sword to the service of his own land'.[5] King Louis had once complained to him that of all the troops in his service, the Irish gave him the most trouble. Dillon replying, 'the enemy make the same complaint, your Majesty.'[6]

Conclusion

The Dillons were close to the Stuart Court, where Arthur Dillon's wife was maid of honour to James's wife, Mary of Modena. Seven members of the family served under French colours in the American Revolutionary War. Edouard Dillon was wounded at Savannah and Billy Dillon was wounded at Yorktown. The Dillons were highly regarded in Ireland; Marmaduke Coghill, the great pillar of Irish Protestantism, described them as 'the persons the Irish have languished for and whom they have always depended on to lead and support them when occasion offered … nobody has been more firmly attached to the Pretender's interest than this family of Dillon.'[7]

Ireland was always the Achilles' heel for any invasion of the British Isles. Historians agree that their greatest chances of success were in 1796 when 15,000 French troops were moored off the Kerry coast and during the 1745 Scottish Rising. The French should have opened a second Jacobite front in Ireland in the '45', in tandem with a landing in Scotland. Charles may then have continued his march to London and not turned back at Derby. The British army in Flanders may have diverted to Ireland, and not to Scotland, thereby giving Charles a greater chance of success.

Irish migration was also part of high adventure; Captain Andrew McDonagh from Co. Sligo was an officer in Dillon's, and became known as the Irish Monte-Cristo. McDonagh's extended family contributed forty-two members to the Irish Brigade of France. He was imprisoned on a trumped-up charge of plotting the murder of an Irish count in Brussels. He made a daring escape in the woods near Dijon while en route to prison in the south of France but was recaptured. He was held for twelve years in a dark, damp cell – six yards by five – in the Isle of St Marguerite, off Cannes, in the south of France. He occupied the same cell as the mysterious state prisoner known simply as 'the Man in the Iron Mask' nearly 100 years previously. That prisoner was thought to be a member of the nobility but his identity was never revealed. Voltaire described him as wearing 'a mask, the chin-piece of which had steel springs to enable him to eat while still wearing it, and the guards had orders to kill him if he uncovered his face.'[8] McDonagh was eventually released during the Revolution, was exonerated of his alleged crime and successfully sued his accusers. He rejoined the French army where he was

John Petrie, *A Portrait of Prince Charles entering Holyroodhouse, 1746*. The return of the Stuart king to the home of his ancestors. (Courtesy of the Royal Collection, HM Queen Elizabeth II)

promoted to lieutenant colonel and was last recorded as having joined Wolfe Tone in the aborted invasion of Ireland in 1796.[9]

The achievements of the Wild Geese were also the very stuff of fairy tales. Chevalier Charles Wogan was a long-standing friend and confidant to James III, 'the Old Pretender', and was chosen to select a suitable bride for James from among the Catholic princesses of Europe. Wogan choose the 16-year-old Princess Maria Clementina, the daughter of the King of Poland. The British were concerned about the prestige this marriage would bring to James and pressured Charles VI of Austria to stop the union. He arrested the princess and put her under guard in Innsbruck Castle in the Austrian Tyrol, where she was persuaded to marry the Prince of Baden-Baden. Like knight-errants in an Arthurian legend, Wogan together with three Irish officers of Dillon's – Captain Lucas O'Toole, Major Richard Gaydon and Captain John Misset – organised the princess's rescue. They set off on horseback from Strasburg, journeying through the Brenner Pass in atrocious weather to Innsbruck. Clementina switched clothes with her maid, who was instructed to stay in bed and feign sickness until the princess was well clear. Wogan and his party arrived in Rome, where the princess married James in a royal wedding. Pope Clement XI made Wogan and his three musketeers Roman Senators for their undertaking –the highest civil honour the city could bestow. James also showered them with military titles. Clementina was the mother of Charles Edward, later known as Bonnie Prince Charlie, and Henry Benedict, the Duke of York.[10] During the French Revolution, other Irish officers devised a plan to 'spring' the French Queen, Marie Antoinette and bring her to safety in the south-west of Ireland. In perhaps the greatest fairy-tale of all, the lifelong dream of many was in restoring to the throne the rightful king who had been removed by an usurper.

Charles Wogan corresponded regularly with Dean Swift in the 1730s and a friendship developed between the two men. Wogan wrote to Swift, concerned that Irish officers were not receiving due recognition in the armies of Europe. The British frequently called upon the French to disband of Irish regiments in their service, and Wogan suspected the British of applying diplomatic pressure in Europe, to favour promotions of Scottish, German and Italian officers at the expense of the Irish. Jonathan Swift (the Irish Voltaire) penned a beautiful reply to Wogan, which perhaps encapsulates Irish military migration abroad:

> I cannot but highly esteem those gentlemen of Ireland who, with all the disadvantages of being exiles and strangers, have been able to distinguish themselves by their valour and conduct in so many parts of Europe, I think, above all other nations.[11]

The Irish revered the Stuarts as their sovereign but also used them for their own political purposes. The Stuarts represented the best hope of restoring Catholic rights and lands back to the Irish. Ironically it was a Stuart King, James I, who advocated colonising Ulster with loyal British subjects in the seventeenth-century Plantation of Ulster to quell rebellion.[12] The French used the Stuarts as pawns in their European strategy by diverting British military resources from the Continent in times of war. Eamonn O'Ciardha described Ireland's association with the Stuarts as a 'fatal attachment', as all attempts of restoring a Stuart to the throne failed and led to Irishmen fighting against Irishmen far away from Ireland. Indeed, the Catholic Stuart king's presence in France and of his army in waiting, the Irish Brigade, threatened the very fabric of the Irish Protestant Ascendency. Both contributed to the maintenance of the Penal Laws and of subsequent British policy in Ireland, which would ultimately result in the Great Famine of the 1840s.

History is of course full of what ifs, but one cannot help wonder how different Ireland's fate would have been, if William's wound at the Boyne had proved fatal, or if the French commander Sainte Ruth had not been decapitated at Aughrim when victory was near. If James himself had been killed at the Boyne, or if his son had been captured in Scotland during the '15, it is probable that the Penal Laws would have been relaxed many years earlier. Catholics and Protestants may have been able to grow and prosper in partnership, presenting a strong, united front to offset and oppose British policies, designed to limit Ireland's economic and political development. No doubt the British would have found formidable political opponents in the likes of the O'Briens, the Dillons, the Lallys, the O'Reillys and the McDonnells to name but a few.[13]

These are the forgotten men (and women) of Irish history, and many thousands lie scattered in forgotten graves: 'For in far foreign fields, from Dunkirk to Belgrade,' wrote Davis, 'lie the soldiers and chiefs of the Irish Brigade.' We should remember the common soldiers and junior officers who would never obtain the glory of the Order of St Louis, the Legion of Honour or high rank; men such as James Russell from Co. Louth, a farrier with twenty-four years' service with Fitzjames' horse who received multiple sabre slash wounds to his head and body at the Battle of Rossbach in 1757; Thomas Kelly, quartermaster with twenty-nine years' service in Fitzjames', still suffering from the effects of an old wound received at Fontenoy, nearly twenty years earlier; Lieutenant John MacHenry, an Ulster Presbyterian serving in Napoleon's Irish Legion, who died in the hospital at Landeneau while undergoing treatment for a swollen knee; Sergeant Hugh Cullen of Berwick's, from Rathfarnham, Dublin, declared medically unfit after sustaining injuries falling down the stairs in the barracks in Lorient;[14] Lieutenant Michael Davoren from Clare's, whose leg was amputated due to a wound received at Fontenoy and who died of his wounds two days later; Lieutenant Thomas Farrell of Dillon's mentioned in the Obituaries of *The Gentleman's Magazine*, having died of fever in Port-au-Prince, Haiti; the two 14-year-old lads, Francois Hickey and Daniel Hagan, attached to Clare's Regiment, who were killed in action in the Battle of Lafelt.

Ireland lost the flower of her nation during the 'long' eighteenth century. The Irish arrived landless and stripped of their titles on the Continent but still managed to hold high civil positions in the courts of Vienna, Madrid or Versailles. Drawing upon a network of kin and patronage, they used their noble background to their full advantage. Their education and their contacts in high places enabled them to springboard themselves into positions of power and influence. This was well demonstrated in the famous St Patrick's Day party held in Vienna in 1766. The Spanish Ambassador to Vienna had invited prominent Irishmen to attend. Among the guests were Field Marshal Count Lacy (President of the Council of War), with Generals Browne, Maguire, McElligott, O'Donnell, O'Kelly and Thomas Plunket.[15] Other Irishmen in attendance were four chiefs of the Grand Cross; two governors; several knights; six staff officers and four privy-counsellors. According to the *Annual Register*, all the officers of state and the whole Court wore Celtic crosses to show their respect, and to honour the Irish nation.[16]

Irishwomen were ladies-in-waiting to Queen Marie Antoinette and mistresses to King Louis. Lady Clare was Lady of the Bedchamber to James's wife, Mary of Modena, after Lord Clare's death in Ramillies. Thérése-Lucy Dillon, the wife of the guillotined General Arthur Dillon, was Lady of the Bedchamber to Marie Antoinette and was reportedly a great favourite of hers.[17] Their daughter, Fanny Dillon, married General Bertrand and accompanied Napoleon as part of his entourage, when he was exiled to Elba and St Helena. Desireé and Julie Clary were daughters of a wealthy Irish merchant in Marseille and in 1794 met the Bonapartes. Desireé was for a time Napoleon's fiancé and her sister Julie married Napoleon's brother, Joseph Bonaparte and became Queen of Spain, while Desireé married Carl XIV of Sweden.[18] Other Irishwomen had boutiques on the fashionable Champs Elysees. Marie Louise O'Murphy was the daughter of a soldier in the Irish Brigade and briefly replaced Madame de Pompadour as Louis's favourite mistress. In 1753 she was installed in rooms at Fontainebleau, and gave birth to Louis's illegitimate daughter, Agathe Louise. But she was banished from Court and was quickly married off to a young officer. She was later imprisoned as a foreigner during the Revolution.[19]

Other Irishmen played a part in the development of newly founded South American countries through their service in Spain. Thomas Wright founded the Ecuadorian navy and William Brown the Argentinian navy. Bernardo O'Higgins is regarded as the co-liberator of Chile and his second in command was Monaghan-born General John McKenna.[20] Lieutenant General Alexander O'Reilly from Co. Meath was regarded as a trouble-shooter in the New World. He was the Spanish governor of Havana, and was a key figure in modernising the Spanish army and establishing Spanish power in Louisiana and New Orleans.[21] Abbé Henry Edgewoth from Co. Longford was the friend and confessor of Louis XVI, and on Louis's request, attended him at the scaffold prior to his execution.[22] He later became chaplain to his successor, Louis XVIII. Richard Wall, an ex-officer of Hibernia's, was Prime Minister of Spain from 1754 to 1763.

They also excelled in medical circles, one of the few professions open to Catholics in Ireland: Dr Moore accompanied the great liberator, Simon Bolivar 'the George Washington of South America' from Venezuela to Peru. Irish exiles were physicians to Philip V of Spain and Sobrieski of Poland. John MacSheedy was described as the *premier medicin* to Louis XVI.[23] Napoleon's doctors in St Helena, Dr Barry O'Meara and Dr James Verling, were also Irishmen.

For many, service in the Irish regiments was a precursor to a career in business. Irish families established the 'wine geese' vineyards in Bordeaux; families such as the Joyces, McCarthys, Bartons, Kirwins and Lynches, many of whom are still operating. In the 1770s, three of the eight largest vineyards were Irish owned, and they controlled one-half of all French wine exported to the British Isles. In 1748, Richard Hennessy from Co. Cork migrated to France following a long family tradition. He served in the Irish Brigade and later established his distillery in Cognac where business bloomed. Irish merchants were active in Nantes, La Rochelle, Cadiz, Saint-Malo, Ostende and Dunkirk where their fluency in English assisted them in establishing colonial trading links between the continental powers and the emerging British Empire and elsewhere.

The Irish punched above their weight on the Continent. The select few held the coveted French marshal's baton, such as Patrick Sarsfield, Henri Clarke and Lord Clare. Many more rose to the highest military rank of field marshal. All over Europe one could find Irish counts and barons, knights of Saint Leopold and of the Order of St Louis, of the Golden Fleece and of the White Eagle, honours awarded by the European monarchs to officers for exceptional merit and bravery. This is perhaps unsurprising as many of these emigrants emanated from the Gaelic aristocracy or from old stock Hiberno-Norman families. If they had stayed at home, they would have remained pariahs in their own country, having to sell their horse to a protestant for £5. By seeking their fortune abroad, over 100 Irishmen became field marshals, generals or admirals in the Imperial Austrian army. During the French Revolution there were ten Irish-born generals serving in France, dispelling claims that the Irish were mainly Royalist. Marshal Henri Clarke was the French Minister of War and was on horseback beside Napoleon at Waterloo. Dubliner General Charles Kilmaine was a close friend to Napoleon and rose to commander-in-chief of the French army in Italy.

There were Irish generals and marshals in Spain, Austria, Russia, France and Sardinia. They were some of the great military minds of the day, men such as Generals O'Mahony, O'Donnell, O'Neill, O'Gara and O'Reilly in Spain, along with Field-Marshal Brown, D'Alton, Taafe and Lacy in Austria and Russia. Franz Moritz von Lacy, the son of Irish-born Field-Marshal Peter de Lacy reformed the Austrian army, which led Austria rivalling Prussia. He was credited with mobilising 300,000 men against Frederick the Great of Prussia during the War of the Bavarian Succession of 1778–79. These men were great military reformers and could rival the great military theorist, Marshal General of France, Maurice de Saxe. What a remarkable feat for a small country like Ireland. What a pity that men of such calibre – the true chieftains of Ireland – had to seek fame and fortune abroad. One wonders what they would have achieved at home if they had not been forced away.

Their descendants were prominent on the Continent right up to the last century. Gottfried Von Banfield was a famous Austrian flying ace during the First World War, who could trace his ancestry back to the Wild Geese of Austria. Some of their descendants achieved high political office. In the nineteenth century, Eduard Counte Taafe von Carlingford became prime minister of Austria and Leopoldo O'Donnell became prime minister of Spain. Marshal of France, Patrice MacMahon was president of the Third French Republic in 1873 and Aristide Briant was president in the 1920s, and both were of Irish descent. The genealogist Chevalier Thomas O'Gorman provided proof of nobility for an ancestor of President MacMahon's and laid out the family's genealogy from the time of the High King of Ireland Brian Boru in the eleventh century.[24]

The most famous president of France – and perhaps the most famous Frenchman of all time – General Charles de Gaulle was also of noble Milesian blood. He was descended from the prominent McCartan clan who ruled part of Co. Down in the north of Ireland.[25] The family later settled in Lille, in northern France – a city with close links with the Irish Brigade – where many practised medicine. de Gaulle's ancestor was Anthony McCartan, who departed Limerick with the Irish army in the Flight of the Wild Geese in 1691 and served as a captain in the Irish Brigade in France. His great-great-grandfather was Dr Andronicus McCartan, who travelled to Dublin in 1837 to check the family's genealogy. De Gaulle's grandmother was a Hibernophile who wrote a biography on Daniel O'Connell. The Battle of Fontenoy and the exploits of the Irish Brigade must have captured the imagination of the young Charles, well known to have a keen interest in history, as he attended boarding school as a teenager in the village where the battle was fought. Charles was proud of his Irish ancestry and one wonders if the battle helped provide the impetus for Charles, a professor's son, to embark on his successful military career.

> To this day, in dusty chateaux in rural France, families proudly maintain genealogical tables which, in many cases, date back to 11th Century High King Brian Boru. Although many of these *Les Oies Sauvages* (Wild Geese) send their children to Ireland for some part of their education, they still retain a romantic view of the motherland that is perhaps as out of touch with Ireland of today as their frequent proclaimed royalist views are out of step with modern France.[26]

Miles Byrne in his *Memoirs* lamented the death of the '98 Kildare rebel leader, William Aylmer, who fought and was killed in South America; 'how melancholy it is to think of such brave men not having a country of their own to fight for!'[27] Alymer had served as a captain in the Austrian army, and recruited a South American legion with the aim of unseating the Spanish in South America. Byrne records that if he had lived, Simon Bolivar would have rewarded him. The Irish had taken part in almost all the theatres of war in Europe in the eighteenth and early nineteenth centuries. They served in the Americas, under General Montcalm; on the banks of the St Lawrence river; in the swamps of Georgia, Louisiana and Florida; and alongside General Washington in Yorktown. They waged a dirty guerrilla war against Spanish nationalists in Spain and saw action against the Cossacks in the east. They besieged fortresses in islands off the coast of Venezuela, in the West Indies and in the Mediterranean. They fought against the British Empire in India; served to protect French slaving interests in Senegal; fought against the Moors in North Africa; and suppressed slave revolts in the islands of the Caribbean. Fate dictated that they would not mount a landing into Ireland; but instead were destined forever to remain, in the words of the poet Emily Lawless 'Fighters in every clime, every cause but their own.'[28]

Notes

Introduction
1. 'The Flight of the Wild Geese' in 1691 is sometimes mixed up with the 'Flight of the Earls' in 1607, where 100 or so of the Gaelic nobility departed from County Donegal, signalling the fall of the Gaelic Order.
2. F. McLynn, *The Jacobites* (London, 1985), p. 85.
3. Charles Forman, *A Letter to the Rt. Hon. Sir Robert Sutton for Disbanding the Irish Regiments in the Service of France and Spain* (Dublin, 1728), p. 17.
4. A brigade is a military formation comprising two or more regiments. A regiment is a military administrative unit of around 1,000 men, commanded by a colonel, typically made up of two battalions (500–600 each) each commanded by a lieutenant colonel. These were broken down into smaller tactical units of companies or cavalry squadrons (around 90 men) led by majors or captains. These were further reduced into cavalry troops or infantry platoons, commanded by lieutenants. Aide-de-camps (ADC) are personal aides to senior officers. Non-commisioned officers (NCO) comprised the ranks of corporal or sergeant.
5. H. Murtagh, 'Irish Soldiers Abroad 1600–1800', in T. Bartlett and K. Jeffreys (eds), *A Miltary History of Ireland* (Cambridge, 1996), p. 304.
6. Lieutenant Colonel W. Cavanagh, 'Irish Knights of the Imperial Order of Maria Therese', *The Journal of Royal Society of Antiquarians of Ireland*, sixth series, vol. 16 (December 1926), pp. 95–105.

7. Cited in William O'Connor, *The Memoirs of Gerald O'Connor* (London, 1903).
8. The fourteenth-century Irish-language *Great Book of Lecan* and the *Book of Ballymote* were brought to France and deposited in the Irish College in Paris for safekeeping. The sixth-century book of psalms known as the Cathach relic (the battle standard of the O'Donnell clan) contains a Latin psalter believed to have been written by St Colmcille, and also left with the Irish army to France. The Ulster O'Donnells raised a regiment for James in 1689 and followed him to France. It was usual for local chieftains to carry relics consecrated by a local saint into battle. The Cathach (an Irish word meaning 'battler') contains an ancient Latin psalm protected in a silver decorated casket. It is thought to be the oldest psalter in Ireland and the second oldest in the world. It was worn around the neck of a holy man who walked clockwise three times around the clan before the battle began in the hope that it would bring victory. The Cathach returned to Ireland later in the eighteenth century. It is now displayed in the National Museum in Dublin. The O'Donnells repaired the Cathach's casket sometime in the mid-eighteenth century and included a dedication to 'James III'. The historian Eamon O'Ciardha finds it fitting that this ancient relic of Irish Christianity and of the Irish military diaspora should be associated with the Stuarts.
9. J.C. O'Callaghan was a Young Irelander and editor of *The Nation* newspaper and memorably wrote: 'I love, not the entremets of literature but, the strong meat of sedition – I make a daily meal of the smoked carcass of Irish history.'
10. Voltaire, *Histoire du siècle de Louis XIV*, vol. 2 (Paris, 1879), p. 20.
11. In 1738, Chevelier Richard Gaydon began a regimental history of Dillon's but it remained unpublished. General Theobald Dillon's grandson started a history of the Irish Brigades, but was unfinished at the time of his death in 1874. The Liberator's son, John O'Connell, had also collected material to write a history of the Irish Brigades before his untimely death aged 48.
12. *The Gentleman's Magazine*, vol. 8 (1837), p. 153.

1. The Recruitment of the Irish Regiments Abroad
1. C. Chenevix Trench, *Grace's Card: Irish Catholic Landlords 1690–1800* (Cork, 1997).
2. J.G. Simms, *The Williamite Confiscation in Ireland, 1690–1703* (London, 1976), p. 160. Taking Daniel O'Connell's Irish Party in 1832 as an example, the party comprised thirty-two members of the Catholic gentry and nine Protestants, eight of whom emanated from converted Catholic families.

3. I. McBride, *Eighteenth Century Ireland* (Dublin, 2009), p. 188.
4. Cited in McBride, *Eighteenth Century Ireland*, p. 188.
5. Cited in E. O'Ciardha, *Ireland and the Jacobite Cause, 1685–1766* (Dublin, 2004), p. 295.
6. Thomas Bartlett, *Ireland: A History* (Cambridge, 2010), p. 203.
7. Edith Mary Johnston (ed.), *Ireland in the Eighteenth Century* (Dublin, 1974), p. 17.
8. Cited in Valerie Pakenham, *The Big House in Ireland* (London, 2000), p. 65.
9. *Ibid.*, p. 69.
10. K. Whelan, An Underground Gentry? Catholic Middlemen in Eighteenth-Century Ireland in *The Tree of Liberty*, 1760-1830 (Cork, 1996), p. 21.
11. Chenevix Trench, *Grace's Card*, p. 101.
12. *Ibid.*, p. 210.
13. L.M. Cullen, 'The Irish Diaspora of the Seventeenth and Eighteenth Centuries', in N. Canny (ed.), *Europeans on the Move: Studies on European Migration, 1500–1800* (Oxford, 1994), p. 134.
14. Chenevix Trench, *Grace's Card*, p. 212.
15. L.M. Cullen, *The Irish Brandy Houses in 18th Century France* (Dublin, 2000), p. 72.
16. Terry Crowdy, *French Warship Crews 1789–1805* (Oxford, 2005), p. 12.
17. M. Culligan and P. Cherici, *The Wandering Irish in Europe* (London, 2000), p. 166.
18. Richard Hayes, *Ireland and Irishmen in the French Revolution* (London, 1932), p. 156. 8. In the 1930s, Dr Richard Hayes MD produced several well-regarded books on the Irish diaspora in France. He was 'out' in the 1916 Easter Rising and was sentenced to death by the British, along with around 100 others. Fifteen rebels were executed, but after the British shot the wounded James Connolly strapped to his chair, international outrage forced the executions to stop. Those that had been sentenced to death had those sentences commuted instead to twenty years' penal servitude. Luckily for us, Hayes lived on to write his extensive work on the Irish in France, for which he received France's *Legion d'honneur*. Michael O'hAnnrachain, who was also 'out' in 1916, wrote a novel centred on the Irish Brigade of France called *A Swordsman of the Brigade* (Dublin, 1914). He was second in command of the rebel garrison that occupied Jacob's factory, Dublin, in 1916 and wasn't as lucky as Hayes, as he was one of the fifteen who were executed by the British.
19. J. DeCourcy Ireland, *Ireland and the Irish in Maritime History* (Dun Laoighaire, 1986), p. 213.

20. J.G. Simms, 'The Irish on the Continent, 1691–1800', in T.W. Moody and W.E. Vaughan (eds), *A New History of Ireland, Volume IV: Eighteenth-Century Ireland 1691–1800* (Oxford, 1996), p. 644.
21. DeCourcy Ireland, *Ireland and the Irish in Maritime History*, pp. 211–12.
22. *Ibid.*, pp. 209, 21.
23. Sir Richard D. Henegan, *Seven Years Campaigning in the Peninsula and in the Netherlands, from 1808 to 1815, vol. 2* (London, 1846), pp. 126–7.
24. Miles Byrne, *Memoirs of Miles Byrne: Chef De bataillon in the Service Of France: Officer of the Legion of Honour, Knight of Saint Louis*, vol. 2 (Paris, 1863), pp. 143–4.
25. Johnston (ed.), *Ireland in the Eighteenth Century*, p. 98.
26. Michael Baigent and Richard Leigh, *The Temple and the Lodge* (New York, 1989), p. 7.
27. Chenevix Trench, *Grace's Card*, p. 221.
28. *The Gentleman's Magazine* (1789).
29. Printed in *Memoirs of the House of Taafe*, p. 74.
30. Daniel O'Connell, 'the Liberator', came from a Catholic aristocratic family in Derrynane in Co. Kerry and was typical of this migration. He was sent to France for his education when he was 14 years old, but narrowly escaped with his life, back to Ireland, when the French Revolution erupted. He witnessed the violence and upheaval of the Revolution, and perhaps this event shaped his desire for peaceful, nonviolent agitation in Ireland.
31. Cullen, 'The Irish Diaspora of the Seventeenth and Eighteenth centuries', p. 23.
32. McBride, *Eighteenth Century Ireland*, p. 188.
33. Cullen, 'The Irish Diaspora of the seventeenth and eighteenth centuries', p. 121.
34. H. Murtagh, 'Irish Soldiers Abroad', p. 312.
35. Cullen, 'The Irish Diaspora of the seventeenth and eighteenth centuries', p. 134.
36. *Ibid.*, p. 124.
37. *Ibid.*
38. Colm James O'Conaill, 'The Irish regiments in France: An Overview of the Presense of Irish Soldiers in French Service, 1716–1791', in E. Maher and G. Neville (eds), *France–Ireland: Anatomy of a Relationship* (Frankfurt, 2004), p. 336. In 1716 a royal decree directed that all French commanders maintain accurate records of rank and file and non-commissioned officers (NCOs).

39. Cullen, 'The Irish Diaspora of the Seventeenth and Eighteenth Centuries', p. 135.
40. *Ibid.*, pp. 139–40.
41. Cullen, 'The Irish Diaspora of the Seventeenth and Eighteenth Centuries', p. 133.
42. Cited in p. Higgins, *The Irish Brigade on the Continent* (London, 1908), p. 58.
43. M. O'Conor, *Military History of the Irish Nation, Comprising a Memoir of the Irish Brigade in the Service of France* (Dublin, 1855), pp. 406–7.
44. O'Conaill, 'The Irish Regiments in France', p. 335.
45. E. O'hAanrachain, 'An Analysis of the Fitzjames Cavalry Regiment, 1737', *The Irish Sword*, vol. 19 (1994), p. 254.
46. R. Hayes, *Irish Swordsmen of France* (Dublin, 1934), pp. 10–11.
47. Higgins, *The Irish Brigade on the Continent*.
48. Cullen, 'The Irish Diaspora of the seventeenth and eighteenth centuries'.
49. K. Whelan, 'The Irish in France in the Eighteenth Century', in J. Conroy (ed.), *Franco-Irish Connections: Essays, Memoirs and Poems in Honour of Pierre Joannon* (Dublin, 2009), p. 316.
50. Cullen, *The Irish Brandy Houses in 18th Century France*, p. 73.
51. Cited in O'Ciardha, *Ireland and the Jacobite Cause*, p. 259.
52. Chenevix Trench, *Grace's Card*, p. 10.
53. J.C. O'Callaghan, *History of the Irish Brigades in the Service of France, from the Revolution in Great Britain and Ireland under James II, to the Revolution in France under Louis XVI* (Glasgow, 1870), p. 263.
54. Dr B. O'Meara, *Napoleon in Exile*, vol. 1 (London, 1822), p. 482.
55. E. Fraser, *The War Drama of the Eagles: Napoleon's Standard Bearers on the Battlefield in Victory and Defeat from Austerlitz to Waterloo, a Record of Hard Fighting, Heroism and Adventure* (New York, 1912), p. 221.
56. Infantry in the period formed hollow squares to impede enemy cavalry charges, and this tactical battle formation was used extensively in Waterloo.
57. Cited in D. and J. Bowen, *Heroic Option: The Irish in the British Army* (Yorkshire, 2005), p. 72.
58. R. Holmes, Redcoat: The British Soldier in the Age of Horse and Musket (London, 2001), p. 63.

2. The Character of the Brigade

1. F.H. Skrine, 'The Irish Brigades, 1689–1750' a lecture delivered before the Irish Literary Society of London, 1 October 1921, p. 91.

2. O. Morales, *Ireland and the Spanish Empire, 1600–1825* (Dublin, 2010), p. 275.
3. *Ibid.*
4. E. O'hAnnrachain, *The Irish Brigade at Lafelt 1747: Pyrrhic Victory and Aftermath*, reprinted from *Journal of the Cork Historical and Archeological Society* (1997), p. 11
5. H. Murtagh, 'Irish soldiers abroad', pp. 313–14.
6. *Ibid.*
7. J. Roche, *Critical and Miscellanous Essays by an Octogenarian* (Cork, 1851), p. 51.
8. One of the prized exhibits in the Irish College in Paris is an English–Irish dictionary signed by Thomas Lally's son, Trophime-Gerard Lally. Although he was the second generation to be born in France, his dictionary suggests that the Irish language was spoken within the Irish community in France.
9. M. Kelly, 'Reminiscences', *The Irish Sword*, vol. 17, no. 66, p. 3.
The D'Alton's were perhaps the most famous Irish military families of Austria. They came from an old Norman family that settled in Ireland in the twelfth century. The family had owned lands at Mount D'Alton in Rathconradh in Co. Westmeath. The D'Alton brothers emigrated to Austria and were clearly men of exceptional ability, as three of them rose to high rank there. Christopher retired to Dublin with the rank of colonel; James was a general and became governor of Gratz, and later retired to Brussels before fleeing to Ireland upon the outbreak of the French Revolution. His brother Richard became a field marshal who commanded the Austrian army in Flanders during the revolt there in the 1790s. He was poisoned and died there shortly afterwards. His cousin Edward D'Alton became a Lieutenant general and was killed in action during the siege of Dunkirk against the British in 1793. His death was also mentioned in the Obituaries of *The Gentleman's Magazine*, where 'the brave Irishman' was buried 'with great military pomp'. Major-General Count O'Donnell was born in Castlebar, Co. Mayo in 1726 and was a descendent of the prominent O'Donnell clan of Tyrconnell, a relation of 'Red Hugh' in Co. Donegal, who were descended from the High Kings of Ireland. O'Donnell married Princess Leopoldine of Constantinople, and their son became the finance minister of Joseph II and President of the Upper House of the Austrian Parliament. Another Kavanagh, General Charles I, held the plum job of governor of Prague and he also emanated from a royal Milesian background – his line extended way back to the MacMurrough Kavanaghs who were kings of Leinster in the first millennium.
10. Culligan and Cherici, *The Wandering Irish in Europe*, p. 155.

11. *Ibid.*
12. Cited in H. Murtagh, 'Irish Soldiers Abroad', p. 313.
13. *Ibid.*
14. Cited in E. O'hAnnrachain, 'Guests of France: A Description of the Invalides with an Account of the Irish in that Institution', in N. Genet-Rouffiac and D. Murphy (eds), *Franco-Irish Military Connections, 1590–1945* (Dublin, 2009), p. 56.
15. Johnston (ed.), *Ireland in the Eighteenth Century*, p. 90.
16. M. Begoña Villar Garcia, 'Irish Migration and Exiles in Spain', in T. O'Connor and M. Ann Lyons (eds), *Irish Communities in Early Modern Europe* (Dublin, 2006), p. 192.
17. Culligan and Cherici, *The Wandering Irish in Europe*, p. 134. O'Reilly emigrated from Baltrasna, Co. Meath as a young man and joined the Regiment of Ultonia of the Spanish Irish Brigade. He was injured during the War of the Austrian Succession and walked with a limp for the rest of his life. He rose to the rank of inspector general in the Spanish army.
18. Forman, *A Letter to the Rt. Hon. Sir Robert Sutton*, p. 17. Forman is referring to the War of the Spanish Succession (1701–14).
19. J. Smith, *The French Nobility in the Eighteenth Century: Reassessments and New Approaches* (Pennsylvania, 2006).
20. J. Barry, 'The Study of Family History in Ireland', McDonnell lectures delivered at UCC on 13 April 1967, p. 14.
21. Cited *ibid.*, p 15.
22. M. O'Connell, *The Last Colonel of the Irish Brigade, Count O'Connell, and Old Irish Life at Home and Abroad, 1745–1833*, vol. 5 (London, 1892), p. 16.
23. *Antrim McDonnells*, p. 150. I am reminded of a story from the Israeli occupied territories of the West Bank and East Jerusalem, seized by the Israelis following the 1948 Arab–Israeli War. The Palestinians were removed from their homes but still kept their front door keys as proof of ownership – and passed them down to the next generation in the hope their homes might yet be recovered.
24. O'Conaill, 'The Irish regiments in France', p. 329.
25. *Ibid.*, p. 329.
26. In 1794 their uniforms were replaced with white, until 1808 when unpopular light blue uniforms exclusive to the three Irish regiments were worn. These were faced with yellow, with different colour collars and lapels to differentiate the regiments.

Notes

27. G.A. Hayes-McCoy, *A History of Irish Flags from Earliest Times* (Dublin, 1979), p. 65. This military motto was first used by the first Christian Roman Emperor Constantine in the fourth century, and was later adopted by the Knights Templar Military Order during the Crusades. It was a very apt motto for the Irish Brigades.
28. The gorget was probably the last relic of armour, originally providing protection to the wearer's neck; it was worn by officers while on duty. The German *Wehrmacht* re-introduced it prior to the Second World War.
29. In 1726, the Irish political writer Jonathan Swift surveyed the eastern part of the country between Drogheda and Dundalk, and provides the extent of the destruction: 'When I arriv'd at this last town [Drogheda], the first mortifying sight was the ruins of several churches batter'd down by that usurper Cromwell, whose fanatick zeal made more desolation in a few days than the piety of succeeding prelates or the wealth of the town have in more than sixty years attempted to repair … Examining all the eastern towns of Ireland and you will trace this horrid instrument of destruction, in the defacing of churches, and particularly in destroying whatever was ornamental, either within or without them. We see in the several towns a very few houses scattered among the ruins of thousands, which he [Cromwell] laid level with their streets. Great numbers of castles, the country seats of gentlemen then in being, still standing in ruin, habitations for bats, daws and owls, without the least repairs or succession of other buildings. Nor have the country churches, as far as my eye could reach, met with any better treatment from him, nine in ten of them lying among their graves, and God only knows when they are to have a resurrection. When I passed from Dundalk, where this cursed usurpers handy-work is yet visible, I cast mine eyes around from the top of a mountain, from whence I had a wide and a waste prospect of several venerable ruins.' T. Sheridan and J. Swift, *The Intelligencer*, edited by J. Wooley (Cambridge, 1992), pp. 87–8.
30. O'Connor, *The Memoirs of Gerald O'Connor*, pp. 289–90.
31. Chenevix Trench, *Grace's Card*, p. 213.
32. Cullen, 'The Irish Diaspora of the Seventeenth and Eighteenth Centuries'.
33. Morales, *Ireland and the Spanish Empire*, p. 232.
34. E. O'hAnnrachain, *'Galériens*: The Irish Galley Slaves of France', *The Irish Sword*, vol. 25, no. 99 (2005–6), p. 2.
35. P. Waldon Bamford, *Fighting Ships and Prisons: The Mediterranean Galleys of France in the Age of Louis XIV* (London, 1973), p. 173.
36. N. Genet-Rouffiac, 'The Irish Jacobite Exile in France, 1692–1715', in T. Barnard and J. Fenlon (eds), *The Dukes of Ormond, 1610–1745* (Suffolk, 2000), p. 200.

37. J. O'Neill, 'Conflicting Loyalties: Irish Regiments in the Imperial Service, 1689–1710', *The Irish Sword*, vol. 17, no. 67 (1987–88), p. 117.
38. Antrim McDonnells, p. 139.
39. Cited in F.H. Skrine, Fontenoy and Great Britain's Share in the War of the Austrian Succession 1741–48 (Edinburgh, 1906), p. 41.
40. C. Jones, *The Great Nation: France from Louis XV to Napoleon 1715–99* (London, 2002), p. 140.
41. Cited in Hayes, *Irish Swordsmen of France*, p. 11. O'Connor remained in the Irish Brigade and rose to captain and, as we shall see, went on to capture the British governor of St Eustatius during the American War of Independence. While serving in the French Caribbean island of Guadeloupe in 1793 he was assassinated by French Revolutionary troops.
42. Morales, *Ireland and the Spanish Empire*.
43. Cited in Chenevix Trench, *Grace's Card*, p. 216.
44. Holmes, *Redcoat*, p. 33.
45. C. Jones, *The Great Nation*, p. 141.
46. Lieutenant John Cooke cited in Holmes, *Redcoat*, p. 165.
47. Holmes, *Redcoat*, p. 33.
48. Cited in Jeremy Black, *Warfare in the Eighteenth Century* (London, 1999), p. 162.
49. Tone took this jingle from a popular barrack-room song of the time, 'How Stands the Glass Around?'
50 J. Norris, *Pistols at Dawn: A History of Duelling* (Gloucestershire, 2009), p. 24.
51. Holmes, *Redcoat*, p. 284.
52. Norris, *History of Duelling*, p. 24.
53. M. de Saxe, *Reveries, or Memoirs upon the Art of War by Field Marshal Count Sax*, vol. 2 (London, 1757), p. 148.
54. C. Jones, *The Great Nation*, p. 141.
55. Humphrey Metzgen and John Graham, *Caribbean Wars Untold: A Salute to the British West Indies* (Jamaica, 2007), p. 46.
56. *Ibid*.

3. The Jacobite War (1689–91)
1. S. O'Callaghan, *To Hell or Barbados* (London, 2000), p. 9.
2. The Stuarts created titles and peers in the Jacobite peerage and continued this tradition while they were in exile. Although these Jacobite titles of sir, viscount, baron, earl, baronet, duke and lord, and their corresponding

female titles, including the chivalric Order of the Thistle, were not recognised under British law, they were recognised within Jacobite circles abroad, in France and Spain and by the Papacy.

3. J.G. Simms, *Jacobite Ireland, 1685–91* (London, 1969), p. 101.
4. *Ibid.*, p. 110.
5. H. Murtagh, 'Franco-Irish Military Relations in the Nine Years War, 1689–97', in Sarah Alyn Stacey and Véronique Desnain (eds), *Culture and Conflict in Seventeenth-Century France and Ireland* (Dublin, 2004), p. 250.
6. J.A. Murphy, 'Justin McCarthy, Lord Mountcashel Commander of the First Irish Brigade in France' an O'Donnell memorial lecture delivered at University College, Cork on 22 May 1958, p. 31.
7. H. Murtagh, 'Franco-Irish Military Relations', p. 251
8. J.A. Murphy, *Lord Mountcashel*, p. 35.
9. *Ibid.*, p. 37.
10. *Ibid.*
11. H. Murtagh, 'Irish Soldiers Abroad', p. 307.
12. J. Fitzjames, *Memoirs of the Marshal Duke of Berwick*, vol. 1 (London, 1779), p. 96.
13. K. Haddick-Flynn, *Sarsfield and the Jacobites* (Cork, 2003), p. 122.
14. D. and J. Bowen, *Heroic Option*, p. 9.
15. D. Murtagh, 'The Jacobite Horse', *The Irish Sword*, vol. 1 (1952–53), p. 320.
16. William Ridgeway, *The Origin and Influence of the Thoroughbed Horse* (Cambridge, 1905), pp. 390–2.
17. P. Lenihan, *1690 Battle of the Boyne* (Gloucestershire, 2003), p. 162. As the name suggests, the matchlock used a lighted cord (which was made more difficult in bad weather) to ignite the powder in the pan, which in turn ignited the main charge and fired the ball. The flintlock used flint to strike a piece of metal, when the trigger was pulled, which caused sparks to ignite the powder in the pan.
18. P. Wauchope, *Patrick Sarsfield and the Williamite War* (Dublin, 1992), p. 49.
19. Simms, *Jacobite Ireland*, p. 145.
20. Wauchope, *Patrick Sarsfield and the Williamite War*, p. 100.
21. The Old Style Julian calendar was in use until it was replaced by the New Style Gregorian calendar in 1752. Under the New Style, 1 July became 12 July.
22. Haddick-Flynn, *Sarsfield and the Jacobites*, p 123.

23. James was said to have been chased off his throne to the tune of 'Lillibulero', which made fun of the Irish brogue and superstitions, and was disrespectful to Richard Talbot the Earl of Tyrconnell, and to King James. The last verse ran as follows: 'Dare was an auld prophesy found in a bog, Ireland would be ruled by an ass and a dog, and now the auld prophesy has come to pass, For Talbot's a dog and James is an ass.'
24. Cited in Wauchope, *Patrick Sarsfield and the Williamite War*, p. 110.
25. O'Connor, *The Memoirs of Gerald O'Connor*, p. 60.
26. Fitzjames, *Memoirs of the Marshal Duke of Berwick*, vol. 1, pp. 75–6.
27. Cited in Wauchope, *Patrick Sarsfield and the Williamite War*, p. 123.
28. After the war, Galloping Hogan joined the Irish Brigade of France, but in 1705 he was forced to leave due to killing a fellow Irish officer in a duel, and he then entered the Portuguese army. He had a distinguished career, where he put his guerrilla skills to good use and rose to the rank of major-general in the Spanish army.
29. Ireland was one of the first countries in Europe to adopt a system of hereditary surnames, as the vast majority of Gaelic Irish surnames date from the eleventh-century. Previously people were known by their first name only, which was only useful when populations were small and the movement of people was uncommon. Under the Gaelic clan system, people adopted the prefix of 'Mac' or 'Mc', meaning the 'son of', or 'O', meaning 'grandson of', indicating kinship and signifying that they belonged to the same family or clan (the Irish word *clann* meaning family). The Irish tribe of 'Scoti' settled in western Scotland and gave the country its name and Gaelic clan system, which they retained along with their Gaelic names partly due to their geographical remoteness and by remaining relatively free of English domination in the early Middle Ages. With the fall of the Gaelic order, much of the Gaelic Irish clan system was gradually wiped out and many Gaelic names were anglicised or translated and lost their 'Mac' and 'O' prefixes.
30. J.A. Murphy, *Lord Mountcashel*.
31. Fitzjames, *Memoirs of the Marshal Duke of Berwick*, vol. 1, p. xiv.
32. Cited in Wauchope, *Patrick Sarsfield and the Williamite War*, p. 15.
33. Fitzjames, *Memoirs of the Marshal Duke of Berwick*, vol. 1, p. 7.
34. M. McNally, *The Battle of Aughrim 1691* (Gloucestershire, 2008), p. 61.
35. Wauchope, *Patrick Sarsfield and the Williamite War*.
36. Lenihan, *1690 Battle of the Boyne*, p. 8.
37. Cited in Wauchope, *Patrick Sarsfield and the Williamite War*, p. 232.

38. James arrived in Dublin short of funds and so melted down various metals such as old cannon and church bells into 'gunmoney'. This token coinage was effectively an IOU and was to be redeemed in their corresponding gold value when James was restored to the throne.

4. The Flight of the Wild Geese (1691)
1. Parallels can be drawn between the Jacobite Wars and the Irish War of Independence in 1921; Tyrconnell as DeValera, the experienced statesman, and Sarsfield as Collins. Sarsfield's guerrilla tactics on destroying the Williamite siege-train mirror Collins' hit-and-run guerrilla tactics in 1921. Both were iconic heroes of their day, and were soldiers sent to broker treaties where statesmen may have been better suited to the task.
2. Wauchope, Patrick Sarsfield and the Williamite War, p 272.
3. Simms, Jacobite Ireland, p. 259
4. C. O'Kelly, *The Jacobite War in Ireland 1688–90* (Dublin. 1894), p. 109.
5. Cited in Wauchope, Patrick Sarsfield and the Williamite War, p. 28.
6. Fitzjames, Memoirs of the Marshal Duke of Berwick, vol. 1, p. 93.
7. Cited in Simms, *Jacobite Ireland*, p. 256.
8. Fitzjames, Memoirs of the Marshal Duke of Berwick, vol. 1, p 329.
9. *Ibid*, p. xiv.
10. Cited in Wauchope, Patrick Sarsfield and the Williamite War, p. 284.
11. Fitzjames, Memoirs of the Marshal Duke of Berwick, vol. 1, p. 98.
12. McLynn, *The Jacobites*, p. 132.
13. Fitzjames, Memoirs of the Marshal Duke of Berwick, vol. 1, p. 100.
14. Cited in Wauchope, Patrick Sarsfield and the Williamite War, p. 293.
15. Patrick Sarsfield lies buried in the grounds of St Martin's Church, Huy, Belgium; a plaque on the wall of this church marks the approximate location of his grave.
16. Fitzjames, Memoirs of the Marshal Duke of Berwick, p. 380.
17. H. Murtagh, 'Franco-Irish military relations', p. 254.
18. E. Carp, 'The Irish at the Jacobite court of Saint Germain en Laye', in Thomas O'Connor (ed.), *The Irish in Europe, 1510–1815* (Dublin, 2001), p. 153.

5. The Day We Beat the Germans at Cremona
1. Daniel Szechi, 1715: The Great Jacobite Rebellion, p. 74.
2. O'Connor, The Memoirs of Gerald O'Connor, p. 30.
3. Cited in J.C. O'Callaghan, *Irish Brigades*, p. 207.

4. Cited in O'Conor, *Military History of the Irish Nation*, p. 250.
5. J.C. O'Callaghan, *Irish Brigades*, p. 216.
6. Arthur Conan Doyle, *The Poems of Arthur Conan Doyle* (London, 1922). The poet Emily Lawless also commemorated the battle:

> Homesick, sad, and weary,
>
> Heartsick, hungry, dreary,
>
> (Shout, boys, Erin's the renown!)
>
> O'Brien, Burke, and Tracy,
>
> MacMahon, Dillon, Lacy,
>
> We watch the town.

E. Lawless, 'Cremona', in *With the Wild Geese* (London, 1902).
7. E. O'hAnnrachain, 'Irish Involvement in Cremona, 1702', in Thomas O'Connor and Mary Ann Lyons (eds), *Irish Communities in Early Modern Europe* (Dublin, 2006), p. 452.
8. J.C. O' Callaghan, *Irish Brigades*, p. 204.
9. Francis Collinson, *The Bagpipe: The History of a Musical Instrument* (London, 1975), pp. 115–16.
10. J.C. O'Callaghan, *Irish Brigades*, p. 218.
11. *Ibid.*, p. 220.
12. Cited *ibid.*, p. 221.
13. Sir Edward Creasy, *The Fifteen Battles That Changed the World from Marathon to Waterloo* (London, 1851), p. 261.
14. O'Connor, *The Memoirs of Gerald O'Connor*, p. 159.
15. Charles Spencer, *The Battle for Europe: How the Duke of Marlborough Masterminded the Defeat of the French at Blenheim* (New Jersey, 2004), p. ii.
16. Thomas J. Mullen, Jr, 'The Seven Years War: Battle of Wandiwash', *Military History Magazine* (February 1994).
17. Cited in J.C. O' Callaghan, *Irish Brigades*, p. 234.
18. *Ibid.*, p. 240.
19. Cited in A.E.C. Bredin, *A History of the Irish Soldier* (Belfast 1987), p. 149.
20. Peter Drake, *The Memoirs of Capt. Peter Drake* (Dublin, 1755), p. 83.
21. A portion of the flag of the Scottish Regiment in the Dutch service survives. It is known as the 'Kylemore flag' and is lodged in Kylemore Abbey in Co. Galway. The surviving flag portion is the Irish harp quarter (in the form of the Maid of Erin) of the Royal Standard of

England, which was carried by the Scottish Regiment. In 1907, an aged Irish nun at the Irish Benedictine Convent in Ieper verified this as she recalled the flag in its original condition and described it to a visiting writer: 'It was attached to a stick, and I remember reading on a slip of paper which was on the flag "Remerciements Refuged at Ypres, 170." The flag consisted of three parts – blue with a harp, red with three lions, and yellow. The red and yellow parts were accidentally destroyed, and all that remains is the blue, as you see it, with a harp; and we have also preserved one of the lions. The story that has come down to us is that it was left here after the battle of Ramillies.' Barry O'Brien (ed.), *The Irish Nuns at Ypres: An Episode of the War* (London, 1915). In 1914, during the First World War, the nuns were evacuated when Ieper (located on the Western Front) was bombarded and flattened by the Germans, and they re-established themselves in Kylemore Abbey, Co. Galway. A modern rendition of the Maid of Erin is famous worldwide today as it has been adopted as Ryanair's logo.

22. P. Nolan, *The Irish Dames of Ypres* (Dublin, 1908), p. 236. The Irish Dominican College in Leuven did not survive the French Revolution, and the Irish Benedictine Convent at Ieper, Belgium was destroyed by German bombardment during the First World War.

23. Drake, *The Memoirs of Capt. Peter Drake*, p. 83. The nineteenth-century Young Ireland poet Thomas Davis commemorated the exploits of Clare's Regiment at Ramillies with the musical air: 'Clare's Dragoons'. Daniel O'Brien, 3rd Lord Clare, raised a mounted dragoon regiment during the Jacobite war. When Clare's Dragoons left Limerick with the Flight of the Wild Geese they became a regiment of infantry. 'Clare's Dragoons' survives today as the regimental march of the 27th Infantry Battalion of the Irish Defence Forces.

23. Drake, *The Memoirs of Capt. Peter Drake*, p. 84.

24. J.C. O'Callaghan, *Irish Brigades*, p. 240.

25. Chevalier Gaydon's Memoir of the Regiment of Dillon, 1738, pp. 120–1.

26. *Ibid.*

27. Nolan, *The Irish Dames at Ypres*, p. 227.

28. J.C. O'Callaghan, *Irish Brigades*, p. 264.

29. John Churchill, *Memoirs of John, Duke of Marlborough*, edited by William Coxe (London, 1819), p. 56.

30. Cited in J.C. O'Callaghan, *Irish Brigades*, p. 267.

31. *Ibid.*, p. 269.

32. McLynn, *The Jacobites*, p. 13.

33. The regiments who transferred from the French to the Spanish army were the Regiments of O'Mahony, Crafton and Fitzharris, followed in 1709 with Castlear, MacAuliffe and Comerford. Some of these regiments were disbanded after the war.
34. Bredin, *A History of the Irish Soldier*.

6. The First Jacobite Rising (1715)

1. Szechi, 1715: *The Great Jacobite Rebellion*, p. 88.
2. *Ibid.*, p. 81.
3. *Ibid.*, p. 46.
4. J.C. O' Callaghan, *Irish Brigades*, p. 302.
5. O'Ciardha, *Ireland and the Jacobite Cause*, p. 295.
6. F. McLynn, 'Ireland and the Jacobite Rising of '45', *The Irish Sword*, vol. 13, no. 53 (Winter 1979), pp. 339–52.
7. M. Ohlmever, *Civil War and Restoration in the Three Stuart Kingdoms: The Career of Randal McDonald, Marquis of Antrim* (Dublin, 2011), p. 7.
8. In the early fourteenth century, Irish chieftains requested assistance from King Robert de Bruce of Scotland (whose ancestor on his maternal side was the Irish High King Brian Boru) in removing the English presence from Ireland. Robert wished to establish a pan-Gaelic kingdom of Ireland and Scotland, and landed 6,000 troops and, together with their Irish allies, succeeded in removing the English from Ulster, pushing them back into fortified strongholds in other parts of the island. Throughout the sixteenth century, the Ulster Irish chieftains built up military, economic and cultural relationships with the Highlanders, and the warrior class of the Highland clans, called *gallowglasses*, were in great demand as mercenaries. T.M. Devine, 'Making the Caledonian connection: the development of Irish and Scottish studies', in L. McIlvanney and R. Ryan (eds), *Ireland and Scotland: Culture and Society, 1700–2000* (Dublin, 2005), p. 249.
9. S.J. Connolly, *Divided Kingdom: Ireland 1630–1800* (New York, 2008), p. 291.
10. O'Ciardha, *Ireland and the Jacobite Cause*, p. 183.
11. McLynn, 'Ireland and the Jacobite Rising of '45', p. 3.
12. Rebecca Wills, *The Jacobites and Russia, 1715–1750* (East Linton, 2002), p. 60.
13 J.C. O'Callaghan, *Irish Brigades*, p. 319.

7. The Battle of Fontenoy (1745)

1. J. White, *Marshal of France, The Life and Times of Maurice de Saxe* (London, 1962).
2. McLynn, *The Jacobites*, p. 13.
3. White, *Marshal Of France*, p. 156.
4. Skrine, *The Irish Brigades, 1689–1750*.
5. M. Walsh, 'Letters from Fontenoy', *The Irish Sword*, vol. 19, no. 78 (Winter 1995), p. 248. The confusion that the Royal Scots had fought in the battle was partly caused by the fact that the regiment's colonel, Sir John Drummond, was present at the battle as an observer with the Irish Brigade.
6. Hayes, *Irish Swordsmen of France*, p. 227.
7. White, *Marshal of France*, p. 159.
8. Voltaire wrote a more picturesque version of this event which has become legend, although it was untrue: that the English officer doffed his hat and offered the French first fire. However, Hay repudiated this and corroborated his less dramatic version of the event in a letter written to his brother.
9. Skrine, *Fontenoy and Great Britain's Share in the War of the Austrian Succession 1741–48*, p. 180.
10. *Ibid.*, p. 160.
11. W. Trowbridge, *A beau sabreur, Maurice de Saxe: Marshal of France, His Loves, His Laurels and His Times 1696–1750* (New York, 1910), p. 296.
12. White, *Marshal of France*, p. 154.
13. W.A. Cumberland, *Historical Memoirs of His Late Royal Highness William-Augustus, Duke of Cumberland* (London, 1767), p. 223.
14. Walsh, 'Letters from Fontenoy', p. 240.
15. The Irish had traditionally gone into battle with bagpipes since ancient times. The English outlawed their use as they were an instrument of war, and they eventually evolved into the less warlike uileann pipes, which are played while seated. In a 1581 volume, the father of the astronomer Galileo, the musician Vincenzo Galileo, wrote that the bagpipe 'is much used by the Irish: to its sound this unconquered fierce and warlike people march their armies and encourage each other to deeds of valor. With it they also accompany the dead to the grave making such sorrowful sounds as to invite, nay to compel the bystander to weep.' The great Irish warpipes were almost identical to

contemporary Scottish Highland pipes, although the Highland pipes would later add a third drone and some Irish pipes followed suit. Bagpipes played at Fontenoy were displayed in the Musee de Cluny, Paris and a colour plate was taken of them in the early twentieth century, but they were last seen in 1936 and have since disappeared without trace. These bagpipes had a green cover, two tenor drones and were nearly identical to the Scottish Highland bagpipes played at Culloden. Fontenoy was the last time Irish pipers played in action, with the exception of the Royal Irish Fusiliers of the British army in Tunisia in the Second World War. The British Prime Minister Sir Winston Churchill brigaded three battalions of Irish regiments in the British army into the 38th Irish Brigade in 1942, evoking their eighteenth-century predecessors in France and Spain. This Irish brigade comprised a battalion of the Royal Irish Fusiliers, the Royal Inniskilling Fusiliers and the Royal Ulster Rifles, served in Algeria, Tunisia and Italy and liberated Brussels in 1944. Sir Winston Churchill would have become well acquainted with the exploits and triumphs of the Irish Brigades of France and Spain when researching his autobiography of his ancestor in the early 1700s the Duke of Marlborough, John Churchill, *The Duke of Marlborough: His Life and Times.*

16. P. Lynch, 'The Battle of Fontenoy', *An Cosantoir*, vol. 1, no. 14 (1941), pp. 441–4.

17. White, *Marshal of France*, p. 162. A fragment of the Dillon colour which is thought to have flown at Fontenoy was presented in 1949 to the National Museum of Ireland by Vicomte Dillon, and is on display in the National Museum, Collins Barracks, Dublin.

18. C. Petrie, 'The Irish Brigade at Fontenoy', *The Irish Sword*, vol. 1, no. 3 (1951–52), pp. 166–72. Many of the wounded were brought to nearby Lille and Tounai. Lille was a long-time garrison town for the Irish regiments due to its proximity to the Channel ports. On a recent visit to Lille, I was dismayed to find little physical evidence that the Irish regiments were ever stationed there. The city's fortress, the Vauban-built La Citadelle de Lille, is not open to the public as it is still a functioning barracks used by the French army. However, I luckily stumbled across a commemorative tablet in the chapel of the Hospital Gomtesse (off the rue Gomtesse) inscribed with the names of officers in the French army who died in the hospital of wounds received, days and weeks after Fontenoy. Of the thirty-two officers listed, four are Irish: Lieutenant Thomas Paye of Fitzjames horse, Captain Christopher Plunket of Clare's, Cadet Etienne Coppinger of Dillon's, and Etienne O'Toole of the King's Household Cavalry of the Garde des Corps.

19. Cited in C. Algrant, *Madame de Pompadour: Mistress of France* (New York, 2002), p. 41.
20. Cited in Trowbridge, *A beau sabreur, Maurice de Saxe*, p. 298.
21. Haddick-Flynn, *Sarsfield and the Jacobites*, p. 211.
22. Cited in *The Celt*, 12 December 1857, p. 316.
23. Cited in John Mitchel, *The History of Ireland, from the Treaty of Limerick to the Present Time* (Dublin, 1868), p. 71.
24. Cited in Walsh, 'Letters from Fontenoy', p. 248.
25. *Ibid.*, p. 240.
26. Lieutenant Colonel A. Burnes, *The Art of War on Land, Illustrated by Campaigns and Battles of All Ages* (London, 1958), p. 123.
27. Cited in Petrie, 'The Irish Brigade at Fontenoy'.
28. J.P. Bois, *Fontenoy, 1745* (Paris, 1996), p. 96.
29. Skrine, *Fontenoy and Great Britain's Share in the War of the Austrian Succession*, p. 189.
30. Cited in M. de Saxe, *Maurice comte de Saxe et Marie-Josephe de Saxe Dauphine de France lettres et Documents inedits des Archives* (Paris, 1867).
31. Walsh, 'Letters from Fontenoy', p. 242.
32. The 1743 Royal Warrant standardised Regimental Colours in the British army such that British line regiments were to carry the Union flag and a regimental flag in the facing colour with a Union in the upper left canton.
33. Standards were the flags carried by cavalry and colours were the flags carried by infantry.
34. Cited in J. O'Donoghue, *Historical Memoirs of the O'Briens* (Dublin, 1860), p. 535.
35. Cited in F. Fitzgerald, 'The Battle of Fontenoy', *An Cosantoir*, vol. 5, no. 12 (1945), pp. 666–67.
36. This event was later commemorated by Horace Vernet's painting *La Bataille de Fontenoy* displayed in Versailles, Paris.
37. Cited in Petrie, 'The Irish Brigade at Fontenoy', pp. 166–72.
38. *Ibid.*
39. *Les Triomphes du Roy Louis le Grand* and *Les Triomphes de Louis XV*, Bibliotheque Nationale, Richelieu Site, Paris. Cabinet de Estampes. The motto of the flag, '*nisi Dominus frustra*' roughly translates as 'Except the Lord in vain'.

40. Also included are regimental colours taken when the Allied garrison surrendered at Ghent, Flanders in July 1745, two months after Fontenoy. These colours are from the Welsh Fusiliers, a Colonel's' colour from Handasyde's, another colour from an unknown Austrian regiment, a few cavalry guidons from Roth's Dragoons, and a couple of other flags I cannot identify. I have contacted the Guards Museum in London and they have confirmed that none of these flags belonged to the Coldstream Guards, or any other Guard's Regiment. This finally dispels the legend that the Coldstream Guards lost colours to the Irish Brigade in the battle.

41. The flag's motto '*nisi Dominus frustra*' is the motto of the city of Edinburgh, which associates it with the Edinburgh regiment of Sempill's foot. The King's Own Scottish Borderers (KOSB) regimental museum (the successor of Sempill's foot) have no reference to colours having been taken in the battle, nor was Sempill's present when the Allies surrendered at Ghent. They have advised that the colour concerned may have been an early regimental or company colour of the regiment. Many British regiments were known by the names of their proprietor-colonels before 1743 and their regimental colours were personal and embellished with elements of the colonel's family coat of arms. In 1745 the Regimental Colour of Sempill's may not yet have faced in the colour of the facings of the Regiment (i.e., yellow). Some regiments owned by proprietor-colonels still carried their own personalised colours; this is borne out by the non-standard personalised flags captured at Ghent and illustrated in the French MSS in Paris. It is also possible that the artist who drew the flag in the French MSS was working from an imperfect memory of the actual flag. The KOSB's regimental museum was intrigued and published my photo and an article over this colour in their 2012 annual regimental magazine *The Borderers*: 'A Colour of the 25th Regiment of Foot'.

42. Sempill's were raised in Edinburgh in 1689 against James's supporters during the Jacobite war and took part in the bloody Irish defeat in Aughrim and in the sieges of Athlone, Galway and Limerick. Sempill's later crossed swords with the Irish Brigade in Culloden when it was shipped from Flanders to serve in the Scottish Rebellion.

43. Fraser, *The War Drama of the Eagles*, p. 334. In 1907, a Celtic cross was erected at Fontenoy by public subscriptions raised in Ireland and America, inscribed: 'To the soldiers of the Irish brigade who on the field of Fontenoy avenged the violation of the Treaty of Limerick.' Thomas Mullins mentioned in his unpublished thesis 'The Ranks of Death' a photograph taken of the unveiling of this cross, which included the Irish-American Fenian leader John O'Leary and John McBride, who had a few years previously raised an Irish brigade

that served alongside the Boers in the South African Anglo-Boer War (1899–1902). The British executed McBride for his part in the 1916 Dublin Rising. Close to the battlefield at Fontenoy, a tablet also exists on the wall of the churchyard nearby: 'In memory of the heroic soldiers who changed defeat into victory at Fontenoy, 11 May 1745. God save Ireland.' In 1995, the Irish contribution to the battle was commemorated on its 250th anniversary with representatives from France, Belgium, England and Ireland, where Ireland was given pride of place. The Belgian and Irish Post Offices also issued a joint stamp of the battle; an exquisite composition, depicting two officers of Clare's and Dillon's standing beside the Celtic cross at Fontenoy. Thomas Davis helped immortalise the battle in Irish nationalist tradition in his epic poem *The Battle of Fontenoy*.

8. The Second Jacobite Rising (1745)

1. Hayes, *Irish Swordsmen of France*, p. 234.
2. Baigent and Leigh, *The Temple and the Lodge*, p 185. Walsh's grandfather had conveyed James II to France after the Jacobite War.
3. J Home, *The History of The Rebellion in 1745* (London, 1822), p26
4. A. and H. Taylor, *1745 and After* (London, 1938), p. 7.
5. *Ibid.*, p. 9.
6. Charles arrived in Scotland dressed in black and later wore tartan 'trews' (trousers) but did not adopt the *feileadh beag* or kilt until after the Battle of Culloden and his time 'in the heather'. The Highland officer class tended to wear tartan jacket and trousers while the ordinary Highland infantryman wore the kilt. The Irish officers who arrived in Scotland and served with Charles wore Highland plaid over their red uniforms for several reasons; for protection from the harsh Highland winter, and for their own safety, so as not to be confused with the redcoated British army. Two Irish officers, Captains McDermot and John Burke, reported that they and some of their fellow Franco-Irish officers wore Highland clothes to 'get protection from the Highlanders who joined us' and to avoid 'danger in travelling in red clothes'. Cited in Bruce Seton, 'Dress of the Jacobite army: the Highland habit', *The Scottish Historical Review*, vol. 25, no. 100 (July 1928), pp. 270–281.
7. Lord Mahon, *The Forty-Five*, vol. 1 (London, 1851), p. 28.
8. *Ibid.*, p. 68.
9. H. McDonnell, *The Wild Geese of the Antrim MacDonnells* (Dublin, 1996), p. 105.
10. A. and H. Taylor, *1745 and After*, p. 159.

11. Lord Mahon, *The Forty-Five*, p. 58.
12. McLynn, 'Ireland and the Jacobite Rising of '45', p. 348.
13. J.C. O' Callaghan, *Irish Brigades*, p. 396.
14. Lord Mahon, *The Forty-Five*, p. 80.
15. The Highlanders' treatment can be compared to the portrayal of the Irish Fenian revolutionaries in the 1850s as half men, half beasts by the notorious *Punch* magazine.
16. Chevalier Johnstone, *Memoirs of the Rebellion in 1745 and 1746* (London, 1820), p. 52.
17. Dudley Bradsheet, *The Life and Uncommon Adventures of Captain Dudey Bradsheet* (Dublin, 1755), p 127.
18. J.C. O'Callaghan, *Irish Brigades*, p. 398.
19. C. Klose, *Memoirs of Prince Charles*, vol. 1 (London, 1846), pp. 345–6.
20. Cited in J.C. O'Callaghan, *Irish Brigades*, p. 400.
21. D. Murphy, *The Irish Brigades 1685–2006* (Dublin, 2007), p. 146.
22. J.C. O'Callaghan, *Irish Brigades*, p. 424.
23. *Ibid.*, p. 420.
24. C. Petrie, 'Irishmen in the '45', *The Irish Sword*, vol 2, no. 8 (Summer 1956), p. 282.
25. McLynn, *1759*.
26. Johnstone, *Memoirs*, pp. 104–5.
27. A. and H. Taylor, *1745 and After*, p. 119.
28. *Ibid.*
29. Cited in Lord Mahon, *The Forty-Five*, vol. 1, p. 113.
30. Klose, *Memoirs of Prince Charles*, vol. 1, p. 409.
31. McLynn, *The Jacobites*, p. 86.
32. Stuart Reid, *Culloden Moor 1746: The Death of the Jacobite Cause* (East Sussex, 2002), p. 63.
33. Black trumpeters were widespread in cavalry regiments, as service in the army was a means of guaranteeing freedom from slavery.
34. A. McKenzie Annand, 'Fitzjames Horse in the '45', *The Irish Sword*, vol. 16, no. 65 (Winter 1986), p. 274.
35. R. Hayes 'Biographical dictionary of Limerickmen in France', *The Old Limerick Journal, French Edition*, vol. 25 (Summer 1989), p. 181.
36. McKenzie Annand, 'Fitzjames Horse in the '45', p. 273.
37. J.C. O'Callaghan, *Irish Brigades*, p. 436.

38. Hector McDonnell, 'Some documents relating to the involvement of the Irish Brigade in the rebellion of 1745', *The Irish Sword*, vol. 16 (1985), pp. 3–21.
39. Cited in J.C. O'Callaghan, *Irish Brigades*, p. 397.
40. J.C. O'Callaghan, *Irish Brigades*, p. 408.
41. Klose, *Memoirs of Prince Charles*, vol. 1 (London, 1846), p. 401.
42. Lord Mahon, *The Forty-Five*, p. 113.
43. Johnstone, *Memoirs*, p. 81.
44. McKenzie Annand, 'Fitzjames Horse in the '45', p. 274.
45. *Ibid.*, p. 275.
46. *Ibid.*
47. A. and H. Taylor, *1745 and After*, p. 155.
48. McKenzie Annand, 'Fitzjames Horse in the '45', pp. 273–76.
49. *Ibid.*, p. 166.
50. *Ibid.*, p. 154.
51. Johnstone, *Memoirs*, p. 13.
52. A. and H. Taylor, *1745 and After*, p. 160.
53. *Ibid.*, p. 161.
54. Johnstone, *Memoirs*, p. 145.
55. McDonnell, 'Some documents relating to the involvement of the Irish Brigade in the rebellion of 1745'.
56. A. and H. Taylor, *1745 and After*, p. 164.
57. Lord Mahon, *The Forty-Five*, p. 125.
58. A flag from Lord Ogilvy's regiment, flown at Culloden, that has managed to survive has only been recently discovered. Local history claims that Captain John Kinloch (who carried the colour at the battle) hid the flag in Logie house, near Kirriemuir. This colour is currently on display at the McManus Gallery in Dundee, Scotland. At the battle site of Culloden, the Military Society of Ireland erected a memorial stone to the Wild Geese who served there: 'The breed of Kings, sons of Mileadh eager warriors and heroes.' In 1994, the White Cockade Society erected a stone to the Scottish troops in France which reads: 'This stone commemorates the French Regiment (Royal Scots) who served under Lord John Drummond.' An English stone also commemorates the memory of government troops killed.
59. Antrim McDonnells, p. 114.
60. Felix O'Neill from Co. Armagh was related to the prominent Ulster

O'Neills who were forced to migrate to Spain in the seventeenth century. He provided the following account of his treatment after his arrest, on board the prison ship HMS *Furnace*: 'I was … brought before Captain Ferguson, who used me with the barbarity of a pirate, stripped me, and had ordered me to be put in a rack, and whipped by his hangman, because I would not confess where I thought the Prince was. As I was just going to be whipped, being already stripped, Lieutenant McGaghan of the Scots Fusiliers, who commanded a party under Captain Ferguson, very generously opposed this barbarous usage, and coming out with drawn sword, threatened Captain Ferguson that he would sacrifice himself and his detachment rather than see an officer used after such an infamous manner.' (Taken from 'Copy of the Declaration of Miss Mac Donald. Apple Cross Bay, July 12, 1746'). He spent three years in captivity, before being exchanged and released. He was promoted to colonel of Hibernia before dying a lieutenant general in 1796 at the ripe old age of 94 years.

61. A. and H. Taylor, *1745 and After*, p. 206.
62. Lord Mahon, *The Forty-Five*, p. 127.
63. A. and H. Taylor, *1745 and After*, p. 206.
64. Lord Mahon, *The Forty-Five*, vol. 1, p. 131.
65. Petrie, 'Irishmen in the '45'.
66. Gearoid Ó hAllmhuráin, *Irish Traditional Music* (Dublin, 1998), p 53. This genre of poetry was led by Aodhagán Ó Rathailleand and Eoghan Rua Ó Suilleabháin, who were obsessed with a Stuart Restoration that would restore lands and rights back to the Catholics and re-establish the old Gaelic aristocracy. The poets also wrote of the situation of the dispossessed Gaelic aristocracy, the proud standard bearers of Milesius for thousands of years, who were once their patrons and voiced their wrongs, reserving their bile for the strangers (the English) who replaced them and took their land and possessions.
67. Cited in D. Dickson, New Foundations: Ireland 1660–1800, p. 93.
68. Christine Kinealy, *A New History of Ireland* (Gloucestershire, 2008), p. 127.
69. J.C. O' Callaghan, *Irish Brigades*, p. 413.
70. W.E.H. Lecky, *A History of Ireland in the Eighteenth Century*, vol. 2 (London, 1892), p. 2027. The Anglo-Irish W.E.H. Lecky's work remains a good, balanced (although anglocentric) authority on eighteenth-century Ireland. It is especially valued today as much of Lecky's primary source material was destroyed when the Four Courts in Dublin was shelled during the War of Independence in 1921.
71. McLynn, 'Ireland and the Jacobite Rising of '45', p. 348.

72. Petrie, 'Irishmen in the '45'.
73. McLynn, 'Ireland and the Jacobite Rising of '45', p. 343.
74. Dickson, *New Foundations: Ireland 1660–1800*, p. 94.
75. Cited in O'Ciardha, *Ireland and the Jacobite Cause*, p. 310.
76. A. and H. Taylor, *1745 and After*. Following the death of Charles's brother, Henry, *Cardinal York*, the last of the Stuart line in 1807, the *Stuart Papers* were purchased by the British Government. Henrietta Taylor wrote in her foreword that O'Sullivan's narrative has been overlooked by Jacobite historians.

9. The decline of Charles Edward Stuart

1. Lord Mahon, *The Forty-Five*, p. 139.
2. George Lockhart, *The Lockhart Papers*, vol. 2 (London, 1817), p. 575.
3. Hayes, *Irish Swordsmen of France*, p. 274.
4. Allan Massie, *The Royal Stuarts* (London, 2010), p. 317.
5. Hayes, *Irish Swordsmen* of France, p. 234.
6. O'Ciardha, *Ireland and the Jacobite Cause*, p. 299.
7. Dickson, *New Foundations: Ireland 1660–1800*, p. 104.
8. *Ibid.*
9. One of their residences, fronting onto Piazza della Pilotta, now houses the Pontificio Istituto Biblico, which was the centre of the Stuart Court. The Stuarts lived in the seventeenth-century Palazzo Muti-Papazurri (also known as the Palazzo dei Santi Apostoli or Palazzo Stuart), located at the north end of Piazza dei Santi Apostoli (no. 49) in Rome. There are no plaques on the outside of the building to commemorate its association with the Stuarts, as if even to this day the Jacobites are still maintaining their intigues and secretly plotting. In the adjoining restaurant (as if in some coded Jacobite message) there hangs a black-and-white engraving of Charles in the '45 by J. Horsburgh captioned 'Prince Charles Edward reading a [captured] despatch from Sir John Cope.' Queen Clementina gave birth to her sons there: Charles in 1720 and Henry in 1725, and she died there in 1735, followed by 'James III' in 1766. Charles died there in 1785, followed by his brother Henry, the Duke of York, in 1807. Sometimes the large door of the palace, fronting onto the Piazza dei Santi Apostoli, is left open and it is possible to enter, and walk down the corridor into the courtyard and climb the stairs of the palace. On the left wall of the corridor there is an Italian inscription:

ABITO QUESTO PALAZZO

ENRICO DUCA POI CARDINALE DI YORK

CHE FIGLIO SUPERSTITE DI GIACOMO III D'INGHILTERRA

PRESE IL NOME D'ENRICO IX

IN LUI NELL' ANNO MDCCCVII

S'ESTINSE LA DINASTIA DE' STUARDI

(There lived in this palace

Henry, Duke later Cardinal of York

who, surviving son of James III of England

took the name of Henry IX.

In him in the year 1807

the House of Stuart expired.)

10. J.C. O'Callaghan, *Irish Brigades*, p. 374.
11. Cited in Lord Mahon, *The Forty-Five*, pp. 140–1.
12. Massie, *The Royal Stuarts*, p. 319. There is a monument erected to the Stuarts in St Peter's Basilica in the Vatican in Rome. In the Vatican Grotto, the Stuart Tomb was erected at George IV's expense; James III and his son, Charles Edward Stuart, together with his brother Henry, Cardinal York, have pride of place together with the Tombs of the Popes.
13. Lord Mahon, *The Forty-Five*, p. 139.

10. The Waning Jacobite Cause

1. W. Augustus Cumberland, *Historical Memoirs of His Late Royal Highness William-Augustus, Duke of Cumberland* (London, 1767), p. 442
2. Cited in J.C. O'Callaghan, *Irish Brigades*, p. 469.
3. E. O'hAnnrachain, *The Irish Brigade at Lafelt* 1747.
4. P. Fagan, *Ireland in the Stuart Papers, 1719–42*, vol. 1 (Dublin, 1995), p. 86.
5. In 1964, a 9-foot Celtic cross commemorating Irish involvement in the battle was erected outside Lafelt by the Cork Choral Society. There is also an outdoor interpretive centre and a small museum in the village. Louis compensated the nearby villages and rewarded the adjacent village of Vlittingen with a gold chalice, which is still used on special occasions in the local church.
6. Cited in J.C. O'Callaghan, *Irish Brigades*, p. 470. O'Callaghan listed a

Captain Wollock from Bulkeley's Regiment was killed in action at Lafelt, and one wonders if this is the same person as Sergeant Wheelock, also from Bulkeley's Regiment with possibly a spelling error, as the French frequently misspelled Irish names. We recall that King Louis promoted Wheelock to sous-lieutenant two years earlier for taking a colour from the British at Fontenoy.

7. W.M. Thackeray, *The Luck of Barry Lyndon* (New York, 1853), p. 115.
8. Cited in Edmund B. O'Callaghan, (ed.) *Documents Relative to the Colonial History of the State of New York*, vol. 10 (Albany, 1853), p. 368.
9. H.R Casgrain (ed.), *Journal du Marquis de Montcalm Durant ses Campagnes en Canada de 1756–1759* (Quebec, 1895), p. 211.
10. Cited in W.A. Cumberland, *Military Affairs in North America, 1748–1765: Selected Documents from the Cumberland Papers in Windsor Castle* (London, 1936), p. 232.
11. J. O'Farrell, *Irish Families in Ancient Quebec Records: With Some Account of Soldiers from Irish Brigade Regiments of France Serving with the Army of Montcalm*, text of address delivered at the annual concert and ball of the St Patrick's Society, Montreal, 15 January 1872 (Montreal, 1872), p. 27.
12. R. Chartrand, 'Montcalm's Irish soldiers, 1756–57', *The Irish Sword*, vol. 26 (2006), p. 1.
13. D. MacLeod, *Memoirs of the Life and Gallant Exploits of the Old Highlander, Sergeant Donald Macleod …* (London, 1791), pp. 70–1. MacLeod returned wounded to England on the same ship as General Wolfe's body. He detailed skirmishes between the Black Watch and the Irish militant group, the Whiteboys, when the regiment was stationed in Ireland from 1746 to 1755.
14. This event became ingrained in American history through James Cooper's book, *The Last of the Mohicans*, and vividly recreated in Michael Mann's historical film *The Last of the Mohicans* (1992).
15. J. O'Farrell, *Irish Families in Ancient Quebec Records*, p. 26.
16. T. Guerins, 'Irish Soldiers of the Old Regime in Canada', *The Irish Sword*, vol. 2, no. 5, p. 59.
17. Abbé MacGeoghegan, *A History of Ireland, Ancient and Modern, Dedicated to the Irish Brigade* (Paris, 1762), translated by Patrick O'Kelly (Dublin, 1844), p. vii.
18. McLynn, 'Ireland and the Jacobite Rising of '45'.
19. McLynn, *1759*, p. 84.
20. Cited in DeCourcy Ireland, *Ireland and the Irish in Maritime History*, p. 186.

21. Cited in J.C. O'Callaghan, *Irish Brigades*, p. 589.
22. *Ibid.*, p. 591.
23. *Ibid.*, p. 587. General Julius Agricola (AD 40–93), who was largely responsible for the Roman conquest of Britannia, was of the opinion that Ireland could be taken with a single Legion (of around 5,000 troops) supported by a few hundred auxilliairies. Following the Roman legions' failed incursions into Scotland, it is doubtful if Agricola's assessment would have proved true.
24. *The London Magazine* (1762), p. 372.
25. J.C. O'Callaghan, *Irish Brigades*, p. 598.
26. *Ibid.*, p. 598.
27. *Ibid.*
28. *The London Magazine* (1762), p. 372.

11. Lieutenant General Thomas Lally's Expedition to India

1. The Lallys were originally the O'Mullallys and according to the *Annals of the Four Masters* (1616) could trace their ancient lineage back to the second-century High King of Ireland 'Conn of the hundred battles'. The Lallys had resided in Castle Tullanadaly in Co. Galway but they were attainted for treason after the Jacobite War and were forced to forfeit their estates. Little remains of the Lallys' ancestral home, Castle Tullendaly, save for the castle's foundations and a small monument, on which is written 'IHS pray for the soul of James Lally, and his family 1673.' The stone is located halfway between Tuam and Tullendaly, 2km from Tuam and about 100 metres from the Claremorris Road.
2. Hayes, Irish Swordsmen of France, p. 229.
3. Eoghan O'hAnnrachain, 'Lally, the Regime's Scapegoat', *The Irish Sword*, vol. 24, no. 96 (2004*)*, p .169.
4. Cited in Hayes, *Irish Swordsmen of France*, p. 240.
5. René Chartrand, *Louis XV's Army (3): Foreign Infantry* (Oxford, 2003), p. 24.
6. T. Lally, *Memoirs of Count Lally,* (London, 1766), p. 2.
7. Mullen, 'The Seven Years War: Battle of Wandiwash'.
8. Cited in E. O'hAnnrachain, 'Lally, the Regime's Scapegoat', p. 170.
9. D. and J. Bowen, *Heroic Option*, p 16.
10. E. O'hAnnrachain, 'Lally, the Regime's Scapegoat', p. 171.
11. *Ibid.*, p. 171.
12. M. Hennessy, *The Wild Geese: The Irish Soldier in Exile* (London, 1973), p. 96.
13. Cited in J.C. O'Callaghan, *Irish Brigades*, p. 570.

14. E. O'hAnnrachain, 'Lally, the Regime's Scapegoat', p. 173.
15. Hayes, *Irish Swordsmen of France*, p. 249.
16. Twenty-five years later, during the French Revolution in 1791, Dr Guillotine invented his contraption for beheading victims in a more humane manner. The victim was beheaded in less than a second, the head falling into a waiting basket. Forty thousand people reportedly 'kissed the blade' in the period.
17. E. O'hAnnrachain, 'Lally, the Regime's Scapegoat', p. 169.
18. Hayes, *Irish Swordsmen of France*, p. 245.
19. McLynn, *The Jacobites*, p. 135.
20. Hayes, *Irish Swordsmen of France*, p. 252.
21. Cited in Hennessy, *The Wild Geese*, p. 98.

12. The War of American Independence (1775–83)
1. D. and J. Bowen, *Heroic Option*, p. 19.
2. Cited in F. Green, *The Revolutionary War and the Military Policy of the United States* (New York, 1911), p. 179.
3. R.F. Foster, *Modern Ireland 1600–1972* (London, 1988), p. 216.
4. Cited in Charles Patrick Niemeyer, *America Goes to War: A Social History of the Continental Army* (New York, 1996), p. 31.
5. Niemeyer, *America Goes to War*, pp. 37, 40.
6. Charles Lucey, *Harp and Sword, 1776: The Irish in the American Revolution* (Washington, 1976), p. 12.
7. H. Murtagh, 'Irish soldiers abroad', p. 307.
8. Washington refused a generalship to Conway in the Continental army on the grounds that he was a foreigner – even though Conway was probably the officer with most military experience among Washington's staff. Conway was furious and wrote to General Horatio Gates, who had just secured a Continental victory at Saratoga, supporting him as commander of American forces and criticising Washington. Conway later apologised to Washington and was promoted by Congress to inspector general against Washington's wishes. He was shot in the mouth in a duel by one of Washington's supporters, but survived and resigned his commission and returned to France. The French occupied Cape Town in South Africa from 1781 to 1783 and Conway played a prominent role in defending the colony from British attack. As commanding officer of the French garrison he built a fort there, a portion of which survives today, known as 'Conway's Redoubt'. He served as Governor General of French India (1788–90) and was Governor of Mauritius when the French Revolution broke out.

He returned to Ireland and formed the royalist Irish Brigade in the British army to restore the French monarchy, dying there in 1800.

9. In 1849, Richard Rush, the then US Minister to France, researched the contribution of foreign regiments in the war. French military researchers assisted him, who after analysing the officer muster rolls in the *Archives de la Guerre* and in the *Ministre de la Marine* found many of the records there to be fragmentary.

10. Cited in P. Clarke de Dromantin, 'Irish Jacobite Involvement in the American War of Independence', in Thomas O'Connor and Mary Ann Lyons (eds), *Irish Migrants in Europe after Kinsale, 1602–1820* (Dublin, 2003). Arthur Dillon was the grandson of his namesake Lieutenant General Arthur Dillon, who served with distinction earlier in the century.

11. P. Clarke de Dromantin, 'The Jacobites in the American War of Independence', in N. Genet-Rouffiac and D. Murphy (eds), *Franco-Irish Military Connections, 1590–1945* (Dublin, 2009), p. 126.

12. W.S. Murphy, 'The Irish Brigade of France at the Siege of Savannah, 1779', *The Irish Sword*, vol. 2, no. 6 (1954–56), p. 95–102.

13. W. Murphy, 'Dillon's regiment was not at Yorktown,' *The Irish Sword*, vol. 3, no. 10 (Summer 1957), pp. 50–4.

14. *Ibid.*

15. David Marley, *Wars of the Americas: A Chronology of Armed Conflict in the Western Hemisphere* (Santa Barbara, Ca., 2008), p. 512

16. Brigadier General. James Collins Jr, 'Irish participation at Yorktown', *The Irish Sword*, vol. 15, no. 58 (Summer 1982), p. 5.

17. D. Doyle, *Ireland and Irishmen in the American Revolution* (Dublin 1981), p. 171.

18. Gilbert du Motier, *Memoirs, Correspondence and Manuscripts of General Lafayette*, vol. 1 (London, 1837), pp. 292–3.

19. Marcus de la Poer Beresford, 'Ireland in French Strategy During the American War of Independence, 1776–83,' *The Irish Sword*, vol 13, no. 50 (Summer 1977), pp. 20–9.

20. Cited in Dickson, *New Foundations: Ireland 1660–1800*, p. 103.

21. Beresford, 'Ireland in French Strategy', p. 23.

22. Cited in Lucey *Harp and Sword 1776*, p. 12.

23. Beresford, 'Ireland in French Strategy'.

24. *Ibid.*

25. *Ibid.*, p. 27.

26. Cited in Doyle, *Ireland and Irishmen in the American Revolution*, p. 171.

27. T. Williams, *America's First Flag Officer: Father of the American Navy* (Bloomington, Ind., 2008), p. 245. Barry came from a Catholic family from County Wexford who emigrated to Philadelphia when he was 15 years old. He then embarked on a career at sea.
28. Lecky, *History of Ireland*, vol. 2, p. 234.
29. In 1992, the United States Senate and House of Representatives acknowledged the part played by the Irish Brigade in naval operations during the Revolutionary War by passing Joint House Resolution 427 commemorating the occasion. The 215-year anniversary of the event on 13 May 1994 was designated as 'Irish Brigade Marines Day' by the Senate, according to which 'the President of the United States is authorised and requested to issue a proclamation calling upon the people of the United States to observe such day with appropriate ceremonies and activities.' During the Second World War, the United States navy named a destroyer USS *Stack* in honour of Edward Stack.
30. John Paul Jones, *John Paul Jones' Memoir of the American Revolution* (Hawaii, 1979), p. 72. The Order was a hereditary decoration founded in 1783 by General Washington to preserve the ideals the American War. A copy of the Dillon flag is still displayed at the Society of the Cincinnati.
31. According to Lieutenant Colonel Charles Niemeyer (the former chief historian of the US Marine Corps), the Continental Marine's uniform was then faced in red in tribute to *Bonhommes* Walsh's Marines who wore red uniforms faced with blue. He has also suggested that in the 1790s the US Marines' dress uniform, blue with red piping which is still worn today, was derived from the colours (in reverse) of Walsh's Irish Brigade.
32. *The Scots Magazine*, 1790.
33. W. Murphy, 'The Irish Brigade of France at the siege of Savannah, 1779', p. 95
34. Cited in *The Scots Magazine* (1779), p. 615.
35. Cited in J. Fielding, *History of the War with America, France, Spain and Holland: Commencing in 1775 and Ending in 1783*, vol. 3 (London, 1785), p. 302.
36. W.S. Murphy, 'The Irish Brigade of France at the siege of Savannah, 1779'.
37. F. Hough, *The Siege of Savannah, by the Combined American and French Forces, under the Command of Gen. Lincoln and the Count D'Estaing in the Autumn of 1779* (Albany, 1866), p. 172.
38. W.S. Murphy, 'The Irish Brigade of France at the Siege of Savannah, 1779'.
39. Hough, *The Siege of Savannah*, p. 174.

40. *Ibid.*, p. 168.
41. W.S. Murphy, 'The Irish Brigade of France at the Siege of Savannah, 1779'.
42. Hough, *The Siege of Savannah*, p. 156. D' Estaing later returned to France and was executed during the French Revolution. His fellow officers all spoke highly of him. Three years later, in July 1782, the British withdrew from Georgia, leaving the fate of 'the colony to its future destiny as one of the states of the new republic.'
43. Many Irishmen served onboard Admiral Rodney's fleet. When Rodney's fleet defeated a French fleet in a later engagement, it was said the French were beaten by a combination of 'Rodney's guns! and Paddy's sons!'
44. Cited in *The Scots Magazine* (November 1779), p. 30.
45. *Ibid.*
46. J.C. O'Callaghan, *Irish Brigades*, p. 627.
47. H. Johnston, *The Yorktown Campaign and Surrender of Cornwallis 1781* (New York, 1971), p. 111.
48. Beresford, 'Ireland in French Strategy'.
49. F.W. Van Brock in *The Irish Sword* mentions an interesting (although historically incorrect) stamp issued in 1980 by the French Post Office commemorating the arrival of Rochambeau's expedition to Rhode Island in 1780, 200 years earlier. The stamp depicts a ship with an ensign clearly carrying the Dillon Regimental flag.
50. W. Murphy, 'Dillon's Regiment was not at Yorktown,' p. 53.
51. S. Scott, *From Yorktown to Valmy: The Transformation of the French Army in an Age of Revolution* (Colorado, 1998), p. 10.
52. List of Regiments at Yorktown, J. Stevens, *Yorktown Centennial Handbook: Historical and Topographical Guide to the Yorktown Peninsula, Richmond, James River and Norfolk* (New York, 1881), p. 36.
53. S. Scott, From *Yorktown to Valmy*, p. 12.
54. F.W. Van Brock, 'Lieutenant General Robert Dillon, 1754–1781', *The Irish Sword*, vol. 14, no. 55 (Winter 1980), p. 173.
55. H. Johnston, *The Yorktown Campaign and the Surrender of Cornwallis, 1781*.
56. Cited in Clarke de Dromantin, 'The Jacobites in the American War of Independence', p. 134.
57. W. Murphy, 'Dillon's Regiment was not at Yorktown'.
58. S. Scott, *From Yorktown to Valmy*.
59. Cited in J. deCourcy Ireland, 'Irish participation in the French naval activities which led to the fall of Yorktown 19 October 1781, and the

independence of the United States', *The Irish Sword*, vol. 14, no. 56 (Summer 1981), p. 221.
60. Doyle, *Ireland and Irishmen in the American Revolution*, p. xvii.

13. The French Revolution (1789)

1. Kavanagh, of Irish parentage, was a district representative and was only one of six representatives who demanded the establishment of a National Guard. His actions were later celebrated in a pamphlet entitled *Les exploits glorieux du célèbreCavanagh. Cause première de la liberté française.*
2. Hayes, *Ireland and Irishmen in the French Revolution*, p. 80.
3. G. Martinez, 'Semper et Ubique Fidelis', in Nathalie Genet-Rouffiac and David Murphy (eds), *Franco-Irish Military Connections, 1590–1945* (Dublin, 2009), p. 148.
4. Baigent and Leigh, *The Temple and the Lodge*, p. 185.
5. A. Mackey and W. Singleton, *History of Masonry* (New York, 2010), p. 273.
6. L. Swords, 'The Irish in Paris at the End of the Ancient Regime', in T. O'Connor (ed.), *The Irish In Europe, 1580–1815* (Dublin, 2001), p. 204.
7. General Daniel O'Connell (the Liberators' uncle) was an ardent royalist. After the French Revolution he joined the army of the émigrés, before being breveted to colonel in the Irish Brigade in the British army that was formed to restore the Bourbons. He returned to France after the Revolution and was appointed Inspector General of French Infantry, before dying in 1833 at the advanced age of 88 years.
8. Hayes, *Ireland and Irishmen in the French Revolution*, p. 78.
9. Lecky, *History of Ireland*, vol. 3, p. 524.
10. Cited in Hayes, *Irish Swordsmen of France*, p. 120.
11. *Ibid*, p. 119.
12. Hayes, *Irish Swordsmen of France*, p. 121.
13. F.W. Van Brock, 'Defeat at les Plantons 1792', *The Irish Sword*, vol. 13 (1979), p. 89.
14. S. Reid, *Armies of the Irish Rebellion 1798* (Oxford 2011), p. 39. O'Gorman had served as a captain in the 88th (Berwick's) and as aide-de-camp to Count d'Argout, the Governor of Haiti, and acquired a substantial sugar plantation on the island. He later became a colonial representative sent to serve in the National Assembly in Paris.
15. Marley, *Wars of the Americas*, pp. 536–7. General Oliver Harty was a resourceful commander and had once declared (with a little arrogance):

'As to my abilities, allow me to say they are solely military … My successful record warrants that I can usefully serve the Nation.' F.W. Van Brock, 'Major General Oliver Harty in Brittany 1799–1800', *The Irish Sword*, vol. 14, no. 57 (Winter 1981), p. 288. Oliver Harty was born in Co. Limerick and was sent to France at the age of 16 and joined Berwick's Regiment as a cadet, and rose to colonel before being breveted to major-general in 1792. He was created Baron de Pierrebourg by Napoleon and owned a substantial castle in the Alsace region of France. While later stationed in Haiti, Harty fell out with the French Commissioner Polveral and was imprisoned for seventy days and shipped back to France. British privateers intercepted his ship and he was imprisoned on the British dominion of Bermuda. He managed to escape to Charleston and made it back to France, where his rank was restored.

16. Hayes, *Irish Swordsmen of France*, p. 27.
17. *Ibid.*, p. 51.
18. Hayes, *Ireland and Irishmen in the French Revolution*, p. 272.
19. *Ibid.*, pp. 81–2.
20. Leslie Stephens, *Dictionary of National Biography*, vol. 15 (London, 1888), p. 83. Edouard became gentleman-in-waiting to the king's brother and was the son of a failed Dublin banker who emigrated to France. It was rumoured that Edouard may even have been romantically involved with Marie Antoinette.
21. Cited in Hayes, *Ireland and Irishmen in the French Revolution*, p. 271.
22. Nolan, *The Irish Dames of Ypres*, p. 250. A replica of this flag, embroidered by the Irish Benedictine nuns in Ypres, was presented to Tipperary-born Major-General Sir William Hickie, GOC of the 16th Irish Division of the British army in 1914 during the First World War. The flag was then presented to the Irish Defence Forces Artillery School in the Curragh Camp in Co. Kildare by Captain Richard Deasy of the Irish army (a nephew of Sir William Hickie), where it is still displayed.
23. Cited in Hennessy, *The Wild Geese*, p. 99.
24. H. Murtagh, 'Irish Soldiers Abroad', p. 303.
25. Cited *ibid.*, p 301.
26. Lecky, *History of Ireland*, vol. 3, p. 525.
27. *Ibid.*
28. W. Tone, *Memoirs of Theobald Wolfe Tone*, vol. 1 (London, 1827), p. 310.
29. The two men later reconciled. Blayney went on to command the British 89th Regiment of Foot and served with distinction in the Peninsular War,

and rose to the rank of major-general. Blayney's family in Castleblayney, Co. Monaghan had received confiscated lands from the McMahan clan after the Elizabethan Wars in the 1600s.
30. *The Gentleman's Magazine* (1783).
31. At this time there were three Dillon's regiments in the British army: Edouard Dillon's Regiment; Henry Dillon's Regiment in the Irish Catholic Brigade; and the 87th (Dillon's), a battalion of which surrendered and changed sides at Haiti in 1792 and entered the British service.
32. Richard Hayes researched Robespierre's Irish connection, and could find no reference to any family called Robespierre in Ireland. He concluded that his name could have been a derivative of the prominent Kilkenny merchant families of Rothe (Rooth) and Fitz Piers (Pierre). There could be currency in this suggestion as it is recorded that a John Rothe Fitz Piers built Rothe House in Kilkenny in the sixteenth century. It was not unusual for many Irish family names to be adapted and gallicised, appearing more French over time. It is also plausible that the surname 'Roth Fitz Piers' could well have been adapted to 'Robespierre'.
33. P. Dwyer, *Napoleon: The Path to Power 1769–1799* (London, 2007), p. 153. Bellew came from a family with a tradition of military service abroad (not unusual in many Catholic gentry families in the period) as eleven of his uncles had also served in the Irish Brigade of France.
34. Hayes, *Irish Swordsmen of France*, p. 91.
35. James O'Moran immigrated from Roscommon at the age of 17 years and joined Dillon's as a cadet. In 1792 he served under General Dumouriez in Belgium and in Champagne, and was appointed lieutenant general (general of division) and captured the town of Tourney in Flanders in command of 16,000 men.
36. Cited in Hayes, *Irish Swordsmen of France*, p. 104.

14. The United Irishmen and France
1. Marianne Elliott, *Wolfe Tone* (London, 1989), p. 11.
2. Bartlett, *Ireland: A History*, p. 169
3. J. Kelly, *Henry Flood, Patriots and Politics in Eighteenth-Century Ireland* (Dublin, 1998), p. 435.
4. Francis Wheatley commemorated this event in a painting; *The Dublin Volunteers on College Green 4th November 1779.*
5. Dissenters were Presbyterian Irish Protestants who also suffered discrimination from the majority established Church of Ireland

(Anglican), but not to the same degree as Catholics.
6. Cited in Lecky, *History of Ireland*, vol. 3, p. 509.
7. Cited in J.A. Murphy, *The French Are in the Bay: The Expedition to Bantry Bay 1796* (Cork, 1997), p. 21.
8. W. Tone, *Memoirs*, vol. 2, p. 141.
9. Van Brock, 'Major General Oliver Harty in Brittany 1799–1800', p. 288.
10. This 'Légion Irlandaise' was deactivated in February 1799 and should not to be confused with Napoleon's Legion that was established later in 1804.
11. Lecky, *History of Ireland*, vol. 3, p. 539.
12. Tone, *Memoirs*, vol. 2, p. 151.
13. Cited in Lecky, *History of Ireland*, vol. 4, p. 531.
14. The 'Bantry boat', still sporting its original tricolor paint, is displayed in the National Museum of Collins Barracks, Dublin.
15. *The Scots Magazine*, vol. 59 (1797).
16. Tone, *Memoirs*, vol. 2, p. 151.
17. Lecky, *History of Ireland*, vol. 3, p. 540.
18. Cited in *The European Magazine, and London Review*, for January 1797, vol. 31, pp. 214–15.
19. R. Hayes *The Last Invasion of Ireland* (Dublin, 1937), p. 28.
20. J. Thompson (ed.), *Napoleon's Letters* (London, 1998), p. 46. Contrary to popular belief, perpetuated by British propaganda, Napoleon, 'the little Corsican' was not low in stature; He was 5 foot 7 imperial inches or 1m 68cm tall, slightly taller than the average Frenchman.
21. Van Brock, 'Major General Oliver Harty in Brittany, 1799–1800', p. 84.
22. Mitchel, *The History of Ireland*, p. 254.
23. *Ibid*.
24. O'Meara, *Napoleon in Exile*, pp. 37, 482.
25. Croppies was the nickname given to the rebels who cropped their hair short, being anti-wig and anti-aristocrat, in the French Revolutionary style. Hundreds were hanged from the Liffey's bridges and dumped into mass graves in an area of waste land fronting Collins Barracks, Dublin known as 'Croppy Acre'.
26. Hayes, *The Last Invasion of Ireland* (Dublin, 1937).
27. S. Reid, *Armies of the Irish Rebellion* 1798, p. 47.
28. H. Murtagh, 'Irish Soldiers Abroad', p. 310.
29. Chenevix Trench, *Grace's Card*.

30. L. Kelly, *A Flame Now Quenched, Rebels and Frenchmen in Leitrim 1793–1798* (Dublin, 1998), p. 79.
31. T. Pakenham, *The Year of the French* (London, 1969), p. 307.
32. L. Kelly, *A Flame Now Quenched*, p 86.
33. Hayes, *The Last Invasion of Ireland,* p. 22.
34. This is the same general who surrendered at Yorktown in 1781 during the American War of Independence.
35. Hayes, *The Last Invasion of Ireland*, p. 148.
36. This colour was produced in Paris by the wives of Irish emigrés, according to the *Journal of the Galway Archaeological and Historical Society*, vol. 50 (1998), and is currently displayed in Armagh Cathedral.
37. L. Kelly, *A Flame Now Quenched*, p. 124.
38. Cited *ibid*.
39. Hayes, *The Last Invasion of Ireland*.
40. Chenevix Trench, *Grace's Card*. Napper Tandy and Blackwell headed back to the Continent by steering north past the Scottish coast and into the North Sea to the northern German city of Hamburg. This was the preferred route instead of the more obvious and shorter (but more dangerous) sea crossing wide of Cork and into the Atlantic and back to France, which was swarming with Royal Navy patrols. Hamburg was a centre of Irish radicalism and was the only city outside the British Isles which had a United Irish Society. Both men were betrayed to the German authorities, who handed them over to the British. Napoleon was furious with the German authorities and fined the city a considerable sum for this. See p. Weber, *On the Road to Rebellion: The United Irishmen and Hamburg* (Dublin, 2007).
41. Kilmaine later offered to adopt Tone's son and gained a captaincy for Tone's brother in the French army.
42. Wolfe Tone is remembered today in his native city with a statue in Bantry Bay and on the corner of St Stephen's Green, Dublin, and lies buried in Bodenstown, Co. Kildare.
43. Jean Agnew (ed.), *The Drennan–McTier Letters*, vol. 2 (1999), p. 147.
44. Cited in Hayes, *Irish Swordsmen of France*, p. xiii.
45. *Irish Independent*, 31 July 2010.
46. J.A. Murphy, *The French Are in the Bay*, p. 63.
47. In the 1790s a popular song connected with ''98' appeared, called the Sean Van Vocht (*an tseanbhean bhocht* is Irish for 'the poor old woman'). It was first printed in 1842 in the Young Irelander's newspaper *The Nation*;

The French are on the sea! Says the Sean Van Vocht;
The French are on the sea! Says the Sean Van Vocht;
The French are on the sea! They'll be here without delay;

And the Orange will decay, says the Sean Van Vocht.
Shall Erin then be free? Says the Sean Van Vocht;
Shall Erin then be free? Says the Sean Van Vocht;
Yes, Erin shall be free, and we'll plant the laurel tree,
And we'll call it Liberty, says the Sean Van Vocht.

15. Napoleon's Irish Legion (1803–15)

1. Dwyer, *Napoleon*, p. 334.
2. *Ibid.*, p. 335.
3. J.M. Thompson (ed.), *Napoleon's Letters* (London, 1998), p. 334.
4. Byrne, *Memoirs*, edited by his widow.
5. T. Bartlett, 'Last flight of the Wild Geese? Bonaparte's Irish Legion, 1803–1815', in T. O'Connor and M. Ann Lyons (eds), *Irish Communities in Early Modern Europe* (Dublin, 2006), p. 197.
6. N. Dunne-Lynch, 'The Irish Legion of Napoleon, 1803–15', in N. Genet-Rouffiac and D. Murphy (eds), *Franco-Irish Military Connections, 1590–1945* (Dublin, 2009), p. 190. General D'Alton was born in France and was descended from an old Hiberno-Norman family. His father also served as an officer in the Irish Brigade. Alexandre D'Alton together with his brother accompanied Wolfe Tone to Bantry Bay in the aborted 1796 invasion. Tone had described them in his *Memoirs* as 'two very fine lads'. Alexandre D'Alton went on to have a brilliant military career, becoming Inspector General of Infantry in the French army and received both the Knight of St Louis and the Legion of Honour. He distinguished himself under Napoleon at the Battle of Austerlitz in 1805, and his name is inscribed in the Arc de Triomphe in Paris.
7. W. Scott, *The Life of Napoleon Bonaparte, Emperor of the French* (Philidephia, 1857), p. 374.
8. Bartlett, 'Last Flight of the Wild Geese?', p. 166.
9. *Idem.*
10. Byrne, *Memoirs*, vol. 2, p. 258.
11. J. Elting, *Napoleonic Uniforms*, vol. 2 (London, 2007).
12. Fraser, *The War Drama of the Eagles*, pp. 50–1.

13. D. Murphy, *The Irish Brigades*, p. 34.
14. L. Swords, *The Green Cockade: The Irish in the French Revolution 1789–1815* (Dublin, 1989).
15. Ó hAllmhuráin, *Irish Traditional Music*, pp. 76–7.
16. Dunne-Lynch, 'The Irish Legion of Napoleon, 1803–15', p. 191.
17. J. Gallagher, *Napoleon's Irish Legion* (Carbondale, Ill., 1993), pp. 110–11.
18. Bartlett, 'Last flight of the Wild Geese?', p. 162.
19. Gallagher, *Napoleon's Irish Legion*, p. 53.
20. *Ibid.*, p. 54.
21. Clifford D. Connor, *Arthur O'Connor: The Most Important Irish Revolutionary You May Never Have Heard Of* (New York, 2009). Arthur O'Connor lies buried in the famous cemetery of Pere Lachaise, Paris.
22. Captain F. Forde, 'Napoleon's Irish Legion', *An Cosantoir* (March 1974), pp. 71–76.
23. Bartlett, 'Last flight of the Wild Geese?', p. 164.
24. Gallagher, *Napoleon's Irish Legion*.
25. Cited in Thompson (ed.), *Napoleon's Letters*, p. 83.
26. M. Byrne, *Memoirs*, p. 331. The Irish Legion could be compared at this point with the *Legion Noire*, made up of criminals and dubious characters, which landed in Fishguard, Wales in 1796.
27. Thompson (ed.), *Napoleon's Letters*, p. 110.
28. De Courcy Ireland, *Ireland and the Irish in Maritime History*, pp. 211–12.
29. H. Murtagh, 'Irish Soldiers Abroad', p. 308.
30. Thompson (ed.), *Napoleon's Letters*, pp. 253–4.
31. Byrne, *Memoirs* p. 27.
32. Gallagher, *Napoleon's Irish Legion*.
33. *Ibid.*
34. Byrne, *Memoirs*, p. 61.
35. Lieutenant Colonel R. Bentley, *A Soldier's Recollections of the West Indies and America* (London, 1834), p. 345. There were no bagpipers as in the Irish Brigade, as they had been replaced by a brass band. Bentley mistakenly refers to the Irish Legion as the Irish Brigade.
36. Lawless's sword is on display in the National Museum in Collins Barracks, Dublin with a pictorial engraving and the inscription 'Flessingue' (Flushing).
37. J. Gallagher, 'William Lawless and the siege of Flushing', *The Irish Sword*, vol. 17, no. 68 (1989), pp. 159–64.

38. Dunne-Lynch, 'The Irish Legion of Napoleon, 1803–15', p. 194.
39. Hayes, 'Biographical dictionary of Limerickmen in France', pp. 181–2. De Lacy was born in Gibraltar and had served as a captain in Ultonia's Regiment of the Spanish Irish Brigade. His father was Lieutenant Colonel Patrick de Lacy in the same regiment and his grandfather had also served in Ultonia. He had quarrelled over a local girl with the governor of the Canary Islands, and in the ensuing duel the governor was injured, resulting in de Lacy being court-martialled and subsequently crossing the border into France and joining the French army in 1803. The French Minister of War, Henri Clarke, introduced him to Napoleon and procured a commission for him in the Irish Legion. The De Lacys came from old Norman stock who settled in the thirteenth-century stronghold of Ballygrennan Castle in Bruff, Co. Limerick. Louis's great-grandfather, Pater De Lacy, had fought with James in the Jacobite War and his estate was confiscated after he followed James to France with the Flight of the Wild Geese.
40. This event is dramatically depicted in Francisco Goya's famous painting *El Tres de Mayo*.
41. B. Clark and K.G. Thompson, 'Napoleon's Irish Legion, 1803–15: The Historical Record', *The Irish Sword*, vol. 12, no. 48 (Summer 1976), pp. 165–72.
42. A. O'Reilly, *The Irish at Home and Abroad, at the Court and in the Camps* (New York, 1856), p. 218.
43. D. Murphy, *The Irish Brigades*, p. 51.
44. O. Breatnach, 'Irish Soldiers at the Sieges of Girona, 1808–1809', *Irish Migration Studies in Latin America*, vol. 7, no. 3 (March 2010), p. 30.
45. The regiment was disbanded in 1818, and in 1960 a new regiment was formed called the Regimiento de Infanteria Ultonia No. 59, eventually dissolved in 1986. The Catalan Volunteer Reserve takes the name of 'Ultonia' today. There is also a Hotel Ultonia operating in the town.
46. Byrne, *Memoirs*, p. 74.
47. *Ibid.*, p 76.
48. A. Wellesley, Duke of Wellington, *Dispatches of Field Marshal the Duke of Wellington during his Various Campaigns, 1799–1815*, edited by John Gurwood, vol. 12 (London, 1838), p. 31. Joseph Lawlor, born in 1776, emigrated from Co. Laois with his brother James to Spain, where they reassumed the family surname of 'O'Lawlor'. It is thought that it was more advantageous for the young Lawlor brothers to adopt the more Irish sounding 'O'Lawlor'. This is in contrast to emigrants in England and later on in America, when Irishness was sometimes frowned upon and as a result many dropped their

'O' and 'Mac' prefixes and adopted more English-sounding surnames. Both Joseph and his brother entered the Military Academy of Artillery in Spain. Upon the outbreak of the Peninsular War, Joseph's brother was killed in 1808. After the war, Joseph continued his successful career and became the military governor of Grenada. He married an heiress from Malaga and one of his daughters married into an Irish banking family, O'Shea and Co., who were based in Madrid.

49. William Grattan, *Adventures of the Connaught Rangers, from 1808 to 1814* (London, 1847), p. 55.

50. Robert Southey, *The History of the Peninsular War* (London, 1837), p. 395. This tune has an interesting history. Irish regiments of the British army played it and Queen Victoria herself was known to be fond of it. There was an account published of the 16th (Irish) Division in the British army during the Somme offensive in 1916: 'The Irish were tired, having been long in action, but they settled grimly to their task. Suddenly there rose up from the trenches the familiar strains of "*St. Patrick's Day*", given with vigour by the pipers. A new spirit entered into the men and a roar of cheers went down the line.'

51. Cited in Holmes, *Redcoat*, p. 65.

52. Byrne, *Memoirs*, vol. 2, p. 68.

53. *New Monthly Magazine and Literary Journal*, part 1. (London, 1829), p. 511.

54. *The Times*, 27 March 1846.

55. *Ibid*.

56. Byrne, *Memoirs*, p. 171.

57. *Ibid*, p. 123.

58. *Ibid*, p. 172.

59. For his exploits in the 1813–14 campaign, Joseph O'Rourke (1772–1849), the celebrated cavalry general, was awarded the Prussian Iron Cross, the Order of the Red Eagle and the Swedish Order of the Sword. His portrait hangs in the Hermitage Museum in St Petersburg and in 1910 a monument was erected to him in Serbia. During his illustrious career he received two golden swords for bravery, one of which was encrusted with diamonds. The O'Rourkes were a prominent Gaelic aristocratic family who lost lands in the Elizabethan and Cromwellian conquests, and several family members emigrated to Russia. The family were descended from the ninth-century kings of Connacht and ruled the ancient kingdom of Breifne in the north-west of the country until they were unseated during the Elizabethan conquest in the sixteenth century.

60. D. Murphy, *The Irish Brigades*, p. 36. The celebrated Marshal of France, Jacques MacDonald, had served in Dillon's; his father was 'out' in the '45 and later served in a Scottish regiment of France.
61. *The Times*, 27 March 1846.
62. Dunne-Lynch, 'The Irish Legion of Napoleon, 1803–15', p. 195.
63. Byrne, *Memoirs*, p. 132.
64. Dunne-Lynch, 'The Irish Legion of Napoleon, 1803–15', p. 195.
65. Cited in Gallagher, *Napoleon's Irish Legion*, p. 191.
66. *The Times*, 27 March 1846.
67. D. Murphy, *The Irish Brigades*, p. 36.
68. R. Maddan, *United Irishmen, Their Lives and Times*, vol. 2 (London, 1843), p. 526.
69. D. Murphy, *The Irish Brigades*, p 36.
70. Cited in Gallagher, *Napoleon's Irish Legion*, p. 209.
71. Bartlett, 'Last flight of the Wild Geese?', p. 170.
72. D. Murphy, *The Irish Brigades*, p. 51.

17. Conclusion

1. Cited in Hayes, *Irish Swordsmen of France*, p. ix.
2. S. de Freine, *The Great Silence* (Dublin, 1978).
3. Cited in Higgins, *The Irish Brigade on the Continent*, p. 66.
4. E. O'hAnnrachain, *The Irish Brigade at Lafelt 1747*, p. 12.
5. Cited in H. Murtagh, 'Irish Soldiers Abroad', p. 308.
6. T.P. Coogan, *Wherever Green Is Worn* (London, 2000), p. 31.
7. Letters of Mamaduke Coghill to Edward Southill, March 1728, in D. Hayton, *Letters of Marmaduke Coghill 1722–1738* (Dublin, 2005). After the American war, Robert Dillon, along with Eugene McCarthy and Edward Stack, were founding members of the prestigious Society of the Cincinnati.
8. Voltaire, *The Age of Louis XIV* (New York, 1961), p. 261. There are many similarities between McDonagh and the character of Alexander Dumas's character, Dantes, in *The Count of Monte Cristo*. Indeed Dumas could have based his book on the Irishman.
9. In 1792, MacDonagh wrote a 157-page account entitled Memoir of Macdonagh, a Native of Ireland, Lieutenant-colonel of the 60th Regiment of Infantry (Royal Marine), Chevalier of the Royal and Military Order of St. Louis. See p. Joannon, 'Andrew MacDonagh: the Irish Monte-Cristo', in T. O'Connor and M.A. Lyons (eds), *Irish Communities in Early Modern Europe* (Dublin, 2006), pp. 145–59.

10. Wogan later wrote a best-selling book about his daring rescue of the princess and became famous for it throughout Europe: *The Narrative of the Escape of Princess Clementina*. It later captured the attention of Hollywood and was made into a 'B' film called *The Iron Glove* (1954) starring Robert Stack. Wogan was later raised to brigadier-general by Philip V of Spain, and went on to lead 1,300 Spaniards against the Moors in Santa Cruz. Richard Gaydon from Irishtown in Dublin was decorated with the Knight of St Louis and rose to Lieutenant Colonel in Dillons and wrote his Memoirs of the Regiment of Dillon's in 1738, but they remained unpublished until they were translated into English and appeared in the 1950s and 1960s *Irish Sword* (The Irish Military History Journal). Lucas O'Toole from County Kildare, was described as being 6-feet tall and 'the finest man in the regiment'. He was killed in action when the French were fighting the Austrians along the Moselle in Germany. I could find no further reference to what happened to John Misset, who also hailed from County Kildare.

11. J. Swift, *The Works of Jonathan Swift* (Edinburgh, 1814), pp. vii–viii.

12. The Plantation of Ulster occurred after the Flight of the Earls from 1607, when land from the Gaelic O'Neill and O'Donnell chieftains was given to Protestant settlers from Scotland and England. This plantation has been a source of conflict between Catholics and Protestants in Northern Ireland ever since.

13. Many Irish Protestants fought for the liberation of Ireland: Wolfe Tone, Robert Emmet, and many others fought in 1916. Thomas Davis, the national poet, was also a Protestant. Davis is commemorated in his native city with a statue occupying close to the same spot on College Green, Dublin, where King William's classical equestrian statue – riding in the guise of a triumphant Roman conqueror – stood for nearly 200 years. It frequently became the target of attacks before it was finally removed.

14. Eoghan O'hAnnrahain has compiled a list of Irishmen admitted to the old soldiers' home, the Invalides, in Paris. O'hAnnrachain, 'Guests of France'.

15. General Thomas Plunket (1716–79) came from Castle Plunket in Co. Roscommon and left Ireland at the age of 12 years and entered the Imperial Austrian service. Plunket concluded his career as military commander of Antwerp in 1770 when it formed part of the Austrian Netherlands. The following year, his only son was killed in action during the Siege of Belgrade in 1780.

16. Simms, 'The Irish on the Continent', p. 642, in *A New History of Ireland* (Oxford, 1996)

17. *The Gentleman's Magazine* (April 1794). Therése-Lucy was the daughter of Lieutenant General Charles deRoth of Kilkenny, whose family left

Limerick in the Flight of the Wild Geese.
18. Hayes, 'Biographical Dictionary of Irishmen in France', p. 35. Her portrait by Baron Francois Gerard, *Julie Bonaparte as Queen of Spain with her daughters Zenaide and Charlotte (1808–9)*, hangs in the National Gallery in Dublin.
19. Algrant, *Madame de Pompadour: Mistress of France*, p. 156.
20. John McKenna was descended from the McKenna chieftains who ruled part of Co. Monaghan from the twelfth to the seventeenth centuries. He was born in 1771 and left Ireland for Spain when 11 years old, and through the patronage of his relative, Alexander O'Reilly, he was enrolled in the Royal Engineering College in Barcelona. He later joined the Irish Regiment of Ultonia of Spain as an engineering officer, and rose further in the Spanish army. He was posted to Santiago and took up the struggle for Chilean independence with the rebels against Spanish rule and was credited with securing notable victories against the Spanish. His demise was perhaps as dramatic as the adventurous life he lived as he was killed in a duel.
21. O'Reilly has a street named after him in Havana, Cuba: 'Calle Oreilly'. Ireland also had other links with Cuba; the revolutionary leader Ernesto Che Guevara had Irish ancestry through Patrick Lynch, who was born in Co. Galway and emigrated to Spain in 1715 and then on to Argentina. His father, Ernesto Guevara Lynch, attributed his revolutionary spirit and ideals to his Irish heritage, and was clearly proud of his Irish ancestry. In 1969, he described his son as follows: 'The first thing to note is that in my son's veins flowed the blood of the Irish rebels.'
22. Chenevix Trench, *Grace's Card*, p. 224. King Louis XVI's young son nominally became the uncrowned King Louis XVII after his father was guillotined. The boy was imprisoned and it was rumoured that he died at the age of ten years of tuberculosis, although the body was never properly identified and some suspect 'the lost dauphin' escaped as the last Bourbon heir.
23. Swords, 'The Irish in Paris at the end of the Ancient Regime', p. 196.
24. John O'Hart, *Irish Pedigrees; Or, The Origin and Stem of the Irish Nation, Second Series* (Dublin, 1876), pp. 122–23. The MacMahons were Gaelic lords in Co. Clare who had their estates confiscated in the Cromwellian conquest. Two MacMahon brothers subsequently emigrated to France, one of whom served in the Ultonia regiment of Spain and fought with Bonnie Prince Charlie in the '45.
25. *Ibid*. The nineteenth-century genealogist John O'Hart traced De Gaulle's ancestry back to their lordship of lands in Co. Down in 1004;

but their estates were reduced in the Elizabethan conquest and in the Plantation of Ulster. In the Jacobite War they were attainted for treason and forfeited their estates. The McCartans were a rebellious clan who fought with the O'Neills in Kinsale (1607) and in the Boyne (1690). A family member, Fergus McCartan, was recorded as being imprisoned in Downpatrick, Co. Down for his part in the 1798 Rising, and another fought in the Battle of Ballinamuck. General de Gaulle (1890–1970) attended the Lycee de Sacre Cour in the village of Antoing from 1907 to 1908. His height, nose and rebellious nature were said to be attributable to his Irish heritage. The MacCartan family shield and a painting of one of his Irish ancestors is displayed in the house in which de Gaulle was born in Lille, France, where it is now a museum. Members of the McCartan clan welcomed him during his visit to Ireland in 1969. In the 1960's, with the threat of World War Three looming, two beacons of western democracy – America and France – held the balance of power, and were presided over by men of Irish descent, Charles de Gaulle and John Fitzgerald Kennedy.

26. Cited in Coogan, *Wherever Green Is Worn*, p. 37.
27. Byrne, *Memoirs*, vol. 2, p. 216.
28. Lawless, *With the Wild Geese* (London, 1902).

BIBLIOGRAPHY

Agnew, J. (ed.), *The Drennan–McTier Letters*, vol. 2 (1999).

Algrant, C., *Madame de Pompadour: Mistress of France* (New York, 2002).

Baigent, M. and Leigh, R., *The Temple and the Lodge* (New York, 1989).

Balch, T., *The French in America during the War of Independence of the United States 1777–83*, vol. 2 (Boston, 1891).

Barnard, T. and Fenlon, J. (eds), *The Dukes of Ormond, 1610–1745* (Woodbridge, 2000).

Barry, J., The Study of Family History in Ireland, McDonnell lectures delivered at UCC on 13 April 1967.

Barthorp, M., *The Jacobite Rebellions 1689–1756* (Oxford, 1982).

Bartlett, T., *Ireland: A History* (Cambridge, 2010).

——, 'Last flight of the Wild Geese? Bonaparte's Irish Legion, 1803–1815', in T. O'Connor and M. Ann Lyons (eds), *Irish Communities in Early Modern Europe* (Dublin, 2006).

Bentley, Lieutenant Colonel R., *A Soldier's Recollections of the West Indies and America* (London, 1834).

Beresford, M. de la Poer, 'Ireland in French strategy during the American War of Independence, 1776–83', *The Irish Sword*, vol. 13, no. 50 (Summer 1977), pp. 20–29.

Black, J., *Warfare in the Eighteenth Century* (London, 1999).

Bois, J.P., *Fontenoy, 1745* (Paris, 1996).

Boswell, J., *The Scots Magazine*, vol. 41 (November 1779).

Bowen, D. and J., Heroic Option: *The Irish in the British Army* (Yorkshire, 2005).

Bradsheet, D., *The Life and Uncommon Adventures of Captain Dudey Bradsheet* (Dublin, 1755).

Bibliography

Breatnach, O., 'Irish Soldiers at the Sieges of Girona, 1808–1809', *Irish Migration Studies in Latin America*, vol. 7, no. 3 (March 2010).

Bredin, A.E.C., *A History of the Irish Soldier* (Belfast, 1987).

Brereton, J.M., *A History of the 4th/7th Royal Dragoon Guards and Their Predecessors* (Catterick, 1982).

Burke, E. (ed.), *The Annual Register for the Year 1782*, vol. 25 (London, 1782).

Burnes, Lieutenant Colonel A., *The Art of War on Land, Illustrated by Campaigns and Battles of All Ages* (London, 1958).

Byrne, M., *Memoirs of Miles Byrne: Chef de Bataillon in the Service of France: Officer of the Legion of Honour, Knight of Saint Louis*, vols 1–2 (Paris, 1863).

Carp, E., 'The Irish at the Jacobite court of Saint Germain en Laye', in Thomas O'Connor (ed.), *The Irish in Europe, 1510–1815* (Dublin, 2001).

Casgrain, H.R. (ed.), *Journal du Marquis de Montcalm Durant ses Campagnes en Canada de 1756–1759* (Quebec, 1895).

Cavanagh, Lieutenant Colonel W., 'Irish Knights of the Imperial Order of Maria Therese', *The Journal of Royal Society of Antiquarians of Ireland*, sixth series, vol. 16 (December 1926), pp. 95–105.

Chandler, D., *The Art of Warfare in the Age of Marlborough* (London, 1990).

Chartrand, R., *The French Army in the American War of Independence*, Osprey series (Oxford, 1991).

———, *Louis XV's Army (3): Foreign Infantry* (Oxford, 2003).

———, 'Montcalm's Irish Soldiers, 1756–57', *The Irish Sword,* Vol. 26 (2006), pp. 1–2.

Chenevix Trench, C., *Grace's Card: Irish Catholic Landlords 1690–1800* (Cork, 1997).

Childs, J., 'The Abortive Invasion of 1692', in E. Cruickshanks, and E.T. Corp (eds), *The Stuart Court in Exile and the Jacobites* (London, 1995), pp. 61–72.

Churchill, J., *Memoirs of John, Duke of Marlborough*, edited by William Coxe (London, 1819).

Clark, B. and Thompson., K.G., 'Napoleon's Irish Legion, 1803–15: The Historical Record', *The Irish Sword*, vol. 12, no. 48 (Summer 1976), pp. 165–72.

Clarke de Dromantin, P., 'Irish Jacobite Involvement in the American War of Independence', in Thomas O'Connor and Mary Ann Lyons, (eds), *Irish Migrants in Europe after Kinsale 1602–1820* (Dublin, 2003).

———, 'The Jacobites in the American War of Independence', in N. Genet-Rouffiac and D. Murphy (eds), *Franco-Irish Military Connections, 1590–1945* (Dublin, 2009).

Clarke, G.B., *Irish Soldiers in Europe, 17th–19th Century* (Cork, 2010).

Collins Jr, Brig. General. J., 'Irish Participation at Yorktown', *The Irish Sword*, vol. 15, no. 58 (Summer 1982), pp. 3–10.

Collinson, F., *The Bagpipe: The History of a Musical Instrument* (London, 1975).

Conan Doyle, A., *The Poems of Arthur Conan Doyle* (London, 1922).

Connolly, S.J., *Divided Kingdom: Ireland 1630–1800* (New York, 2008).

Connor, C.D., *Arthur O'Connor: The Most Important Irish Revolutionary You May Never Have Heard Of* (New York, 2009).

Conroy, J. (ed.), *Franco-Irish Connections: Essays, Memoirs and Poems in Honour of Pierre Joannon* (Dublin, 2009).

Conway, S., *War, State, and Society in Mid-Eighteenth-Century Britain and Ireland* (Oxford, 2006).

Coogan, T.P., *Wherever Green Is Worn* (London, 2000).

Creasy, Sir E., *The Fifteen Battles That Changed the World from Marathon to Waterloo* (London, 1851).

Crowdy, T., *French Warship Crews 1789–1805: From the French Revolution to Trafalgar* (Oxford, 2005).

Cruickshanks, E. and Corp, E.T. (eds), *The Stuart Court in Exile and the Jacobites* (London, 1995).

Cullen, L.M., *The Irish Brandy Houses in 18th Century France* (Dublin, 2000).

——, 'The Irish Diaspora of the Seventeenth and Eighteenth centuries', in N. Canny (ed.), *Europeans on the Move: Studies on European Migration, 1500–1800* (Oxford, 1994).

Culligan, M. and Cherici, P., *The Wandering Irish in Europe: Their Influence from the Dark Ages to Modern Times* (London, 2000).

Cumberland, W.A., *Historical Memoirs of His Late Royal Highness William-Augustus, Duke of Cumberland* (London, 1767).

——, *Military Affairs in North America, 1748–1765: Selected Documents from the Cumberland Papers in Windsor Castle* (London, 1936), p. 232.

D'Arcy McGee, T., *A History of the Irish Settlers in North America. From the Earliest Period to the Census of 1850* (Boston, 1831).

Davis, T., 'The Battle of Fontenoy, 1745', in W. Kenealy, *The Ballads of Ireland*, vol. 1 (London, 1855).

De Courcy Ireland, J., *Ireland and the Irish in Maritime History* (Dun Laoighaire, 1986).

——, 'Irish Participation in the French Naval Activities which led to the fall of Yorktown 19 October 1781, and the independence of the United States', *The Irish Sword*, vol. 14, no. 56 (Summer 1981), pp. 221–29.

——, 'Irish Soldiers and Seamen in Latin America', *The Irish Sword*, vol. 1, no. 4 (1952–53), pp. 296–303.

——, 'Thomas Charles Wright: Soldier of Bolivar; Founder of the Ecuadorian Navy', *The Irish Sword*, vol. 6, no. 25 (Winter 1964), pp. 271–75.

De Freine, S., *The Great Silence* (Dublin, 1978).

Devine, T.M., 'Making the Caledonian Connection: The Development of Irish and Scottish studies', in L. McIlvanney and R. Ryan (eds.), *Ireland and Scotland: Culture and Society, 1700–2000* (Dublin, 2005), pp. 248–59.

Bibliography

Dickson, D., Keogh, D. and Whelan, K. (eds), *The United Irishmen, Republicism, Radicalism and Rebellion* (Dublin, 1993).

Dowling, B., 'The Brigade at Fontenoy, 11 May 1745', in W. Kenealy, *The Ballads of Ireland*, vol. 1 (London, 1855).

Doyle, D., *Ireland and Irishmen in the American Revolution* (Dublin, 1981).

Drake, P., *The Memoirs of Capt. Peter Drake* (Dublin, 1755).

Duffy, S. (ed.), *Atlas of Irish History* (Dublin, 2000).'

du Motier, G., *Memoirs, Correspondence and Manuscripts of General Lafayette*, vol. 1 (London, 1837).

N. Dunne-Lynch, 'The Irish Legion of Napoleon, 1803–15', in N. Genet-Rouffiac and D. Murphy (eds), *Franco-Irish Military Connections, 1590–1945.* (Dublin, 2009).

Dwyer, P., *Napoleon: The Path to Power 1769–1799* (London, 2007).

Elliott, M., *Wolfe Tone* (London, 1989).

Elting, J., *Napoleonic Uniforms*, vol. 2 (London, 2007).

Fagan, P., *Ireland in the Stuart Papers, 1719–42*, vol. 1 (Dublin, 1995).

Ffrench-Devitt, M., *A Short History of Ireland, Her Literature and Ancient Monuments* (Cork, 1983).

Fielding, J., *History of the War with America, France, Spain and Holland: Commencing in 1775 and Ending in 1783*, vol. 3 (London, 1785).

Fitzgerald, F., 'The Battle of Fontenoy', *An Cosantoir*, vol. 5, no. 11 (1945), pp. 599–607; vol. 5, no. 12 (1945), pp. 666–7.

Fitzjames, J., *Memoirs of the Marshal Duke of Berwick*, vol. 1 (London, 1779).

Forde, Captain F., 'Napoleon's Irish Legion', *An Cosantoir* (March 1974).

Forman, C., A Letter to the Rt. Hon. Sir Robert Sutton for Disbanding the Irish Regiments in the Service of France and Spain (Dublin, 1728).

Foster, R.F., *Modern Ireland 1600–1972* (London, 1988).

Fraser, E., *The War Drama of the Eagles: Napoleon's Standard Bearers on the Battlefield in Victory and Defeat from Austerlitz to Waterloo, a Record of Hard Fighting, Heroism and Adventure* (New York, 1912).

Gallagher, J., 'Conflict and Tragedy in Napoleon's Irish Legion: The Corbett/Sweeney Affair', *The Irish Sword*, vol. 16, no. 64 (1986).

——, *Napoleon's Irish Legion* (Carbondale, Ill., 1993).

——, 'William Lawless and the Siege of Flushing', *The Irish Sword*, vol. 17, no. 68 (1989), pp. 159–64.

Gandilhon, D., *Fontenoy, La France domine l'Europe* (Paris, 2008).

Garcia, M.B.V., 'Irish Migration and Exiles in Spain', in T. O'Connor and M. Ann Lyons (eds), *Irish Communities in Early Modern Europe* (Dublin, 2006), pp. 172–99.

Genet-Rouffiac, N., 'The Irish Jacobite Exile in France, 1692–1715', in T. Barnard and J. Fenlon, *The Dukes of Ormond, 1610–1745* (Suffolk, 2000), pp.195–211.

———, 'Jacobites in Paris and Saint Germain-en-Laye', in E. Cruickshanks and E.T. Corp (eds), *The Stuart Court in Exile and the Jacobites* (London, 1995).

Genet-Rouffiac, N. and Murphy, D. (ed.), *Franco-Irish Military Connections, 1590–1945* (Dublin, 2009).

Grattan, W., *Adventures of the Connaught Rangers, from 1808 to 1814* (London, 1847).

Green, F., *The Revolutionary War and the Military Policy of the United States* (New York, 1911).

Griffith, P., *French Napoleonic Infantry Tactics 1792–1815* (Oxford, 2007).

Guerins, T., 'Irish Soldiers of the Old Regime in Canada', *The Irish Sword*, vol. 2 (1954–56), no. 5, pp. 57–61.

Haddick-Flynn, K., *Sarsfield and the Jacobites* (Cork, 2003).

Hayes, R., 'Biographical Dictionary of Limerickmen in France', *The Old Limerick Journal, French Edition*, vol. 25 (Summer 1989), pp. 181–87.

Ireland and Irishmen in the French Revolution (London, 1932).

———, 'Irish Casualties in French Military Service', *The Irish Sword*, vol. 1 (1949), pp. 198–201.

———, *Irish Swordsmen of France* (Dublin, 1934).

———, *The Last Invasion of Ireland* (Dublin, 1937).

———, *Old Irish Links with France: Some Echoes of Exiled Ireland* (Dublin, 1940).

Hayes-McCoy, G.A., *A History of Irish Flags from Earliest Times* (Dublin, 1979).

Hayton, D.W., *Letters of Marmaduke Coghill 1722–1738* (Dublin, 2005).

Henegan, Sir R. D., *Seven Years Campaigning in the Peninsula and in the Netherlands, from 1808 to 1815*, vol. 2 (London, 1846).

Hennessy, M., *The Wild Geese: The Irish Soldier in Exile* (London, 1973).

Henty, G.A., *In the Irish Brigade: A Tale of War in Flanders and Spain* (London, 1901).

Higgins, P., *The Irish Brigade on the Continent* (London, 1908).

Hogan, P., 'The Regiments of Dillon and Walsh in the American War of Independence', *The Irish Sword*, vol. 14, no. 54 (Summer 1980), p. 106.

Holmes, R., *Redcoat: The British Soldier in the Age of Horse and Musket* (London, 2001).

Holohan, R., *The Irish Chateaux: In Search of the Descendants of the Wild Geese* (Dublin, 2008).

Hough, F., *The Siege of Savannah, by the Combined American and French Forces, under the Command of Gen. Lincoln and the Count D'Estaing in the Autumn of 1779* (Albany, 1866).

Joannon, P., 'Andrew MacDonagh: The Irish Monte-Cristo', in T. O'Connor and M.A. Lyons (eds), *Irish Communities in Early Modern Europe* (Dublin, 2006), pp. 145–59.

Johnston, E.M. (ed.), *Ireland in the Eighteenth Century* (Dublin, 1974).

Johnston, H., *The Yorktown Campaign and the Surrender of Cornwallis, 1781* (New York, 1971).

Bibliography

Johnstone, C., *Memoirs of the Rebellion in 1745 and 1746* (London, 1820).

Jones, C., *The Great Nation: France from Louis XV to Napoleon 1715–99* (London, 2002).

Jones, J.P., *John Paul Jones' Memoir of the American Revolution* (Hawaii, 1979).

Journal of Army Historical Research, vol. 16, no. 64 (1937), p. 87.

Joyce, P.W., *A Concise History of Ireland from the Earliest Times to 1908* (Dublin, 1912).

Kelly, J., Henry *Flood, Patriots and Politics in Eighteenth-Century Ireland* (Dublin, 1998).

Kelly, L., *A Flame Now Quenched: Rebels and Frenchmen in Leitrim 1793–1798* (Dublin, 1998).

Kelly, M., 'Reminiscences', *The Irish Sword*, vol. 17, no. 66, p. 3.

Killeen, R., *A Timeline of Irish History* (Dublin, 2003).

Kinealy, C., *A New History of Ireland* (Gloucestershire, 2008).

Klose, C., *Memoirs of Prince Charles*, vols 1–2 (London, 1846).

Lally, T., *Memoirs of Count Lally* (London, 1766).

Lawless, E., *With the Wild Geese* (London, 1902).

Lawson, C., *A History of Uniforms of the British Army*, vol. 2 (London, 1940), p. 168.

Lecky, W.E.H., *A History of Ireland in the Eighteenth Century* (London, 1892).

Lenihan, P., *1690 Battle of the Boyne* (Gloucestershire, 2003).

Lockhart, G., *The Lockhart Papers*, vol. 2 (London, 1817).

Lucey, C., *Harp and Sword, 1776: The Irish in the American Revolution* (Washington, 1976).

Lynch, P., 'The Battle of Fontenoy,' *An Cosantoir*, vol. 1, no. 14 (1941), pp. 441–4.

Lyons, M.A. and O'Connor, T., *Strangers to Citizens: The Irish in Europe 1600–1800* (Dublin, 2008).

MacGeoghegan, A., *History of Ireland, Ancient and Modern, Dedicated to the Irish Brigade* (Paris, 1762), translated by Patrick O'Kelly (Dublin, 1844).

MacKay, D., *Flight from Famine: The Coming of the Irish to Canada* (Ontario, 2009).

Mackey, A. and Singleton, W., *History of Masonry* (New York, 2010).

Mackinnon, D., *Origin and Services of the Coldstream Guards*, vol. 1 (London, 1883).

MacLeod, D., *Memoirs of the Life and Gallant Exploits of the Old Highlander, Sergeant Donald Macleod …* (London, 1791).

Maddan, R., *United Irishmen, Their Lives and Times*, vol. 2 (London, 1843).

Maguire, W.A. (ed.), *Kings in Conflict: The Revolutionary War in Ireland and Its Aftermath 1689–1750* (Belfast, 1990).

Mahon, Lord, *The Forty-Five* (London, 1851).

Marley, D., *Wars of the Americas: A Chronology of Armed Conflict in the Western Hemisphere* (Santa Barbara, Ca., 2008).

Martinez, G., 'Semper et Ubique Fidelis', in Nathalie Genet-Rouffiac and David Murphy (eds), *Franco-Irish Military Connections, 1590–1945* (Dublin, 2009).

Massie, A., *The Royal Stuarts* (London, 2010).

McBride, I., *Eighteenth Century Ireland* (Dublin, 2009).

McCracken, J.L., 'The Political Structure, 1714–60', in T.W. Moody and W.E. Vaughan (eds), *A New History of Ireland* (Oxford, 1986), pp. 57–83.

McDonnell, H., 'Some Documents Relating to the Involvement of the Irish Brigade in the Rebellion of 1745', *The Irish Sword*, vol. 16 (1980), pp. 3–21.

——, *The Wild Geese of the Antrim MacDonnells* (Dublin, 1996).

McIlvanney, L. and Ryan, R. (eds), *Ireland and Scotland: Culture and Society, 1700–2000* (Dublin, 2005).

McKenzie Annand, A., 'Fitzjames Horse in the '45', *The Irish Sword*, vol. 16, no. 65 (Winter 1986).

McLaughlin, M., *The Wild Geese: The Irish Brigades of France and Spain* (London, 1980).

McLynn, F., 'Ireland and the Jacobite Rising of '45', *The Irish Sword*, vol. 13, no. 53 (Winter 1979), pp. 339–52.

——, *The Jacobites* (London, 1985).

——, *1759: The Year Britain Became Master of the World* (London, 2004).

McNally, M., *The Battle of Aughrim 1691* (Gloucestershire, 2008).

——, *Battle of the Boyne 1690: The Irish Campaign for the English Crown* (Oxford, 2005).

——, *Ireland 1649–52: Cromwell's Protestant Crusade* (Oxford, 2009).

Metzgen, H. and Graham, J., *Caribbean Wars Untold: A Salute to the British West Indies* (Jamaica, 2007).

Mitchel, J., *The History of Ireland, from the Treaty of Limerick to the Present Time* (Dublin, 1868).

Mokyr, J., and Ó Gráda, C., 'The Height of Englishmen and Irishmen in the 1770s: Evidence from the East India Company Army', *Eighteenth-Century Ireland*, vol. 4 (1989), pp. 83–92.

Moody, T.W. and Vaughan, W.E. (eds), *A New History of Ireland, Volume IV: Eighteenth-Century Ireland 1691–1800* (Oxford, 1986).

Morales, O., *Ireland and the Spanish Empire, 1600–1825* (Dublin, 2010).

Mullen Jnr, T., 'The Seven Years War: Battle of Wandiwash', *The Military History Magazine* (February 1994).

Murphy, D., *The Irish Brigades 1685–2006* (Dublin, 2007).

Murphy, J.A., *The French Are in the Bay: The Expedition to Bantry Bay 1796* (Cork, 1997).

——, Justin McCarthy, Lord Mountcashel commander of the first Irish Brigade in France, an O'Donnell memorial lecture delivered at University College, Cork on 22 May 1958.

Murphy, W., 'Dillon's Regiment was not at Yorktown', *The Irish Sword*, vol. 3, no. 10 (Summer 1957), pp. 50–4.

Murphy, W.S., 'The Irish Brigade of France at the siege of Savannah, 1779,' *The Irish Sword*, vol. 2, no. 6 (1954–56), pp. 95–102.

Murtagh, D., 'The Jacobite Horse', *The Irish Sword*, vol. 1 (1952–53).

Murtagh, H., 'Franco-Irish Military Relations in the Nine Years War, 1689–97', in S.A. Stacey and V. Desnain (eds), *Culture and Conflict in Seventeenth-Century France and Ireland* (Dublin, 2004).

——, 'Irish Soldiers Abroad 1600–1800', in T. Bartlett and K. Jeffreys (eds), *A Military History of Ireland* (Cambridge, 1996), pp. 294–315.

Niemeyer, C.P., *America Goes to War: A Social History of the Continental Army* (New York, 1996).

Nolan, P., *The Irish Dames of Ypres* (Dublin, 1908).

Norris, J., *Pistols at Dawn: A History of Duelling* (Gloucestershire, 2009).

O'Brien, B. (ed.), *The Irish Nuns at Ypres: An Episode of the War* (London, 1915).

O'Callaghan, E.B. (ed.), *Documents Relative to the Colonial History of the State of New York*, vol. 10 (Albany, 1853).

——, Papers Relating to the First Settlement and Capture of Fort Oswego: 1727–1756 (Albany, 1849).

O'Callaghan, J.C., *The Green Book; or, Gleamings from the Writing-desk of a Literary Agitator* (Dublin, 1842).

——, *History of the Irish Brigades in the Service of France, from the Revolution in Great Britain and Ireland under James II, to the Revolution in France under Louis XVI* (Glasgow, 1870).

—— (ed.), *Macariæ Excidium or The Destruction of Cyprus, Being a Secret History of the War of the Revolution in Ireland* (London 1850).

O'Callaghan, S., *To Hell or Barbados* (London, 2000).

O'Ciardha, E., *Ireland and the Jacobite Cause, 1685–1766* (Dublin, 2004).

O'Conaill, C.J., 'The Irish Regiments in France: An Overview of the Presence of Irish Soldiers in French Service, 1716–1791', in E. Maher and G. Neville (eds), *France–Ireland: Anatomy of a Relationship* (Frankfurt, 2004).

O'Connell, M., *The Last Colonel of the Irish Brigade, Count O'Connell, and Old Irish Life at Home and Abroad, 1745–1833*, vol. 5 (London, 1892).

O'Connor, W., *The Memoirs of Gerald O'Connor* (London, 1903).

O'Conor, M., *A Military History of the Irish Nation, Comprising a Memoir of the Irish Brigade in the Service of France* (Dublin, 1855).

O'Donoghue, J., *Historical Memoirs of the O'Briens* (Dublin, 1860).

O'Donovan, P. Clifford, *The Irish in France* (London, 1992).

O'Farrell, J., Irish Families in Ancient Quebec Records: With Some Account of Soldiers from Irish Brigade Regiments of France Serving with the Army of Montcalm, text of address delivered at the annual concert and ball of the St Patrick's Society, Montreal, 15 January 1872 (Montreal, 1872).

Ó hAllmhuráin, G., *Irish Traditional Music* (Dublin, 1998).

O'hAnnrachain, E., 'An Analysis of the Fitzjames Cavalry Regiment, 1737', *The Irish Sword*, vol. 19 (1995), pp. 253–76.

———, 'Casualties in the Ranks of the Clare Regiment at Fontenoy', *Journal of the Cork Historical and Archeological Society*, vol. 99 (1994), pp. 96–110.

———, *Galériens*: The Irish Galley Slaves of France', *The Irish Sword*, vol. 25, no. 99 (2005–6), pp. 23–49.

———, 'Guests of France: A Description of the Invalides with an Account of the Irish in that Institution', in N. Genet-Rouffiac and D. Murphy (eds), *Franco-Irish Military Connections, 1590–1945* (Dublin, 2009).

———, The Irish Brigade at Lafelt 1747: Pyrrhic Victory and Aftermath, reprinted from *Journal of the Cork Historical and Archeological Society* (1997).

———, 'Irish Involvement in Cremona, 1702', in Thomas O'Connor and Mary Ann Lyons (eds), *Irish Communities in Early Modern Europe* (Dublin, 2006).

———, 'The Irish Prisoners in the Bastille', *The Irish Sword*, vol. 26, no. 103 (2008–9), pp. 57–78.

———, 'Lally, the Regime's Scapegoat', *The Irish Sword*, vol. 24, no. 96 (2004), pp. 164–76.

O'hAnnrachain, M., *A Swordsman of the Brigade* (Dublin, 1914).

O'Hart, J., *Irish Pedigrees; Or, The Origin and stem of the Irish Nation*, Second Series (Dublin, 1878).

Ohlmever, M., *Civil War and Restoration in the Three Stuart Kingdoms: The Career of Randal McDonald, Marquis of Antrim* (Dublin, 2011).

O'Kelly, C., *The Jacobite War in Ireland 1688–90* (Dublin, 1894).

O'Meara, B., *Napoleon in Exile*, vol. 1 (London, 1822).

O'Neill, J., 'Conflicting Loyalties: Irish Regiments in the Imperial Service, 1689–1710', *The Irish Sword*, vol. 17, no. 67 (1987–88).

O'Reilly, A., The Irish at Home and Abroad, at the Court and in the Camps (New York, 1856).

Pakenham, T., *The Year of the French* (London, 1969).

Pakenham, V., *The Big House in Ireland* (London, 2000).

Parker, R., *Memoirs of the Most Memorable Military Transactions …* (Dublin, 1746).

Pawly, R., *Napoleon's Scouts of the Imperial Guard* (Oxford, 2006).

Petrie, C., 'The Irish Brigade at Fontenoy', *The Irish Sword*, vol. 1, no. 3 (1951–52), pp. 166–72.

———, 'Irishmen in the '45', *The Irish Sword*, vol. 2, no. 8 (Summer 1956), pp. 275–82.

Reid, S., *Armies of the Irish Rebellion 1798* (Oxford, 2011).

———, *Culloden Moor 1746: The Death of the Jacobite Cause* (East Sussex, 2002).

Ridgeway, W., *The Origin and Influence of the Thoroughbred Horse* (Cambridge, 1905).

Roche, J., *Critical and Miscellaneous Essays by an Octogenarian* (Cork, 1851).

Roscoe, T. (ed.), *The Works of Jonathan Swift: Containing Interesting and Valuable Papers, Not Hitherto Published*, vol. 2 (London, 1843).

Sankey, M., *Jacobite Prisoners of the 1715 Rebellion: Preventing and Punishing Insurrection in Early Hanoverian Britain* (Hampshire, 2005).

Saxe, M. de, *Maurice comte de Saxe et Marie-Josephe de Saxe Dauphine de France lettres et Documents inedits des Archives* (Paris, 1867).

———, *Reveries, or Memoirs upon the Art of War* by Field Marshal Count Sax (London, 1757).

Scott, S., *From Yorktown to Valmy: The Transformation of the French Army in an Age of Revolution* (Colorodo, 1998).

Scott, W., *The Life of Napoleon Bonaparte, Emperor of the French* (Philadelphia, 1857).

———, *The Works of Jonathan Swift* (Edinburgh, 1814).

Seton, B., 'Dress of the Jacobite Army: The Highland habit', *The Scottish Historical Review*, vol. 25, no. 100 (July 1928), pp. 270–281.

T. Sheridan and J. Swift, *The Intelligencer*, edited by J. Wooley (Cambridge, 1992).

Simms, J.G., 'The Irish on the Continent, 1691–1800', in T.W. Moody and W.E. Vaughan (eds), *A New History of Ireland, Volume IV: Eighteenth-Century Ireland 1691–1800* (Oxford, 1996), pp. 629–56.

———, *Jacobite Ireland 1685–91* (London, 1969).

———, *The Williamite Confiscation in Ireland, 1690–1703* (London, 1976).

Skrine, F.H., *Fontenoy and Great Britain's Share in the War of the Austrian Succession 1741–48* (Edinburgh, 1906).

———, The Irish Brigades, 1689–1750: a lecture delivered before the Irish Literary Society of London, 1 Oct, 1921.

———, The Irish Brigades, 1691–1791, lecture delivered in Dublin in January 1914.

Smith, J., *The French Nobility in the Eighteenth Century: Reassessments and New Approaches* (Pennsylvania, 2006).

Southey, R., *The History of the Peninsular War* (London, 1837).

Spencer, C., *The Battle for Europe: How the Duke of Marlborough Masterminded the Defeat of the French at Blenheim* (New Jersey, 2004).

Stanhope, P.H., *History of England from the Peace of Utrecht to the Peace of Versailles, by Lord Mahon*, vol. 3 (Boston, 1853).

———, *The Forty-Five*, vols 1 and 11 (London, 1851).

Stevens, J., *Yorktown Centennial Handbook: Historical and Topographical Guide to the Yorktown Peninsula, Richmond, James River and Norfolk* (New York, 1881).

Story, G., *A True and Impartial History* (London, 1691).

Swords, L., *The Green Cockade: The Irish in the French Revolution 1789–1815* (Dublin, 1989).

———, *The Flight of the Earls: A Popular History* (Dublin, 2007).

——, 'The Irish in Paris at the End of the Ancient Regime', in T. O'Connor (ed.), *The Irish In Europe, 1580–1815* (Dublin, 2001).

Taylor, A. and H., *1745 and After* (London, 1938).

Thackeray, W.M., *The Luck of Barry Lyndon* (New York, 1853).

Thompson, J.M. (ed.), *Napoleon's Letters* (London, 1998).

Tone, W., *Memoirs of Theobald Wolfe Tone*, vols 1 and 2 (London, 1827).

Trowbridge, W.R., *A beau sabreur, Maurice de Saxe: Marshal of France, His Loves, His Laurels and His Times 1696–1750* (New York, 1910).

Urban, S., *The Gentleman's Magazine*, vol. 67 part 2 (London, 1797).

Van Brock, F.W., 'Defeat at les Plantons 1792', *The Irish Sword*, vol. 13 (1979).

——, 'Lieutenant General Robert Dillon, 1754–1781', *The Irish Sword*, vol. 14, no. 55 (Winter 1980), pp. 172–87.

——, 'Major General Oliver Harty in Brittany 1799–1800', *The Irish Sword*, vol. 14, no. 57 (Winter 1981), pp. 287–315.

Voltaire, *The Age of Louis XIV* (London, 1751).

——, *The Age of Louis XV, Being the Sequel to Louis XIV* (London, 1774).

Waldon Bamford, P., *Fighting Ships and Prisons: The Mediterranean Galleys of France in the Age of Louis XIV* (London, 1973).

Walsh, M.K., 'Letters from Fontenoy', *The Irish Sword*, vol. 19, no. 78 (Winter 1995), pp. 238–48.

Wauchope, P., *Patrick Sarsfield and the Williamite War* (Dublin, 1992).

Weber, P., *On the Road to Rebellion: The United Irishmen and Hamburg* (Dublin, 2007).

Wellesley, A., *Dispatches of Field Marshal the Duke of Wellington during his Various Campaigns, 1799–1815*, edited by John Gurwood, vol. 12 (London, 1838).

Whelan, K., 'The Irish in France in the Eighteenth Century', in J. Conroy (ed.), *Franco-Irish Connections: Essays, Memoirs and Poems in Honour of Pierre Joannon* (Dublin, 2009).

——, *The Tree of Liberty, Catholic Middlemen in Eighteenth-Century Ireland* (Cork, 1996).

White, J., *Marshal of France: The Life and Times of Maurice de Saxe* (London, 1962).

Williams, T., *America's First Flag Officer: Father of the American Navy* (Bloomington, Ind., 2008).

Wills, R., *The Jacobites and Russia, 1715–1750* (East Linton, 2002).

INDEX

18th Royal Irish Regiment of Foot, 196
27th (Iniskilling's) Foot, 29, 115, 146
4th Royal Regiment (French Foreign Legion), 213
87th (Royal Irish Fusiliers) Regiment of Foot, 207
87th (The Prince of Wales Own) Irish Regiment of Foot, 28-9
87th Regiment d'Infanterie, 167, 179, 205
88th Foot (Connaught Rangers), 'The Devil's Own', 201, 207
88th Regiment d'Infanterie, 167, 179, 205
92nd Regiment d'Infanterie, 167, 179, 205

Act of Union (1707), England and Scotland, 84
Act of Union (1801), Ireland and Great Britain, 187-8
Agincourt, Battle of (1415), 70
Allen, Captain John, 205
Almanza, Battle of (1707), 82
Almeida, Siege of (1810), 206
American War of Independence 13, 20, 27-8, 104, 151-62
Astorga, Siege of (1810), 205, 206
Asturias, 203
Athlone, 55, 57, 59
Atholl, duke of, 106
Aughrim, Battle of (1691), 36, 59-60, 66, 68, 70, 220
Austerlitz, Battle of (1805), 102, 104, 198
Avignon, 127, 130

Badojaz, Siege of (1812), 204
Baggot's Hussars, 117, 119, 120
Ballina, 186
Ballinamuck, Co. Longford, 186, 189, 269
Bannockburn, Battle of (1314), 120
Bantry, 180
Barcelona, Siege of (1707), 82, 144
Barker, William, 185, 201
Barossa, Battle of (1811), 28
Barrell's, Regiment of Foot, 121
Barry, Commodore John, 155
Bautzen, Battle of (1813), 210
Belgrade, Siege of (1789), 185
Bellow, Matthew, 185
Berwick, duke of, see Fitzjames, 36, 52-4, 57-8, 66-70, 73, 82, 86
Berwick's, Regiment of 10, 36, 74, 76, 82, 93, 99, 111, 118, 153, 162, 167, 205, 221
Berwick's. Regiment of (Royalist, émigré army of the princes), 169
Black Watch, Highland Regiment of, 91, 94, 98, 138, 158
Blackwell, General, 187
Blake, George, 185
Blenheim, Battle of (1704), 77-8, 216
Bligh's, Regiment of Foot, 121
Boissleau, marquis de, 56
Bonaparte, Joseph, 202, 222
Bos, Jean, 101
Bourke's, Regiment of, 9, 10, 74, 76, 78
Boyne, Battle of (1690), 8, 52-3, 220
Brown, Field-Marshal Maximilian von, 39, 221

Browne, Colonel of Dillon's, 158
Bulkeley's, Regiment of, 36, 93, 111, 119
Busaco, Battle of (1810), 207
Bussy, comte de, 145, 146
Butler, James the Duke of Ormond, 86, 90
Byrne, Miles, 20, 192, 197, 200, 204-6, 208, 210, 225
Byron, Admiral John, 157

Calcinato, Battle of (1706), 80
Carrrickfergus, 51, 125, 140, 181
Cashel, 55, 58
Cassano, Battle of (1705), 78, 216
Castiglione, Battle of (1706), 78
Castlebar Races, 186
Castlereagh, Lord Robert, Chief Secretary, 193
Chambery, 48
Charles II of England, 46-7, 50
Charles II of Spain, 73
Charles VI of Austria, 219
Charles XII of Sweden, 90
Chateau-Renaud, Admiral, 65
Cherin, Bernard, French herald, 35
Chesapeake, Battle of (1781), 160
Chesterfield, Lord, 125, 126
Chiara, Battle of (1701), 74
Choiseul, duc de, 139, 148
Churchill, Sir Winston, 73
Churchill's, (the buffs) Regiment of, 79
Clare, County, 18, 20, 24, 58
Clare's, Regiment of, 10, 36, 37, 48, 77-80, 93, 106, 111, 113-15, 165, 177, 221
Clarke, Marshal Henri, due de Feltre, 104, 168, 177-8, 193, 199, 205, 208, 209, 223
Clary, Desire and Julie, 222
Coldstream Guards, 94, 98, 102-3
College of Surgeons, Dublin, 211
Compagnie des Indes (French East India Company), 143, 145, 148
Conti, Prince de, 139
Conway, General Count Thomas, 152, 170
Coote, Lieutenant Colonel Eyre, 146
Cope, Sir John, 108, 109
Corbett, Captain Thomas, 197
Corbett, Captain William, 194
Corcoran, James, 189
Cornwallis, General Charles, 160, 186
Costello, Sergeant, 209-10 ,211
Cremona, Battle of (1701), 39, 74-6
Cromwell, Oliver, 47

Culloden, Battle of (1746), 119, 120-2, 126, 141, 189
Cumberland, Prince William Augustus, duke of, 7, 92, 94, 96-8, 102, 113, 116, 118-23, 134, 137, 189

d'Ache, Admiral, 144, 145, 146, 148
Dalrymple, Lieutenant General Hew, 180
D'Alton, General Alexandre, 192, 193, 224
D'Alton, Major-General James, 32
d'Arcy, Captain, 158
d'Argenson, comte, 100-2, 125, 129, 135, 144
Darragh, Captain, 137
Davis, Thomas, 221
Davoren, Lieutenant Michael, 221
de Bellefonds, Marshal Bernardin, 33
de Vaudreuil, Marquis, 137
DeCourcy Ireland, John, 160, 198
DeGaulle, President Charles, 224, 268
d'Eguilles, Marquis, 111, 120
DeLacy, Captain Louis, 202
Derby, 112, 116, 124, 128, 217
de Roqueville, Admiral, 105
Desbureaux, General Charles-Francois, 209
d'Estaine, Admiral, 157, 158
Dettingen Agreement (1743), 43
Dettingen, Battle of (1743), 41, 93
Dillon, Colonel Barthemy, 161
Dillon, Colonel Edouard, 156, 169, 172, 217
Dillon, Colonel James, 97
Dillon, Colonel Robert, 161
Dillon, Fanny, 222
Dillon, Gauillaine (Billy), 161, 217
Dillon, General Count Arthur (1750-94), 149, 153, 156, 158, 161, 166-8, 174, 216, 222
Dillon, General de Brigade Count Theobald, 165, 167, 168
Dillon, Henry, 170
Dillon, James, 216
Dillon, Lieutenant Francois (Frank), 161
Dillon, Lieutenant General Arthur (grandfather of Count Arthur, Richard, Theobald), 48, 76, 78, 80, 89, 217
Dillon, Regiment of (Royalist émigré army of the princes), 169
Dillon, Richard, Archbishop of Narbonne, 216
Dillon, Therese-Lucy, 222
Dillon's, Regiment of Foot (British Army), 172
Dillon's, Regiment of, 10, 18, 21, 23-4, 36, 48, 74, 75, 76, 78, 80, 82, 93-4, 97, 100, 111, 124-5, 143, 153, 155-6, 158, 160-1, 164, 167, 170, 177, 217, 219, 221
Dorrington's, Regiment of, 10, 77-8, 80-1

Index

Douglas, John (alias of Prince Charles Edward Stuart), 129
Douglas, Major-General James, 55
Doyle, Sir Arthur Conan, 76
Drake, Captain Peter, 79
Drogheda, 47, 55
Drummond, Lieutenant Colonel John, 111, 114-5
Duhesme, General Guillaume, 204
Duleek, 53
Dumas, Alexander, 171
Dundas, General David, 201
Dundee, Viscount, 54, 88
Dwyer, Michael, 190

East India Company (British), 139, 143, 146
Edgeworth, Abbe Henry, 222
Elbe River, 209, 213
Emmet, Robert, 190, 267
Emmet, Thomas, 192, 196
Erskine, John the 6th Earl of Mar, 86
Ettlingen, Battle of (1734), 143
Eugene, Prince of Austria, 73-6
Evans, Captain, 211
Expedition d'Irlande, 178

Falkirk, Battle of (1746), 114-15, 120, 125-6
Farrell, Lieutenant Thomas, 221
Finglas Declaration, 53
Fitzgerald, Captain, 123
Fitzgerald, Lord Edward, 184
Fitzgerald, Regiment of, 76, 78, 80
Fitzhnery, Colonel, 208
Fitzjames 2nd duc de, 144
Fitzjame's horse, Regiment of, 10, 18, 26, 33, 36, 45, 95, 97, 106, 110-11, 116, 119-22, 134, 139, 141
Fitzjames, Edward, 5th duke of Berwick, 166
Fitzjames, James, 1st duke of Berwick, (illeg. son of James II), 50, 52-4, 56-8, 62, 66-71, 73, 82, 86
Fitzmaurice, Colonel Thomas, 159-60
Fitzpatrick, Dragoon, 207
Fizhenry, Commandant, 203
Flamborough Head, Battle of (1779), 156
Flight of the Earls, 9, 11, 125
Flight of the Wild Geese, 8, 9, 11, 24, 65, 125, 224
Flushing, 200, 201, 202
Fontenoy, Battle of (1745) 8, 25, 26, 31, 43, 141, 144, 216, 225
Foreman, Charles, English pamphleteer, 10, 34, 76, 216

Forrester, Sir John, 85
Foster, R.F., 152
Francis I of Austria, 169
Franco-Dutch War, 50
Franklin, Benjamin, 153, 155, 164
Frederick the Great of Prussia, 41, 104, 138, 224
Freemasonry, 139, 164, 165
French and Indian War, 28
French Revolutionary Wars (1793-1801), 28
Freron, E.C., 103

Gallagher, John, 193
Galmoy's, Regiment of, 10, 74, 76, 78, 80
Galway, 20, 56, 60, 61, 90, 177, 125
Gardes Francaises, Regiment of, 43, 96
Gauillemin, Sous-Lieutenant Edme, 29
Gaydon, Major Richard, 23, 80, 219
George I of England, Hanovarian Prince George Ludwig, 23, 72, 85
George II of England, 7, 92, 99, 112, 128, 131, 134
George III of England, 151, 156
George IV of England, Prince Regent, 29
Gerona, Siege of (1808), 204-5
Gibraltar, 82, 104, 153, 165
Ginkel, General Godard Van, 59, 61-4
Glasgow, 13
Glenfinnan, 108
Glenshiel, Battle of (1719), 91
Grand Army, 200, 209, 212
Grasse, Admiral de, 160
Grassins, Regiment de, 98
Grattan, Henry, 170, 188
Grattan, Lieutenant William, 207
Grebenstein, 141
Grenada, 156-7, 174, 265
Guichen, comte de, 159

Hagan, Daniel, 135, 221
Haiti, 108, 158, 167, 172, 221
Hamilton, Archibald Rohan, 176
Hamilton, Lieutenant General, 52
Hancock, President John, 164
Harty, General Oliver, 167-8, 172, 179, 181, 187, 192, 195-6
Harvey, Bagenal, 184
Hawley, General Henry, 114
Hay, Lord Charles, 96
Hayes, John, 185
Hayes, Richard, 168, 172, 179, 182

Heidelberg, Siege of, 48
Hennessy, Richard, 18, 23, 31, 223
Henry V of England, 70
Henry VII of England, 51
Heraldic King of Arms in Dublin, 34
Hibernia, Regiment of, 9, 31, 36, 81, 82, 123, 130, 154, 204-5, 222
Hickey, Francois, 135, 221
Highland Charge, 110, 121
Hoche, General Lazare, 178-81, 183
Hogan, Michael 'galloping', 55
Holmes, Richard, 29
Hooke, Nathanial, 84
Huguenots, 40, 59
Humbert, General Jean Joseph, 33, 184-7, 189, 192, 195
Hundred Years War, 99

Ibernian Peninsula, 202
Imperial Eagle, 193, 194, 199, 201, 212, 213
Ingoldsby, Brigadier, 96
Innocent XII, Pope, 72
Inverness, 85, 87, 116, 118-19,122
Irish battalion in Canada, 137-8
Irish Brigade in American Civil War, 152
Irish Brigade in British service, 170-2
Irish Brigade in the Second World War, 242
Irish College, Leuven, 12, 134
Irish College, Paris, 16
Irish College, Salamanca, 208
Irish Dominican College, Leuven, 79
Irish Famine of 1740, 27
Irish Famine of 1840s, 189, 220
Irish Rising of 1641, 47, 50, 57
Irish Rising of 1798, 91
Irlanda, Regiment of, 9, 36, 81, 39, 154, 204
Isle of Man, 141
Italy, 108, 155, 169

Jamaica, 158, 172
James I, 12, 220
James II, 7, 8, 10, 12, 39, 46-8, 51, 52-3, 68, 72-3, 76, 105, 109, 129, 132, 216, 220
James III, 10, 12, 16, 22, 23, 46, 72, 81, 85-7, 89, 90, 126, 128, 129, 135, 165, 219
Jemappes, Battle of (1792), 177
Jena, Battle of (1806), 102, 104, 199
Johnstone, Chevalier, 112, 114-15, 120, 126
Jones, Captain John Paul, 155
Joseph II, Emperor of Austria, 32
Jumet, General, 208

Katzbach, Battle of (1813), 211
Kavanagh, General Charles, 32
Keating, General Thomas, 168, 172
Kehl, Siege of (1703), 77
Kelly, Michael, 31
Kelly, Reverend George, 106, 110, 129
Kelly, Thomas, 221
Kenmare, Lord, 154, 182
Kent, 112, 113, 118
Keogh, Ensign Edward, 28
Kerry, County, 35, 217
Killala, 184
Killiecrankie, Battle of (1689), 54
Kilmaine, General Charles, 161, 168, 172-3, 177, 183, 187, 223
Kilmainham Gaol, Dublin, 187
Kilmarnock's horse, 116
King's Own Scottish Borderers, 103
King's Royal Irish Hussars, 114
Kinsale, 51, 53, 180

La Terreur, 172, 177
Lachaber No More, 131
Lacy, Field-Marshal Count Franz Moritz von, 221, 224
Lacy, Field-Marshal Peter de, 224
Lafayette, marquis de, 152, 154, 156, 164
Lafelt, Battle of (1747), 7, 25, 26, 133-4, 141, 144, 216
LaHogue, Battle of (1692), 69-70
Lake, General Gerard, 186
Lally de Tollendal, Lieutenant General Thomas, comte de, 31, 94, 97, 99, 114-15, 125, 143-50
Lally, Sir Gerald (father of Thomas), 143
Lally, Trophime-Gerald (son of Thomas), 149
Lally's, Regiment of, 10, 36, 93, 111, 113, 118, 144
Landen, Battle of (1693), 71, 82
Lauzon's Legion (American War), 161, 177
Lauzun, duc de, French Brigade commander, 50-2, 54, 56
Lauzun's French Brigade, 48, 51, 56, 58
Lawless, Commandant William, 192, 200-2, 209, 211
Lawless, Emily, 225
Lawless, Peter, 90
Lee, Andrew, colonel and lieutenant general in French service, 77-8, 80, 82
Lee, Regiment of (newly formed in 1796), 179
Lee's, Regiment of, 10, 77, 80, 82
Legion Noire, 178, 181, 185

Index

Les Invalides, 31, 103, 104, 232, 267
Lillibulero', 52, 236
Limerick, 20, 53, 56, 57, 60
Lisbon, 82, 207
Lochiel, chief of, 109, 111, 121
Louis XIV of France, 10, 31, 39, 47-8, 54, 69, 72-4, 76, 78, 84, 85, 166
Louis XV of France, 10, 31, 93, 97, 99, 102, 105, 127, 139, 143, 148, 216
Louis XVI of France, 16, 149, 167, 222, 223
Louis XVIII of France, comte de Provence, 169, 174, 213, 222
Louis, Dauphin of France, 93, 99
Louisbourg, 138
Louisiana, 142, 222, 225
Lowenberg, 1st Battle of (1813), 210
Lowenberg, 2nd Battle of (1813), 211
Lowendahl, comte de, 101
Luxembourg Gardens, Paris, 31
Luxembourg, Marshal de, 70, 71
Luzzara, Battle of (1702), 75, 76, 83, 141, 216
Lynch, Lieutenant Colonel Dominic (at Lafelt), 134
Lynch, Major-General Isodare, 161, 168

MacCartan, Captain Anthony, 224
MacCartan, Doctor Andronicus, 224
MacCarthy, Eugene, 155, 156
MacCarthy, Governor of Fort Charles, Illinois, 138
MacCarthy, Justin (Lord Mountcashel), 47, 48, 50, 83
MacCarthy, Lord, 157
MacDermott, Colonel Thomas, 172
Macdonald of Clanranald, 106
Macdonald of Sleat, 106
MacDonald, Aeneas, 106
MacDonald, Lieutenant Colonel Sir John, 106, 110, 120
MacDonald, Marshal Jacques, 210, 211
MacDonnell, Captain Enrique, 198
MacDonnell, Captain Francis, 75
MacDonnell, Colonel Daniel, 39
MacDonnell, Enrique, 19
MacGeoghegan, Captain Francis, 111, 112, 114, 116, 118
MacGeoghegan, Chaplain Abbe, 23
MacHenry, Lieutenant John, 221
MacLachlann, Chief, 121
MacMahon, Captain, 123
MacMahon, President Patrice, 224
MacNamara, Admiral John, 18, 137

MacNamara, Henry, 19
Macpherson, James, 176
MacSheedy, (engineering officer at Kehl in 1703), 77
MacSheedy, Adjutant-General Bernard, 192, 196-7
Madame Buonaparte, 195
Madame de Pompadour, 149, 222
Madrid, 90, 202, 203, 221
Magrath, Captain Marcus, 89
Maguire, General, 221
Maillebots, Marshal de, 108
Mainz, 199, 200
Maison du Roi, Regiment de, 97
Mallorca, 139
Malplaquet, Battle of (1709), 8, 80-81, 83, 92, 99, 141, 216
Marengo, Battle of (1800), 200
Marie-Antonitee, Queen of France, 168, 219, 222
Marlborough, John Churchill, the Duke of, 58, 73, 77, 81
Marseille, 222
Marsigila, 83
Martinique, 158, 162
Mary of Modena, 39, 84, 217, 222
Masterson, Sergeant Patrick, 28
McAuley, Captain, 211
McCann, Captain, 201
McCool, Finn, 110, 141
McDonagh, Captain of Dillon's Regiment, 75
McDonagh, Lieutenant Colonel Andrew, 98, 179, 217
McDonnell, James, 185
McDonnell, Reynaldo, 35
McDonough, Captain Anthony, 25
McElligott, General, 221
McGregor, Robert 'Rob Roy', 87
McKenna, Father Charles, 93
McKenna, General John, 222
McLynn, Frank, 149
Michelet, Jules, 101, 172
Misset, Captain John, 219
Mitchel, John, 183
Moidart, the seven men of, 106
Monro's, Regiment of Foot, 121
Montcalm, General Louis-Joseph, 137-8, 225
Montreal, 138
Montreuill-Sur-Mer, 212, 213
Mooney, Sergeant, 204
Moore, Doctor, 223
Moore, General John, 204

Mountcashel's Irish Brigade, 8, 10, 24, 32, 48, 49, 58, 70, 82
Moylan, Dr, Catholic Bishop of Cork, 182
Murphy, Lieutenant Colonel, 146
Murray, John, 117
Murray, Lord George, 90, 108, 112-16, 119-20, 123, 126-7

Nantes, 48, 106, 223
Napoleon (Napoleon Bonaparte), 11, 13, 28-9, 103-4, 164-8, 177, 178, 182-3, 187, 191-202, 204, 207-13, 222, 223
Napoleonic Wars (1803-15), 28, 104
Napoleon's Farewell to Paris', 195
Napoleon's Imperial Eagle, 28, 29, 193-4, 201-2, 212-3,
Nelson, Admiral, 183, 198
New France (Quebec), 136, 137
New Ross, Battle of (1798), 184
Ney, Marshal Michel, 209
Nile, Battle of (1798), 183
Nivelle, Battle of (1813) 19
Normandie, Regiment de, 97, 100
Nugent, Captain Francis, 117
Nugent's horse, Regiment of, 10, 71, 80, 86, 90

O' Brien, Charles, 5th Lord Clare, 64, 77, 79, 83
O'Brien, Charles, 6th Lord Clare, 16, 93, 101, 135, 139, 144, 223
O'Brien, Daniel, 4th Lord Clare, 83
O'Callaghan, John Cornelius, 12, 25, 103, 109, 118
O'Carrol, Major John, 79
O'Ciardha, Eamon, 220
O'Connell, Captain Maurice,18
O'Connell, Daniel 'the liberator', 18, 225
O'Connell, General Count Daniel, 34, 165, 170, 188
O'Connell, Lieutenant Richard, 155
O'Connor, Arthur, 196
O'Connor, Captain, 159
O'Connor, Daniel, 26, 39
O'Connor, Major Gerald, 37, 38, 53, 78
O'Donnell, General, 221, 224
O'Donnell, Hugh 'balldearg', 61
O'Donnell, Hugh, 8
O'Donnell, Leopoldo, 224
O'Donnell, Lieutenant Colonel (at Louisbourg), 138
O'Donnell, Major-General Henry, 32
O'Dowd, James, 185
O'Farrell, Major Denis, 167

O'Flynn, Chef d'escadron, 207
O'Gara, General, 224
Ogerlau, village of, 77
Ogilvy, Regiment of, 141
O'Gorman, Chevalier Thomas, 16, 224
O'Gorman, Count Victor, 167
O' hAnnrachain, Eoghan, 31
O'Hamsey, Denis (harpist), 109
O'Hare, Colonel Jose, 30
O'Heguerty, Dominic, 106
O'Higgins, Bernardo, 222
O'Kelly, Colonel Anthony, 204, 205
O'Kelly, Colonel Charles, 60, 65-7
O'Kelly, James, 155, 156
O'Kennedy, Colonel, 146
O'Keon, Henry, 185
O'Kuoney, Admiral Daniel, 19
O'Lawlor, Brigadier-General Joseph, 206
O'Mahony, Colonel (Napoleon's Legion), 205, 213
O'Mahony, Lieutenant General Daniel, 75-7, 224
O'Meara, Colonel Daniel, 208
O'Meara, Doctor Bernard, 28
O'Moran, Lieutenant (son of James), 192
O'Moran, Lieutenant Colonel James, 161, 172, 174
O'Murphy, Marie Louis, 222
O'Neill, Captain Felix, 123
O'Neill, Colonel Artura, 154
O'Neill, General, 224
O'Neill, Gordon, 52, 59
O'Neill, Owen Roe, 9
Order of the Cincinnati, 156
O'Reilly, Field Marshal Alexander, 33, 154, 201-2, 222
O'Rourke, Major-General Cornelius, 11, 210
O'Rourke, Major-General Joseph, 11, 210
O'Shea, Captain Robert, 116, 120, 122
O'Shea, Général de Brigade Richard, 179
Osmond, Lieutenant, 210
O'Sullivan, Sir John, 106, 108, 109, 113, 119, 121-3, 126, 215
O'Toole, Captain Lucas, 219
Oudenaarde, Battle of (1708), 80, 83

Paris, 10, 16, 17, 25, 31, 47, 68, 72, 100, 101, 103-4, 123, 127-8, 132, 148, 150, 154, 168, 171-2, 179, 182, 185-6, 192, 194-5, 202, 215, 216
Parrot, Captain, 210

Index

Peace of Ryswick (1697), 33, 72-4
Penal Laws, 15, 28, 125, 154, 220
Peninsular War (1808-414), 28, 172, 202-09
Pensacola, Siege of (1791), 154
Perth, 109, 111
Perth, duke of, 108, 121
Peter the Great of Russia, 90
Petrezzoli, Colonel Antoine, 197, 199
Petrie, Sir Charles, 103
Philip V of Spain, 73, 81, 82, 90, 223, 267
Philipsberg, Siege of, 71
Pitsligo, Lord, 117
Pitt, Prime Minister William, 148, 170
Plantation of Ulster, 220
Pluassey, Battle of (1757), 145
Plunket, General Thomas, 221
Pondicherry, 145, 146, 148, 149
Pope Clement XI, 129
Pope Clement XIII, 129
Post traumatic stress disorder, 44
Pratt, Viceroy John, 182
Preston, Battle of (1715), 87, 90
Prestonpans, Battle of (1746), 109-10, 120
Prince Charles Edward Stuart, 'Bonnie Prince Charlie', 12, 105, 108, 110, 121, 139, 215
Prince Charles Volunteers, 114

Quebec, Siege of (1759), 138
Queen Anne of England, 85
Quiberon Bay, Battle of (1759), 140

Ramillies, Battle of (1706), 78-9, 83, 141
Reichenbach, Battle of (1812), 209
Rice, Captain james, 168
Rich, Lieutenant Colonel, 121
Richelieu, duc de, 97
Robespierre, Maximilien de, 164, 172
Rochambeau, comte de, 160, 161
Rodney, Admiral, 159
Roi, Regiment de, 96
Rooth's, Regiment of, 36, 93
Rossbach, Battle of (1757), 138, 221
Royal (Collin's) Barracks, 188
Royal Scots (Royal Ecossais), Regiment of 10, 93, 111-12, 114, 119, 123, 126
Russia, 11, 19, 136
Rutledge, Walter, 106
Ryan, Captain, 212
Ryan, Luke, 20

Saint George, Madras, 145
Saint Germain, Paris, 47
'Saint Patrick's Day in the Morning', 7, 98, 199, 207
Saint-Cyr, Lieutenant General Claude, 41, 205
Sainte Ruthe, Marquis de, 48, 58
Saint-Leger, Captain, 210, 212
Salamanca, 207
Saratoga, Battle of (1777), 153, 162
Sarrazin, Colonel Jean, 185-6
Sarsfield, James (son of Patrick), 71, 83, 90, 223
Sarsfield, Patrick, earl of Lucan, 11, 24, 50, 57, 60, 63, 70-1, 82, 223
Savannah, 157, 158, 172, 174, 217
Saxe, Marshal Maurice de, 14, 43, 48, 92-4, 97-9, 100-1, 105, 128, 133, 144, 224
Schomberg, Duke of, 52
Sempill's Regiment, 94, 103, 121
Senegal, 158, 161, 225
Seven Years War (1754-63), 13, 29, 123, 136, 142, 153
Sheares, Henry and John, 184
Sheldon, Captain Dominic (of Lauzen's Legion), 161
Sheldon, Major-General Dominic, 52
Sheldon's horse, Regiment of, 10, 74, 76, 77
Sheridan, Sir Thomas, 106, 116, 123-4, 130
Sheriffmuir, Battle of (1715), 87
Sherlock, Colonel Juan, 204
Simms, J.G., 54, 61
Skrine, Francis, 101, 102
Sligo, Siege of, 61
Smith, Adjutant-General James (alias of Wolfe Tone), 187
South America, 27, 153, 225
Speyer, Battle of (1703), 77, 141
St Barbara, Company of, 205
St Peter's Basilica, Rome, 132
Stack, Edward, 155, 156
Stapleton, Lieutenant Colonel Walter, 99, 111, 122
Steenkirk, Battle of (1692), 70-1, 104
Stirling Castle, 108, 114, 116
Stolberg-Gedern, Princesss Louis of, 131
Story, George, 65
Strickland, Colonel Francis, 106
Stuart, Captain, of Dillon's, 75
Stuart, Charlotte (illeg. Daughter of Prince Charles Edward Stuart), 131
Stuart, Henry Benedict, Cardinal Duke of York, 110, 219

Stuart, Mary, 46
Sweeney, Captain John, 197
Swift, Dean Jonathan, 164, 219-20
Swiss Guards 96, 97, 165

Taafe, Count Eduard, 224
Taafe, Nicholas 21, 224
Talbot, Richard, see Tyrconnell, earl of, 47-8, 50, 53, 57-8, 61-2, 68
Tallard, Marshal, 78
Tandy, Napper, 176, 187, 197
Tarleton's Cavalry, 161
Tarragonna, Battle of (1642), 19
Tate, William, 181
Teeling, Bartolomew, 185
Tennant, Commandant John, 194, 210-11
Thackery, W.M., 136
The Troubles, 8
The White Cockade, 98
Thirty Years War (1618-48), 11, 19
Thurot, Captain Francois, 140, 181
Tobago, 158
Tone, Matthew, 185
Tone, Theobold Wolfe, 42, 170, 175, 177, 178, 179, 181, 183-4, 187, 197, 219
Tone, Wolfe, 42, 158, 175, 177-8, 197
Torres Vedres, 204, 207
Toulon, 213
Tournai, 92, 93
Tourville, Admiral, 69
Townley, Francis, 116
Trafalgar, Battle of (1805), 19, 104, 198
Trant, Chevalier, 168
Treaty of Aix-la-Chapelle(1748), 128, 136
Treaty of Amiens (1802), 191
Treaty of Compo Formio (1797), 178
Treaty of Limerick (1691), 62-3, 100
Treaty of Paris (1783), 142, 162
Treaty of Utrecht (1713), 82, 90
Trinity College, Dublin, 18, 28, 89, 176, 187
Tyrconnell, Lord, 171
Tyrconnell, 1st earl of, see Talbot, Richard, 47-8, 50, 53, 57-8, 61-2, 68

Ulster, 48, 51, 89, 152, 180, 182, 220
Ultonia (Ulster), Regiment of, 9, 36, 81, 153, 204, 205
United Irishmen, Society of, 174-7, 180-4, 203
Urgel, Siege of, 49

Vachot, General Martial, 210
Vaisseaux, Regiment de, 97, 100
Valencienne, 128
Valladolid, 206
Valmy, Battle of (1792), 174, 200
Vauban, Marshal Sebastien, 70, 80, 242
Velletri, Battle of (1744), 36, 39
Vendome, duc de, 73, 77
Venezuela, 223, 225
Verdun, 7, 199
Vernon, Admiral, 111
Vezon, village of, 93-4
Vienna, 32, 221
Villars, duc de, 73
Villeneuve, General, 198
Villeroi, duc de, 75
Villinghausen, 141
Vinegar Hill, Enniscorthy, 60, 184
Vlissingen, see Flushing
Voltaire, Francois-Marie, 12, 93, 99, 100, 148-9, 163-4, 217
Volunteer Movement, 176

Wade, General, 91
Walcheren Island, 178, 201
Walkinshaw, Clemintina, 131
Wall, Richard (Ricardo), 31, 142, 222
Walsh, Anthony, 106, 108
Walsh, Viscount, 170
Walsh's, Regiment of (Royalist émigré army of the princes), 169
Walsh's, Regiment of, 10, 153, 158-61, 167, 201, 205
Wandiwash, Battle of (1760), 146
War of Austrian Succession (1740-48), 92, 105, 133
War of the Grand Alliance (1688-97), 46
War of the Polish Succession (1735), 27
War of the Spanish Succession (1701-14), 73, 85
Ward, Brigadier General Thomas, 168, 174
Ware, Colonel Hugh, 205, 206, 211, 212, 213
Washington, General George, 13, 104, 152-5, 160, 162, 164, 223, 225, 253
Waterloo, Battle of (1815), 13, 29, 102-3, 178, 213, 223
Wellington, General Sir Arthur Wellesley, duke of, 28, 29, 103, 204, 206-8
Wexford, 55, 155, 172, 184-5, 192
Wheelock, Sergeant, 99, 102, 103
White, Chevalier F.X., 164